Elements of
Weaving

Elements of Weaving

A Complete Introduction to the
Art and Techniques

BY AZALEA STUART THORPE
AND JACK LENOR LARSEN

EDITED BY MARY LYON

DOUBLEDAY & COMPANY, INC.

GARDEN CITY, NEW YORK

ISBN: 0-385-03473-3
Library of Congress Catalog Card Number 67-11164
Copyright © 1967 by Doubleday & Company, Inc.
All Rights Reserved
Printed in the United States of America

9   8   7

ACKNOWLEDGMENTS

The authors would like to acknowledge their colleague and classmate Win Anderson, who so sympathetically and sensibly read the final manuscript. We are in her debt also for the final formulation of the chapter on drafting.

We also thank Merdeces Hensley, who taught design classes at the University of Washington and who made available works of her students, George William Fagan, Diane Glen, Carolyn Hopkins, Bill Knox, James Richardson, and Jerome Yatsunoff. We are grateful to Fan K. Mason, who wove the special samples, and to those weavers near and far who submitted their work to our terrible scrutiny. We praise our illustrators, artist Don Wight and photographer Ferdinand Boesch, for tempering their obvious talent with patience.

We would honor our distinguished editor, Mary Lyon, who so bravely charted this book through long and harrowing rewrites. This gracious lady brought to amateur authors a professional regimen as well as a rich experience of writing for craftsmen.

Finally, kudos to our own teachers, who allowed us the privilege of remaining in classes meant only for those manually dextrous and socially amenable.

Bless you all!

AZALEA STUART THORPE

JACK LENOR LARSEN

CONTENTS

Elements of
Weaving

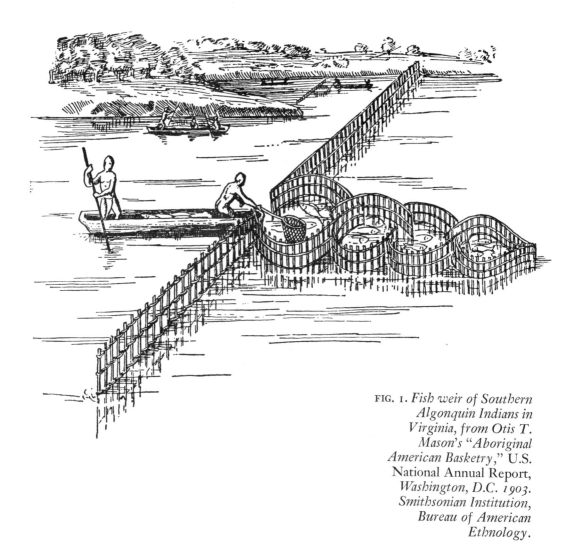

FIG. 1. *Fish weir of Southern Algonquin Indians in Virginia, from Otis T. Mason's "Aboriginal American Basketry,"* U.S. National Annual Report, *Washington, D.C. 1903. Smithsonian Institution, Bureau of American Ethnology.*

CHAPTER ONE

Introduction

IN THE BEGINNING

Most sources mark the emergence of weaving in the new Stone Age when Neolithic man wove mats, baskets, possibly fish traps and some forms of shelter. M. D. C. Crawford* tells us that, prior to this, Paleolithic man used pliable materials to bind points and cutting edges to wooden shafts. The first materials used for this purpose probably were sinews and strips of rawhide from slaughtered animals, as well as the fibers of plants. It is possible that the invention of *interlacing* evolved from this manipulation of materials. Or perhaps man observed the Old World weaver bird attaching its nest to the branch of a tree, and was inspired thereby to adapt the principle of that structure to his own needs.

No one really knows when, where or how weaving began, but it is generally believed that it developed at about the same time in many parts of the world.

PRINCIPLE OF WEAVING

Whatever the beginning may have been, the basic principle of weaving is the same today as it was in prehistoric times. Woven goods, whether baskets of the ancients or products of the power loom, are made by *interlacing* a *lengthwise set* of *material* with a *crosswise set* of *material*.

*The Heritage of Cotton, Fairchild Publications, New York, 1924.

FIG. 2. *Weaver bird and nest which it has woven of grasses, fibers, twigs in a sketchy, free-hand or free-neb plain weave. Drawing, Don Wight.*

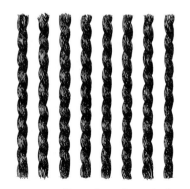

FIG. 3. *Drawing of vertical warp ends. Don Wight.*

FIG. 4. *Drawing of weft, or horizontal filling picks. Don Wight.*

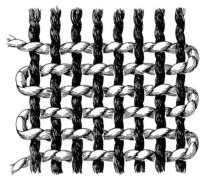

FIG. 5. *Diagram of warp and weft interlaced to form a web of plain weave. Don Wight.*

The lengthwise element is called the *warp* and is composed of many strands of material, which usually is pliable, such as yarn. Each single strand in the warp is called an *end*.

The crosswise element is called the *weft*, or the *filling*, which also is composed of many strands of material. Each single strand in the filling is called a *pick*.

The warp is stretched lengthwise and made taut to form a structure into which the filling is woven crosswise. The movement of a filling pick as it weaves over and under the warp ends—much as in darning—is called *interlacing*. This interlacing of warp ends and filling picks forms a relatively flat-surfaced structure called the *web*.

A web woven of yarns such as are used in making cloth is pliable. However, there are webs woven of wire, strips of wood and various other materials which are comparatively rigid.

The order of interlacing, that is, the particular way in which the ends and picks intersect in the process of weaving is called a *weave*, a *technique* or sometimes a *construction*. For example, the filling may interlace through the warp in the order of *under-one, over-one*, this order being alternated on each successive pick, as shown in Fig. 5. Beginning at the lower left corner, filling pick number one weaves under warp end number one, over end number two, under end number three, over end number four and so on. The order of interlacing alternates on the next pick so that filling pick number two weaves over warp end number one, under end number two, over end three, under end four, and so on. This, the simplest order of interlacing is a *basic weave*, or a *basic construction*, called *plain weave*. In making cloth, it is used more than any other weave.

There are many weaves that are derivations of plain weave, and these, along with weaves in different classifications, together with their derivatives, are explained in Chapter 5.

EVOLUTION OF WEAVING DEVICES

Long before the invention of the loom, various methods and devices were employed to keep warp materials taut and in place in order to facilitate the interweaving or interlacing of filling material.

In some instances the very nature of the material obviated the need to do more than devise a method of handling it. For example, the material used for the warp element in basket weaving, although having some degree of pliability, had sufficient rigidity to remain relatively stationary and in order, once the warp spokes were bound into position at the base of the basket.

The first tensioning device no doubt was gravity. Soft, pliable warp materials, such as yarns, were attached to or looped over a tree branch with the strands hanging vertically from the branch toward the ground. Later the warp strands were made taut by tying stone weights to the free warp ends which hung close to the ground, or by tying them to pegs or to a weighted pole. This arrangement may have been the

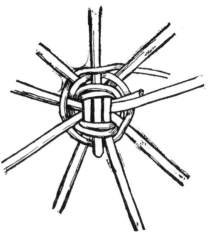

FIG. 6. *Warp stems crossed in pairs, from Otis T. Mason, "Aboriginal American Basketry," Smithsonian Institution, Bureau of American Ethnology.*

FIG. 7. *Gravity and relatively rigid material hold warp ends taut in picture of Virginia Indian woman weaving a basket. From W. H. Holmes's* Prehistoric Textile Art. *Smithsonian Institution, Bureau of American Ethnology.*

predecessor of the single-rod weaving device, which consisted of two vertical ground sticks supporting a horizontal rod to which the warp yarns were attached. With the addition of a second rod to which the bottom or free ends of the warp were attached, the double-rod weaving device evolved, a familiar example being the Navajo rug loom.

For another method the warp was stretched obliquely, with one end tied to a tree or some other support and the other end secure to stakes at a point close to ground level, or to a belt passed around the body of the seated weaver. Various other means were used to support the warp horizontally.

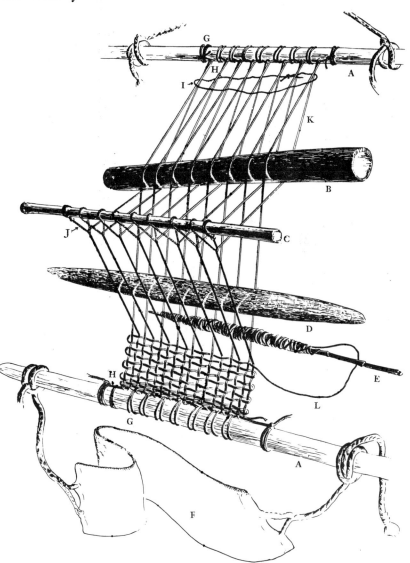

FIG. 8. *A weaving device, one end of which is attached to a support, with warp stretched obliquely to a belt around the waist of the weaver, an Indian girl at Santiago de Atitlán, Guatemala. Courtesy of United Fruit Company.*

FIG. 9. *Diagrammatic representation of a loom with backstrap, showing shedding device and other parts. A type used in Peru (and elsewhere in America).* Andean Culture History, Bennett and Bird, Courtesy of The American Museum of Natural History. (A-A) *cloth stick and warp stick* (B) *lease stick* (C) *heddle rod* (D) *beater, or sword stick* (E) *bobbin, shuttle* (F) *backstrap* (G-G) *lacing cords* (H-H) *lacing cords* (I) *lease cord* (J) *heddles* (K) *warp* (L) *filling.*

The earliest weaving on these primitive devices was done by hand. The warp ends were raised or picked up with the fingers and the filling inserted according to the required order of interlacing. Needlelike tools to which the filling yarn was attached and various other implements were devised for interlacing the filling into the warp, in the manner of darning. The most significant change in the performance of this task came with the introduction of hand operated devices for raising or lowering certain warp ends, while leaving others in place, thus creating a space or opening between the raised or lowered yarns and those which remained stationary. This space or opening, called the *shed*, created by means of various kinds of *shedding devices*, made it possible to pass the filling material through the open shed across the full breadth of the warp instead of interweaving it tediously, strand by strand. Also, the shed made it possible to use *battening* devices which could be inserted into the open shed and used to pack the filling material firmly into place.

The shed doubtless gave rise to the invention of various kinds of *shuttles*. The contemporary shuttle is a hollowed-out wooden device which holds filling material and can be shot or thrown through the open shed. This method of inserting the filling greatly increased the speed at which weaving could be done and facilitated the production of wider fabrics.

Simple Looms in Current Use

Despite their lack of mechanical aids, the simple weaving devices described in Chapter 2 are adequate in that they provide a means for controlling the warp—holding it taut and in place—so that the warp ends can be manipulated, either by the fingers or by a shedding device, to allow the insertion of the filling element.

It should not be surprising, therefore, to learn that such devices are in current use, particularly in places where mechanized equipment is unavailable or impractical. Even in our own highly mechanized era the simple weaving device has its place, serving, for certain purposes, to better advantage than more complicated or expensive equipment.

Wherever such factors as low cost, portability, minimum space requirements, and easy storage are more important than speed of production, the use of a simple weaving device is indicated. Such equipment is particularly appropriate for group work.

A variety of small devices is offered by manufacturers and, fortunately, these are easily obtained, at least by mail order. Also, a very simple weaving device can be constructed by anyone who is able to use a hammer and has at hand a few pieces of wood. The experience of building a simple weaving device is, in fact, an aid to understanding the how and why of weaving.

Perhaps there is no better way to improve this understanding than by weaving on a device that provides few, if any, mechanical aids. It is then that the weaver is closest to his materials. He has the opportunity to become familiar with the feel of yarns as he manipulates and controls them with his hands, and to learn how various constructions result from different techniques. His attention can be focused wholly on the rudiments of weaving, leaving the mastery of loom operation to a time when he has acquired an intimate comprehension of the process of weaving.

Since weaving is learned through doing rather than reading, work projects are suggested as the best means of getting under way. Several of these are outlined in the following pages. The simplest kind of equipment and equally simple projects have been chosen to enable the person with no previous experience in weaving, and with little or no equipment, to follow the outlines with relative ease and at minimum expense.

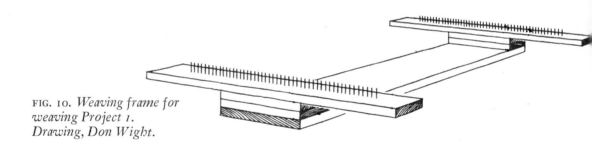

FIG. 10. *Weaving frame for weaving Project 1. Drawing, Don Wight.*

FIG. 11. *Project 1, a place mat 12 by 18 inches, woven of black synthetic raffia and bamboo on a weaving frame, shown in Fig. 10. Photo, Ferdinand Boesch.*

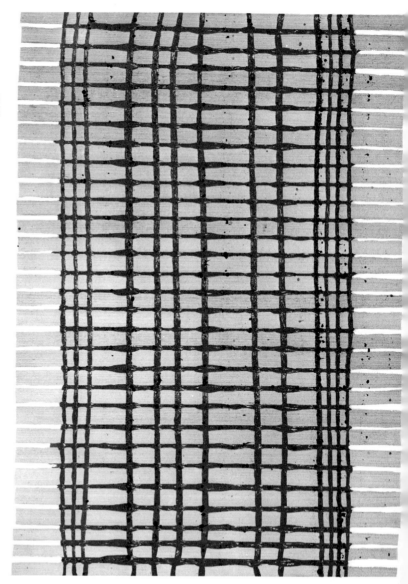

CHAPTER TWO

Getting Started— Two Projects

THE WEAVING FRAME

PROJECT 1, WEAVING A PLACE MAT

The first project is for place mats, to be done on the weaving frame shown in Fig. 10, or on any other simple device that the weaver chooses to use.

The frame shown is easily constructed at low cost, and the materials are in ready supply. This device has the advantage of having no side pieces to interfere with the insertion of filling material. It can be built in any reasonable size, depending only on the requirements of the piece to be woven and the weaver's arm span. The specifications given will accommodate a 12-by-18-inch place mat, or any article of similar dimensions. Of course the dimensions may be varied; the essential requirements are that the baseboard be made long enough to allow the end boards to be placed sufficiently far apart to accommodate the length of the material to be woven, plus an allowance for shrinkage, loom waste, and finishing; and that the end boards be long enough to fit the required width of the material.

For complete specifications—materials, dimensions, and instructions for putting together the frame loom— turn to Appendix B, page 225.

The place mat shown in Fig. 11 is woven of wide black synthetic raffia and half-inch-wide bamboo strips in natural color. The only additional materials required are two strips of stout cardboard or two thin slats of wood measuring one inch by twelve, which are used as a heading at the beginning of the weaving to provide a firm base against which the filling materials are beaten, and a smooth stick or ruler with which to do the beating and to aid in making a shed. This beater, or sword, should be at least 15 inches long and will be easier to grasp and use if it is somewhat longer. A stick 22 to 23 inches long will be found most suitable.

Calculating Materials for Warp and Filling

Calculating the materials for a project is an essential procedure, which involves nothing more than a simple step-by-step thought process. In general one needs to determine the number of ends of each kind of material to be used in the warp and the length of the fabric to be woven; the number of picks per inch of each kind of filling material and the width of the fabric to be woven. If a small sample swatch has been woven prior to the setting up of the project, it will serve as a basis for these calculations. If this has not been done, then the calculations must be based either on one's own experience or on information obtained from other sources. In any event, it is always wise to calculate generously and to buy somewhat more material than is needed. To run short of material when a project is all but finished is one of the most frustrating events that a weaver can experience. With forethought, this can be avoided.

In the warp arrangement for the place mats shown in Fig. 12, there are 25 warp ends. Each end is roughly 30 inches long. Therefore the amount of black raffia required for the warp is 25 times 30 inches, or 750 inches. Since the purchase of yarns is usually based on the ratio of yards to the pound, it is necessary to divide 750 inches by 36 inches in order to determine that, in round figures, 21 yards of raffia will be needed for one place mat. These calculations are based on the length of material required to span the distance between the two sets of nails in the end boards, rather than on the length of the finished piece. It is unnecessary to allow extra material for tying the warp onto the loom, an allowance which would be made if one were using a loom with movable warp and cloth beams. However,

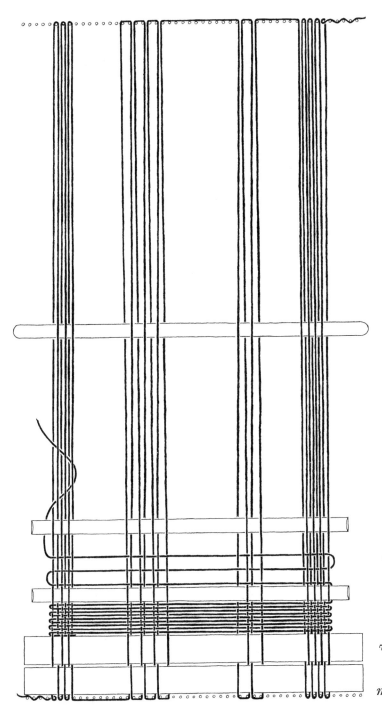

FIG. 12. *How twenty-five warp ends for place mat are wound on frame and weaving begun. First warp end, lower left, is secured by weaving it over and under first four nails, hitching it to fifth nail. At upper right corner, last warp end is hitched to sixth nail from edge and wound over and under remaining nails. Drawing, Don Wight.*

all calculations include an allowance for some waste as well as for extra material to be put into the weaver's stock of yarns for future experiments and projects. The allowance made for waste depends on the project, the kind of materials and equipment used, as well as on the experience of the weaver.

For the place mat project outlined here, an allowance of 20 per cent was made to cover waste. Therefore, .20 × 21 yards equals 4-1/5 yards. Since it is easier to deal with round figures than with fractions, and better to order more rather than less material, the calculation for waste was changed to 5 yards. This figure, added to the 21 yards required for the warp itself, brings the total requirement to 26 yards of raffia for each place mat. This figure should, of course, be multiplied by the number of mats to be woven.

For the filling, thirty-six 12-inch lengths of bamboo a half-inch wide are required to weave a mat 18 inches long. Since 3 picks of raffia are woven in between each pick of bamboo, it is obvious that something less than 36 lengths of bamboo will be used. However, this figure was used as a base because bamboo usually comes in stock sizes which are longer than the 12-inch length required for this project, and waste is inevitable in cutting these longer strips to the desired size. Since the 3 raffia interlacings follow each strip of bamboo, except the last one, there would be 36 such interlacings. The total number of raffia picks is 35 times 3, which equals 105 picks of raffia in each mat.

Fig. 12 shows that the 12-inch strips of bamboo extend an inch beyond each side of the warp, which is set 10 inches wide on the frame. Therefore, each raffia pick covers a 10-inch width rather than the 12-inch over-all width. The width of each pick multiplied by the number of picks gives the amount of material required for one place mat which, in this case, would be 10 inches times 105, a total of 1050 inches. To convert to yards, 1050 inches is divided by 36, which equals approximately 30 yards of raffia needed for the filling. Twenty per cent of 30 yards, the amount allowed for waste and the interlacing movement of the yarns, equals 6 yards, which, added to 35, results in a total of 41 yards of raffia required for the filling material in each mat.

Forty-one yards of filling added to the 26 yards required for the warp give a total requirement of 67 yards of raffia for each place mat. Four mats would require 4 times 67, or 268 yards of raffia.

Since yarns are sold by the pound, the final calculation to be made is that of converting yards into pounds. This is usually based on the numbering system or system of yarn counts which applies to a particular yarn. Raffia, however, unlike most yarns, is not governed by such a system. It is available in various widths and the number of yards to a pound depends on the width of the material. The finer it is, the more yards per pound. The simplest solution to this problem is to ask the vendor how many yards per pound there are in the material he is selling. If, for example, there were 1000 yards in a pound of raffia, it would take a little more than a quarter-pound to weave the four place mats, as calculated. However, it would be advisable to buy at least a half-pound and not amiss to buy a full pound.

Usually raffia is put up in hanks or skeins and before beginning to wind it onto the frame, the skein will need to be opened out on a chairback, a floor swift or an umbrella swift (Fig. 30, Nos. 1 and 3), or held by whatever other means is at hand to keep the skein taut. This facilitates the warping process, making it possible to unwind the material as needed without tangling it. Occasionally a vendor will wind materials from skeins onto cardboard spools especially made for holding yarns. This service is well worth the small fee charged for it. In warping, the spool can be placed in a container, such as a cardboard box, a bowl or a cooking pot, or on a *spool rack* (Fig. 30, No. 2) to keep it from rolling away during the warping process.

The Warping Process

To start winding the warp onto the frame, weave it alternately over and under the first four nails and then hitch it securely around the fifth nail, at the lower left corner of the frame as shown in Fig. 12, page 11. The strand of raffia, which is being pulled from the skein or the spool, is then drawn straight across to the opposite end of the frame where it is hitched around the sixth nail. Next, it is carried back to the end of the frame on which the warp was started and hitched around the sixth nail there. Continue the warping, as shown, taking care to keep the warp at a taut, even tension as it is being wound from one end of the frame to the other and hitched around the nails. The last warp end, shown at the upper right corner of Fig. 12, is hitched to the sixth nail from the edge of the frame, at the end of the frame opposite to that on which the warping was started. The last end is secured, as was the first one, by winding it over and under the remaining nails.

Pick-by-Pick Instructions for Weaving

To begin weaving, follow the pick-by-pick instructions given below, and refer as often as necessary to Figs. 12 and 13.

CARDBOARD OR WOOD SLAT 1: Insert from right to left, *over* the first warp end, *under* the second end, *over* the third end; continue weaving over and under alternate ends until the cardboard is interlaced through all of the warp ends.

BEATING STICK: With one hand, tip on edge the strip of cardboard just inserted so that a space is cleared between the warp ends. Half the warp ends will lie over the tipped stick while the other half lie under it. This is the first shed. Insert the beating stick through the shed so that it lies between the cardboard strip and the far end of the frame. The strip of cardboard and the beating stick are now lying in the same shed. Push the beating stick to the far end of the frame until needed, pull the strip of cardboard forward and press it firmly against the row of nails.

CARDBOARD OR WOOD SLAT 2: Insert, from right to left, immediately following slat No. 1, under the first warp end, over the second end, under the third end, and continue the alternate interlacing until the strip is interlaced through all the warp ends.

FIG. 13. *Weaving of place mat has reached forty-sixth filling pick (bamboo); three raffia picks are being inserted. Beater, above, is ready to beat raffia picks into place. Photo, Ferdinand Boesch.*

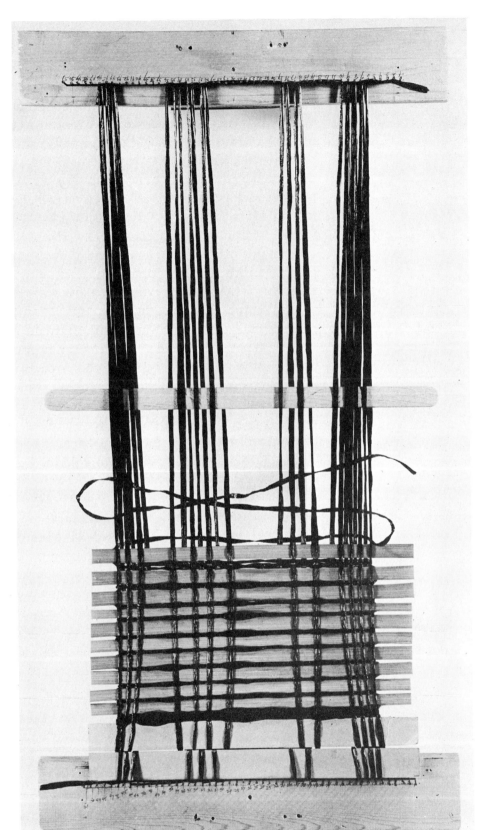

PICK 1, RAFFIA: Reel off about 5 yards of raffia, a comfortable amount to handle, and, holding it at one end, interweave from left to right *over* the first warp end, under the second, over the third end, continuing this over-under alternation until raffia has been interlaced through all the warp ends. Pull the end of the raffia through the warp so that it extends about 2 inches beyond the last warp on the *left*. Turn this excess length of raffia back toward the warp and tuck it in, weaving it from left to right, under the first warp end, over the second, and so on until it has been interlaced through the first group of six ends on the left of the frame. Pull the raffia through these ends until no loop is left at the edge of the warp. The end of raffia will protrude on the surface between the sixth and seventh warp ends; this will be removed later. Now grasp the beating stick with both hands and pull it forward, firmly, forcing the raffia as close as possible to the cardboard strip. However, the stick and the first pick of raffia are in the same shed, and the raffia will not remain tightly in place. It will remain in place when the next pick is inserted and beaten in the opposite shed.

This first pick of raffia has been described as being interlaced by hand, over and under the warp ends, so that the weaver will understand the process of interlacing that is taking place. On future picks, when the raffia is to be placed in the same shed as the beater stick, it is only necessary to tip the beater stick on edge so that the shed is opened; the raffia is then inserted into the open shed and pulled through it, across the entire width of the warp to the opposite side of the frame.

PICK 2, RAFFIA: Pick up the raffia left hanging at the right side of the frame and interlace it, right to left, *under* the first warp end, over the second end, continuing this under-over interlacing until the raffia has been interlaced through all the warp ends. The beating stick is used again to press the raffia into place against the first pick of raffia.

PICK 3, RAFFIA: The length of raffia now lies on the left side of the frame. Interlace it from left to right, *over* the first warp end, *under* the second, and so on, until interlaced through all the warp ends. Beat the raffia into place with the beater stick.

PICK 4, RAFFIA: Interlace this pick from right to left, just as the second pick was interlaced—*under* the first warp end, *over* the second end, and so on. Beat into place.

PICKS 5, 6, 7, 8, AND 9, RAFFIA: Continue the interlacing procedure described for the first four picks, alternating the order of interlacing on each pick. Remember that all odd-numbered picks, such as 3 and 5, can be interlaced by opening the shed with the beater stick.

These first nine picks are called the *heading* and will be removed when the weaving is finished. As the heading is woven in, the warp yarns will pull together slightly at the edges so that the warp is narrower at the line of weaving than at the line of nails to which they are attached. This pull-in is natural but should not be allowed to exceed half an inch or at the most an inch. As the weaving proceeds, a tape measure should be used frequently to check the width of the last few rows of weaving. If the pull-in is excessive, take out the filling to the point where the width is correct. Then, reweave the material, making sure that the filling is not pulled too taut through the warp. Remember that in the process of interlacing through the warp yarns the filling yarns must go over a warp end and then move downward between two ends in order to go under the next end; from its position under a warp end, the filling moves up between two warp ends in order to go over the next end. Therefore, to allow enough yarn for the interlacing motion, the filling should lie in the shed in a slack curve before being beaten into place. With a little practice, one learns to adjust the filling yarns correctly.

PICK 10, BAMBOO: Interlace the strip of bamboo from right to left, under the first warp end, over the second, and so on. Pull bamboo forward, firmly, against preceding picks of raffia.

PICK 11, RAFFIA: Carry raffia, which is at the right of the frame, under the bamboo just inserted and interlace from right to left, *over* the first warp end, under the second end, and so on. The shed can be made with the beater stick for this interlacing.

PICK 12, RAFFIA: Interlace left to right, *under* the first warp end, over the second, and so on. Beat into place.

PICK 13, RAFFIA: Use the beater stick to make the shed, insert raffia from right to left, close the shed and beat into place. (*Note:* This pick will lie over the first end, under the second end, and so on across the warp.)

PICK 14, BAMBOO: Interlace, right to left, under and over.

PICK 15, RAFFIA: Carry raffia under the end of the preceding pick of bamboo and proceed with the proper interlacing.

Continue interlacing the material as described, one bamboo pick and three raffia picks, until the material measures 20 inches, or slightly more, from the first bamboo pick to the last one. The 2 inches added to the 18-inch length required are woven to keep the picks from raveling when the mat is cut from the frame.

FINISHING: With scissors, carefully cut each loop of raffia as close as possible to the row of nails. As the mat is cut from the frame, take care to see that the filling material does not ravel any more than can be helped. Place the mat, underside up, on a flat surface such as a table or a desk and measure the mat to determine how many picks of filling material must be removed to leave the required 18-inch length intact.

The ends of the mats may be finished in any way the weaver chooses to finish them provided the method used will lock the filling in place and produce neat ends. In one method, commonly used, the warp ends are tied in groups which then are cut to an even length and allowed to extend from the ends, as part of the mat. The sparse warp spacing for the mats described here does not lend itself to that particular method, since the warp ends are too far apart in the open areas. It is better in this case to tie two warp ends together on the underside of the mat so the knot will not be seen when the mats are in use. Or, the knots may be covered by binding the end strips of bamboo, over and over from warp edge to warp edge, with raffia. Another method is to leave in, at each end of the mat, one bamboo strip beyond the required 18-inch length. The raffia warp ends are tied in pairs on the underside of the mat, as described above. The extra bamboo strip, coated on the underside with a good grade of waterproof glue, is turned to the back of the mat and pressed against the bamboo pick lying adjacent to it. The two strips of bamboo should be placed under books or some other weight until the glue is completely dry. In this method, the raffia knots are hidden between the glued bamboo strips. These glued ends can also be bound with raffia if desired.

NOTES ON THE FRAME LOOM PROJECT: The place mat shown in Fig. 11, page 8, was woven with "bark" or outside peel of bamboo sticks placed raw side, or wrong side, up. The other side, which is smoother, may be used if preferred. Or, plain wood slats purchased at a hobby shop or lumber yard may be used instead of bamboo. Also, natural raffia or other materials may be used in place of synthetic raffia. And, of course, the color scheme can be varied according to one's own taste.

It is recommended that when one length of raffia filling is used up another length be tied to it and the interlacing continued. The knots should be pulled tight to make them as small as possible; the ends should be clipped about a quarter-inch from the knot. The knot will be hidden if care is taken to see that it is tied in position to interweave with the closely grouped warp ends either at the right or left edge of the warp. A knot should not be tied in a position which puts it in the open spaces of the warp, nor should it be placed in the center groups of yarns which, being set further apart than the groups at the edges, would give insufficient coverage to hide the knot.

It also is recommended that the raffia used for the filling be left unwound, in a free strand. This can be done with raffia because it has little tendency to tangle.

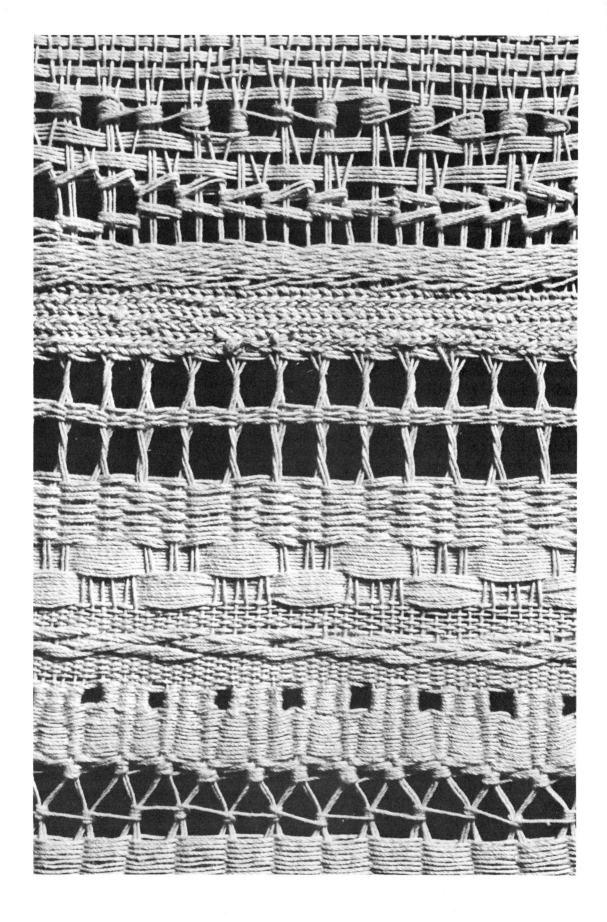

FIG. 14. Left, *experiment in design woven on a frame loom in a single material, natural cotton cord. Leno and other gauze weaves are combined with plain weave and twill, in bands of filling on twisted warp ends, by James Richardson. Photo, Ferdinand Boesch.*

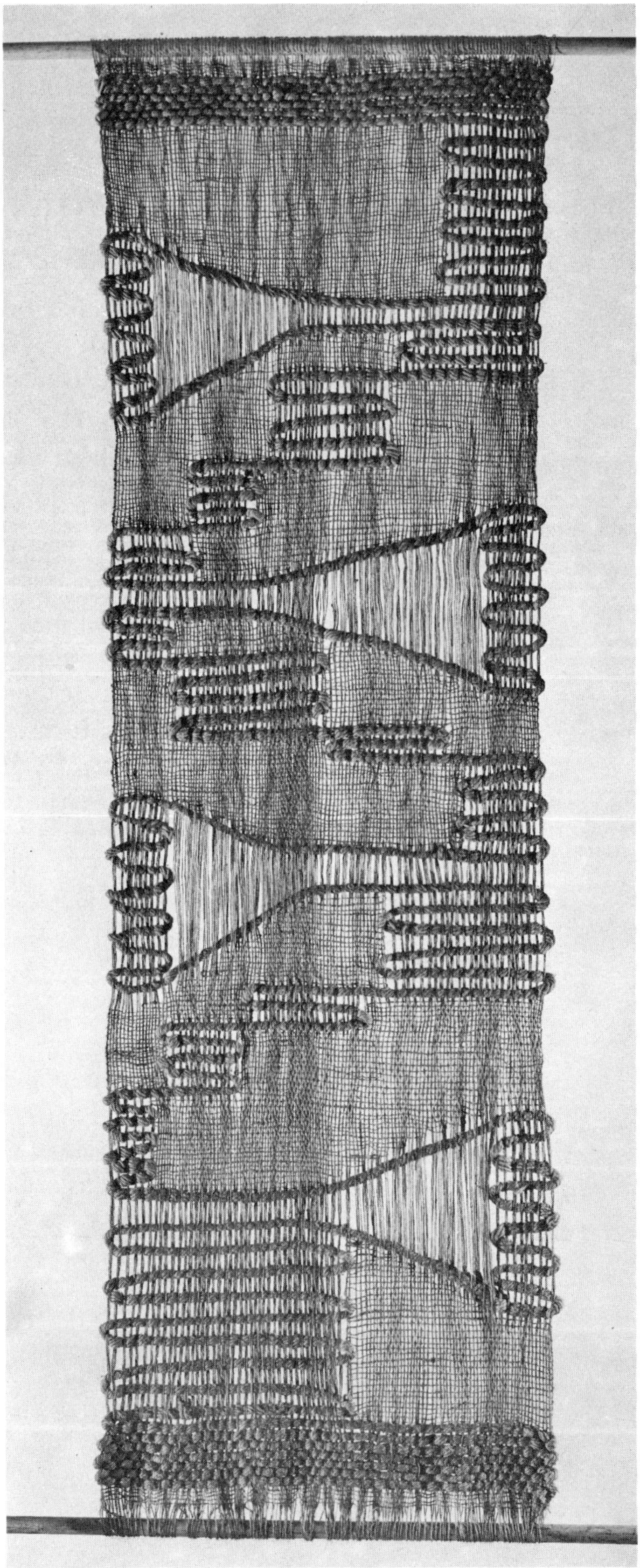

FIG. 15. Right, *tapestry of jute and heavy cotton roving, red on red; roving has been used to outline transparent sections of pattern which was woven on frame similar to that in Fig. 10. Designed by Alice English.*

When interlacing raffia, it is easier to pull a single strand through the warp by hand than to work with it on a bobbin or shuttle.

THE BACKSTRAP LOOM WITH RIGID HEDDLE. PROJECT 2, WEAVING A BELT

The backstrap loom, in one form or another, has been in use from early days in the history of weaving to the present time. It is known by various names. Sometimes it is called after a race or group of people who use it, as with the Ainu loom of Japan; sometimes it is described as the stick loom or the waist loom. Many authorities do not classify it as a loom at all. However, the various parts of the backstrap loom have their functional counterparts in the contemporary hand loom.

The survival of the backstrap loom to this day is not without reason. Its parts are simple, economical and readily available. It is portable and can be used indoors or out of doors. It can be rolled up, complete with its warp, and tucked away when not in use.

Without its warp, the backstrap loom consists of nothing more than a collection of sticks and a length of pliable material to encircle the weaver's waist, plus implements for shedding and beating. The weaver himself becomes a very important part of the loom since it is the force exerted by the weight of his body against the backstrap that gives tension to the warp. (See Figs. 8 and 9, page 5.)

The backstrap loom is particularly useful for making narrow fabrics. These include not only belts, ties, and scarves but also a great variety of decorative ribbons, bands, and cords. The wall hanging shown in Fig. 16 was woven on the same device.

THE RIGID HEDDLE

The rigid heddle, also known as a heddle-reed, is recommended here as a shedding device because it has the advantages of serving to space out warp yarns and can be used to beat in filling picks as well. In weaving

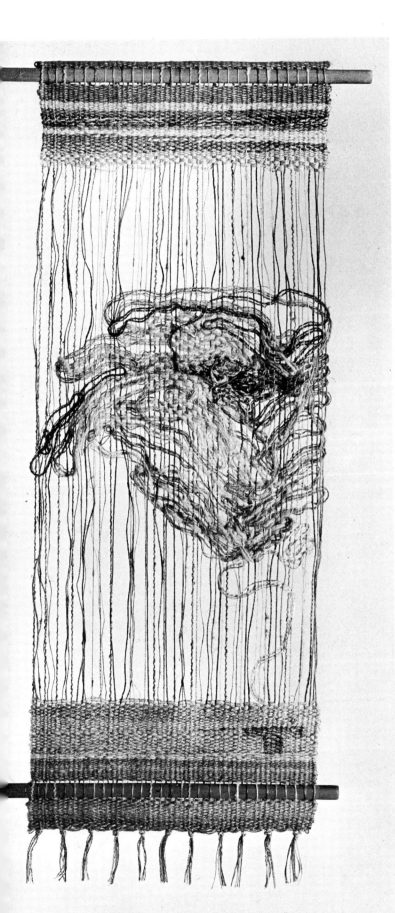

FIG. 16. *Small wall hanging,
free-form design, woven on
backstrap loom with rigid
heddle by Lenore Tawney.
Photo, Ferdinand Boesch.*

which requires shaping, as done with the neckties shown in Fig. 17, the rigid heddle can be used primarily as a shedding device, with the beating done by a stick. This allows the warp yarns to be pulled in by the filling yarns, thus narrowing the fabric as required.

FIG. 17. *Neckties woven and shaped on a backstrap loom. For this, the rigid heddle has been used primarily as a shedding device; beating done by a stick so that the warp yarns can be pulled in by the filling, as required for narrowing.*

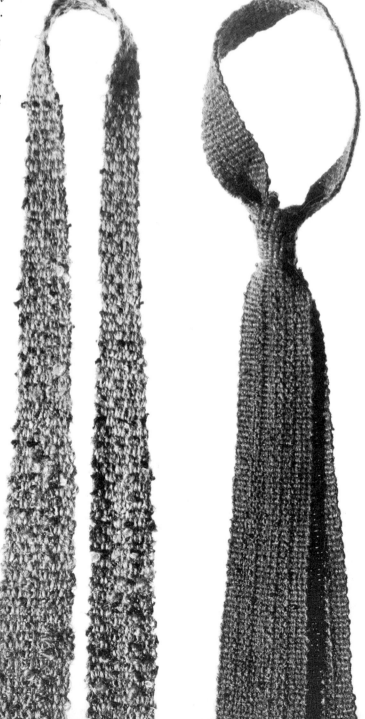

The rigid heddle, as shown in Fig. 18, is an arrangement of vertical parallel bars each of which has a hole in the center. The bars are evenly spaced with a narrow slit between them. Once the principle of operating the rigid heddle is understood there should be no problem in setting it up.

Setting Up the Backstrap Loom, with Rigid Heddle

As shown in Fig. 19, the setup consists of (1) a hitching point to which one end of the warp is secured; (2) a cloth stick, in this case made of a wooden dowel, to which the other end of the warp is tied; (3) a cord or backstrap which goes around the weaver's waist and is attached to each end of the cloth stick, and (4), the rigid heddle through which the warp ends are threaded. The method of threading the warp ends alternately through the holes and slits of the heddle, thus creating the shed, is explained on page 29.

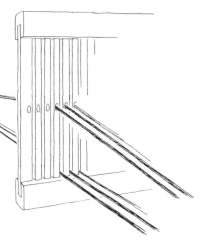

FIG. 18. *Rigid heddle with warp yarns inserted through holes at center and, below, through narrow slits. Drawing, Don Wight.*

FIG. 19. *As set up, the backstrap loom has (1) hitching point; (2) cloth stick; (3) backstrap going around weaver's waist and attached to each end of cloth stick; and (4) the rigid heddle. Drawing, Don Wight.*

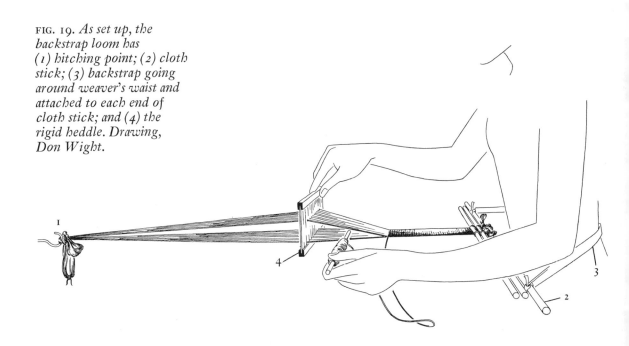

Equipment for Project 2

For the second Project, a belt to be woven with the aid of a rigid heddle, the following very simple equipment is required: (See Fig. 20.)

A rigid heddle, 2 inches wide or wider

Three wooden dowels, 18 to 22 inches wide

One slat of wood, 1 to 1-1/2 inches wide, and from 15 to 22 inches long

One length of cord or tape for the backstrap, long enough to attach to the dowel ends and to go around the weaver's waist, approximately 4 feet

Calculating Material for the Project

Specifications and Calculations:

4/8 wool in any desired color

Length of belt: *2 yards* (allowing for tie at waist and fringe)

Waste: 50 per cent, *1 yard* (see page 27)

Total warp length: *3 yards*

Width of warp: 2 inches

Number of ends per inch: 10

Total number of ends: 10 per inch, multiplied by 2-inch width of warp, or 20 ends

Total yardage: 20 ends multiplied by 3 yards for each end, or 60 yards.

In this project, the number of ends per inch is governed by a rigid heddle, which has 5 holes plus 5 slits per inch, or a total of 10 places per inch through which warp ends can be drawn. Since the size of the holes and slits cannot be changed, the device serves as something of a guide in the choice of material. Wool in 4/8 size fits the holes nicely and, if set at 10 ends per inch, has sufficient size to produce a firm weave without needing to be pulled in by the filling yarn, as is done often in order to get a firm hand when fine yarns are used for the warp, or when shaping is required.

The number of filling picks per inch is adjustable and so determines the hand of the finished fabric. The fewer picks per inch, the looser the fabric. A belt of firm hand will result if the filling picks are put in at 14 or 15 to the inch. The amount of filling yarn required for this project was calculated on the basis of 15 picks to the inch.

In the specifications for planning the width of the warp, as set in the heddle, note that it cannot exceed the capacity of the heddle. Otherwise, the width of the warp is a matter of choice: a belt can be very narrow, or as wide as the heddle or somewhere in between.

The length of the warp was based on the length of belt required to encircle an average waist, with allowance for a knot tie and a generous fringe drop. For a tall person, or for a very ample waist, a longer belt would be needed. In such a case adjust the calculation according to the length of the belt required.

The amount of fabric to be woven, and the amount to be left for the fringe, is a matter of preference and personal measurements. The calculations given allow one yard of woven material for the waist and a knot tie, and 1 yard of unwoven warp for 18-inch fringes.

Based on the figures given, the total number of filling picks would be 15 picks per inch multiplied by 2 (the warp for the belt is 2 inches wide). This equals 30 inches required per inch of woven material. Multiply this by 36 inches of woven material, equaling 1080 inches per yard. Converted to yards, 1080 inches divided by 36 inches equals 30 yards of filling yarn required to weave 1 yard of fabric. (Obviously, since the number of yards of yarn required to weave 1 yard of fabric is equal to the number of inches required to weave 1 inch of fabric, calculations involving multiplication by 36 followed by division by 36 may be omitted.)

There are now 30 yards of filling yarn plus 60 yards of warp yarn, giving a total requirement of 90 yards of yarn to weave the belt as calculated.

In these yarn calculations, the allowance of 50 per cent for waste was made so that there would be an ample amount of warp for tying onto the dowel and for the loop needed at the hitching point. It is well to remember that the shorter the warp, the higher the percentage allowed for waste. If, for example, two belts instead of one were planned, the yardage required for the belts themselves would double, but the yardage

FIG. 20. *Project 2, a belt with knotted fringe, woven on a backstrap loom. Photo, Ferdinand Boesch.*

allowed for waste would remain the same. Therefore, the percentage of waste would decrease.

At this point it is necessary to determine in pounds the amount of wool yarn needed for the project in hand. For this specific calculation the weaver is referred to page 229, in the Appendix, in which various numbering or count systems are explained. Suffice it to say that for this project the equation indicates about a quarter pound of wool for the 90 yards. It is possible to buy as little as quarter-pound lots from some dealers but, again, the suggestion is made that an extra amount be bought to build up the weaver's stock of yarn.

Winding the Warp

Wool sold to the retail trade is usually put up in skeins, sometimes in balls. If the vendor has facilities for winding it from the skein onto spools, the weaver is urged to avail himself of this service. If not, he probably will find his work easier if he winds the yarn into a ball before warping it.

The 20 3-yard lengths of yarn required for the belt warp may be wound with whatever equipment is at hand. The winding may be done between any two pegs or points such as two door knobs or, say, the backs of two chairs. Or two nails can be set 3 yards apart in a board so that each yarn length between the nails measures 3 yards. See Fig. 21.

FIG. 21. *Board with nails set three yards apart, at A and B, for winding the warp of Project 2. Drawing, Don Wight.*

TO BEGIN THE WARPING: The ball of yarn may be placed in a container such as a cooking pot or a box. This will keep the yarn from tangling and prevent the ball from rolling away while the yarn is being reeled off.

To begin the warping, tie one end of the yarn to point A, which is the first of the stationary hitching points shown in Fig. 21. Wind the yarn back and forth between point A and point B, which is the second hitching point, set 3 yards distant. The twentieth warp end, the last one needed, will end at point A, where the warp was started. Tie a piece of stout cord very tightly around all the yarns at point B in Fig. 21. Remove the warp by cutting through all the yarns at point A.

With one hand, hold the warp at the place where it is tied with cord; with the other hand, bring all the yarns together so that they are parallel, pulling them almost taut between the two hands to make certain that they are lying straight. Loop this end of the warp, the cord or uncut end, into a hard knot, as shown in Fig. 22.

Threading the Warp

To begin threading the warp through the rigid heddle, tie this hard-knotted end of the warp just referred to, to a stationary hitching point—a point secure enough to remain firm against the pull of the warp. Then to prevent the warp ends from getting tangled and to keep them off the floor, the warp yarns can be bundled together and tied in a series of slipknots that will pull out easily when necessary. (See Figs. 34-40, page 53.)

Now, measure the rigid heddle from end to end and mark the center of its width. From the center mark, measure one inch to the right or left, depending upon the direction in which the warp will be threaded, and make another mark at this point.

To facilitate the threading process, the rigid heddle frame may be held between the weaver's knees, or it may be propped upright on a table between two heavy books. If the weaver is right-handed, he probably will find it most convenient to sit at the side of the warp with his left shoulder toward the tied end of it. In this position he will be able to reach out, pick up each yarn with his left hand, and pull the end through the heddle with a crochet hook or a bent piece of fine wire held in his right hand.

With the heddle frame in position, pick up the warp and release the soft loops or slipknots in the body of the warp. Then, using both hands and working from

FIG. 22. *After warp for Project 2 has been reeled and cut from warping board at point A, it is tied into a hard knot just below point B. Drawing, Don Wight.*

29

the tied end toward the cut or free end, pull the warp yarns as smooth and straight as possible.

Free one warp end from the group of yarns and pull it through the heddle frame at the mark made to indicate the point one inch from the center of the frame. This may be either a hole or a slit. Free the second yarn from the group of yarns and pull it through the next threading place, moving toward the center of the frame. If the first yarn was threaded through a hole, the second yarn will be threaded through a slit, or vice versa. Thus, the threading is continued until a total of twenty warp ends have been drawn alternately through holes and slits in the frame. Then gather all the cut ends together and pull them taut. Push the heddle frame back toward the tied end of the warp and tie the cut ends into a firm slipknot to keep them from slipping out of the heddle frame.

The Backstrap

Tie one end of the backstrap cord to one end of the dowel which is to serve as the cloth stick. The backstrap then is circled loosely around the weaver's waist and tied to the other end of the cloth stick.

While tying on the warp, the weaver must sit in a position that will stretch the warp taut throughout its length. Before tying the groups of warp ends to the dowel, smooth the yarns and work them forward, using both hands, until they are at equal tension.

Sit facing the warp, pick up all the yarns and untie the slipknot that was tied to secure the warp ends in the heddle frame. Pull the warp taut and divide it into two groups of ten ends each. Tie one group into a slipknot that can be pulled out easily and let it hang free while the other group is being tied onto the dowel. (The tie-on must be made a half yard from the ends of the yarn to allow for the fringe.) Tie the first group onto the cloth stick with the tie-on knot, also called the girth hitch, described on page 72. (See Figs. 45-52.) Then tie the second warp group onto the dowel alongside and parallel to the first group. Fig. 23, series 1 through 8, shows clearly how to make the tie-on knot.

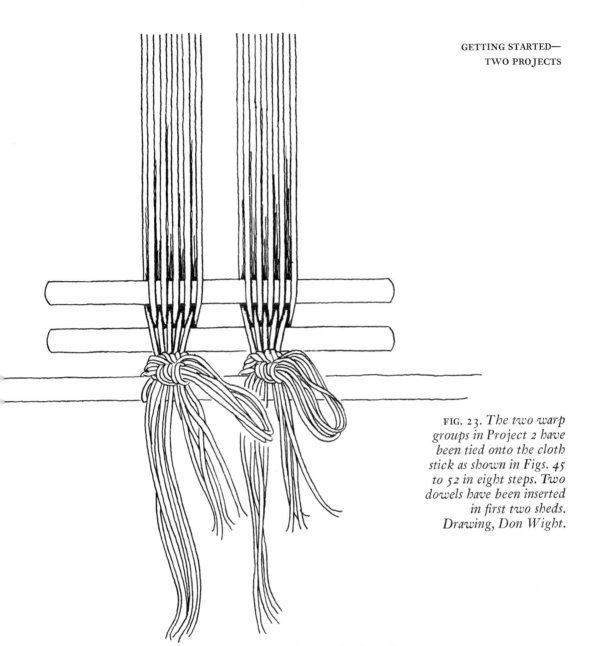

FIG. 23. *The two warp
groups in Project 2 have
been tied onto the cloth
stick as shown in Figs. 45
to 52 in eight steps. Two
dowels have been inserted
in first two sheds.
Drawing, Don Wight.*

Fig. 23 shows the two warp groups tied onto the dowel
in this manner. When the warp is tied on, slip the backstrap off one end of the cloth stick and let the warp
hang free while preparing yarn for the filling.

Making a Butterfly

A yarn butterfly is often used to carry the filling
through the warp shed instead of a bobbin or shuttle,
especially for narrow warps. A butterfly is soft and
light in weight and will not roll away when laid down.

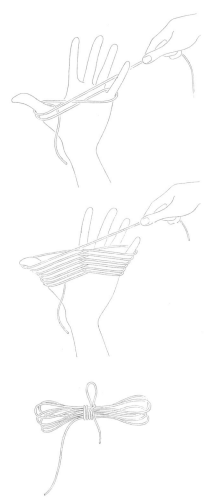

If the butterfly should fall off the warp it would not unwind as it fell, nor would it exert the pull on the warp of a heavier device, such as bobbin or shuttle, should it fall. In fact, it is customary to let the butterfly dangle at the side of the warp whenever the weaver finds it necessary to free both hands.

As shown in Figs. 24, 25, and 26, the weaver makes a butterfly by hitching the end of the yarn several times around his thumb, and then carrying it across his outstretched, open palm to loop it around his little finger; the yarn then is carried back and forth in figure-eight fashion until the butterfly is wound to the desired size. The yarn is cut, leaving an end that is long enough to wrap—firmly but not tightly—around the center of the bundle of yarn on the hand, making the butterfly shape from which it takes its name. The end of the wrapping yarn is tucked into itself to prevent the butterfly from unwinding, and the butterfly is removed from the hand. The end of the yarn that was hitched to the weaver's thumb now hangs longer than the butterfly loops; this end is pulled out from the body of the butterfly as yarn is needed for weaving. It is wise to wind several butterflies at a time to avoid interrupting the weaving each time one runs out.

The Weaving Starts

With the butterflies wound and a pair of scissors at hand, the weaver is ready to begin weaving. He must again put the backstrap around his waist and attach it to the cloth stick. The backstrap must be placed at an equal distance from each end of the cloth stick so that the weaving will be in a straight line.

When the warp is under tension, adjust the rigid heddle so that it is a sufficient distance from the cloth stick to allow for a shed between the heddle and the dowel. Push the top of the rigid heddle down with one hand, forcing the yarns in the holes to a lower position than those in the slits. This opening between the upper and lower yarn levels is the first shed. Slip a dowel through the shed and pull it forward, close against the cloth stick. Then, pull the rigid heddle up so that the position of the yarns is reversed, those in the holes now

FIGS. 24, 25, 26. *A butterfly, to be used instead of a shuttle for Project 2: 24, how to start winding; 25, completing the winding; 26, butterfly ready to use. Drawings, Don Wight.*

being higher than those in the slits. This is the second shed. Slip the remaining dowel through this opening and pull it forward. The next shed, into which the first pick of yarn will be inserted, is made by pushing the heddle frame down, again forcing the yarns threaded through the holes to a lower position than those in the slits. Push the butterfly into the open shed and pull it out at the opposite side of the warp, leaving an end of yarn extending about two inches from the selvage at the side where the butterfly was entered. This end should be wound once around the last warp end and then tucked back into the open shed so that, for a distance of four or five warp ends, it lies alongside the first filling pick. Pull the tucked-in end up between two warp ends, the fourth and fifth, for example, and close the shed. Leave this end of filling yarn on the surface of the warp until several filling picks have been beaten into place; then it may be cut as close as possible to the surface of the web, leaving it clean.

Pull the rigid heddle forward and use it to beat the first filling pick against the dowel. The warp now is ready to receive the second filling pick. Pull the heddle frame up, insert the butterfly into the open shed and pull it through to the opposite side of the warp; close the shed. Grasp the top of the rigid heddle and beat it firmly against the second filling pick. Continue the weaving in this manner. The weaver should expect to use up several inches of warp before he establishes a regular rhythm and an evenly measured beat. Even the most experienced weaver must find the rhythm of beating that is best suited to the particular piece he is weaving.

Measuring the belt length will begin at the point where the weaving becomes even. At this point, insert into the regular shedding sequence two picks of yarn in a color which contrasts with the belt yarn. These are called *felling marks* and indicate the beginning of the belt. Do not tuck the ends of these yarns into the shed; allow them to hang free from the edges of the warp so they can easily be pulled out later. To keep count of the amount of weaving done, pin a tape measure to the woven material at the felling marks. Each time the weaving builds up to a point which is uncomfortable for the weaver to reach, the woven area must be wound forward onto the dowels. Prior to this *take-up*, the tape measure is stretched forward and pinned close to the *fell*, or last woven picks of the cloth; then the pin previously inserted is removed. When the fabric is being wound forward, take care that the tape measure is not wound in with it.

To roll the woven cloth forward, unfasten the backstrap and straighten the knots and ends at the warp stick. They should be stretched out along the dowel so that they will not bunch up and affect the tension of the warp ends. Holding the tied warps in this position, roll the dowels toward the top side of the warp. When the fell of the cloth is within two or three inches of the cloth stick, place the slat of wood (mentioned on page 26) along the underside of the roll of woven material, parallel with the dowels. Approximately midway between the edges of the warp and the ends of the dowels, put a piece of cord around the slat of wood and tie it to the cloth stick; then circle the cord around the whole group of dowels and tie it in place, as shown in Fig. 27. Adjust the backstrap, bringing it around the waist and attaching it to the cloth stick, and continue with the weaving as before.

FIG. 27. *The slat of wood, mentioned on page twenty-six, is slipped under roll of woven material and tied to cloth stick and dowels in a parallel position. Drawing, Don Wight.*

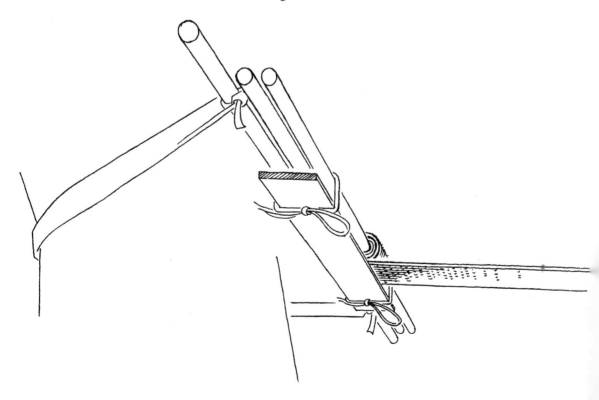

When the one-yard mark on the tape has been reached, the belt is finished. The last pick of filling should be wound once around the warp end at the selvage, on whichever side the filling ends, and tucked into the shed for a distance of four or five warp ends. This end of filling is pulled up between two warp ends to the surface of the cloth. It should be left lying free, to be cut away later.

Taking the Belt from the Loom

When the weaving is finished, do not cut the *thrums*, or excess warp, left at the beginning and end of the warp; this will make the fringe.

Unroll the belt and pull out the dowels that are between the tie-on knots and the beginning of the weaving. Then untie the warp ends from the cloth dowel. Carefully ravel the filling picks up to and including the felling marks that were inserted to indicate the start of the belt. Remove the warp from its hitching point and untie the knot at this, the uncut, end. Pull the warp ends even, cut through the looped yarns at the end of the warp and remove the rigid heddle. The belt is now ready to be fringed.

Making the Fringe

There are many methods of making fringe; perhaps the simplest is tying groups of warp ends together to form a row of simple knots at the line of weaving. Fig. 20 shows the warp end tied in groups of four. The knots should be pushed as close as possible to the last filling pick so that the weaving will be kept in place.

Knot-tying is made easier if the belt is laid flat on a table and weighted down with some object heavy enough to hold the belt securely while the warp ends are pulled even and taut. Pull the belt forward until the line of weaving, where the knots are to be made, is a few inches beyond the edge of the table. Gather together the first group of warp ends at one edge of the warp, pull them evenly taut and make the knot, pushing it tight against the filling yarns. When all the warp ends have been knotted, smooth out the fringe and cut it to the desired length.

CHAPTER THREE

The Four-Harness Foot-Power Loom

Hand-weaving looms have undergone many changes since the invention of the shedding device, but these have been in the nature of structural improvement rather than functional invention.

The foot-powered hand loom most in use today is not so far removed in function from its primitive counterpart as it might seem. Instead of a tree branch or a pair of ground stakes, it has two rotary beams between which the warp yarns are stretched. Instead of a stick or a single frame, the shedding mechanism consists now of a series of frames, or *harnesses*, attached to and controlled by the *lams* which, in turn, are operated by *treadles*. (Hand levers on a table loom serve the same purpose as treadles on the floor loom.) The *beater* still is a comblike device, but usually is made of metal instead of wood or reeds. These working parts are contained in a free-standing frame which has no function other than that of supporting the loom parts.

The foot-controlled mechanism which leaves the weaver's hands free to operate the shuttle and beater is undoubtedly the most significant change.

LOOM PARTS AND LOOM MOTIONS

Each part of the loom performs a specific function and all of these are interrelated. However, in the course of familiarizing himself with the total operation of a loom, the weaver will find it helpful to classify the parts by groups which relate in general to the following loom motions:

(1) let-off motion, (2) shedding motion, (3) beating, or beat-up motion, and (4) take-up motion.

Following the method for dressing the loom in Project 3, beginning on page 52, the description here of loom parts starts at the back of the loom and progresses to the front.

The parts of the loom are shown in Figs. 28 and 29. The first is a diagrammatic sketch showing a side view of a counterbalanced foot-powered hand loom. The other is a perspective drawing which shows the moving parts of the loom, with the warp in place. The numbers in these illustrations correspond with those in the description of loom parts that follows.

Loom Parts Related to Let-Off Motion

Beginning at the back of the loom, the loop end of the wound warp is slipped onto the *warp stick* which is secured to the *warp beam* (1) by cords, or a piece of

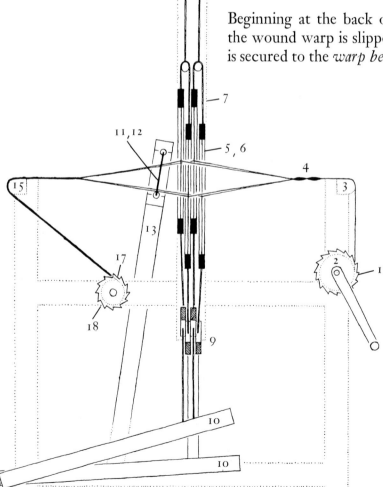

FIG. 28. *Diagram showing side view of working parts of counterbalanced foot power loom: (1) warp beam (2) ratchet (3) back beam (4) lease sticks (5 & 6) heddles and heddle eye (7) harnesses (8) castle (9) lams (10) treadles (11 & 12) reed and dents in reed (13) beater (14) cloth stick (shown in Fig. 29) (15) breast beam (16) cloth beam apron (shown in Fig. 29) (17) cloth beam (18) ratchet at front of loom. Drawing, Don Wight.*

canvas called the *warp apron*. The warp apron and the warp stick, not shown in Figs. 28 or 29, correspond with the *cloth apron* (16) and the *cloth stick* (14) shown at the front of the loom on Fig. 29. The *warp beam* (1) is a cylinder of wood or metal which can be revolved, and around which the warp yarns are wound. It is held stationary by a notched device called a ratchet (2) which can be released, thereby allowing the warp yarns to be rolled forward toward the front of the loom. This releasing of the warp is called the let-off motion. From the warp beam the warp ends go up and over the stationary *back beam* (3) which rests horizontally on the two side posts at the back of the loom. The back beam supports the yarns at the same level as does a corresponding beam, parallel to it, at the front of the loom, thus maintaining the horizontal position of the warp.

The Cross

In the process of making a warp, as explained on page 48, the warp yarns are wound alternately over and under a series of pegs on the warping reel, or warping

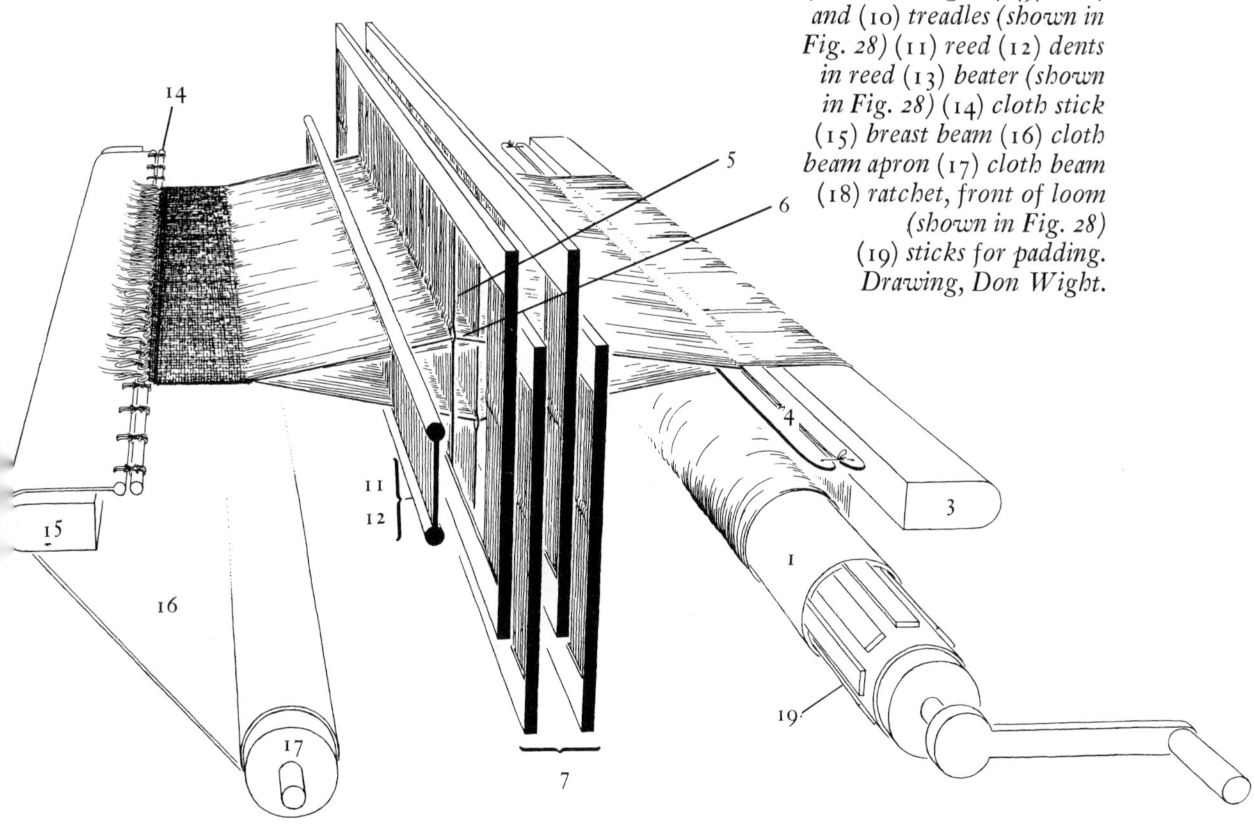

FIG. 29. *Perspective drawing of moving parts of loom with warp in place: (1) warp beam (2) ratchet (shown in Fig. 28) (3) back beam (4) lease sticks (5 & 6) heddles and heddle eye (7) harnesses (8) castle (shown in Fig. 28) (9) lams, and (10) treadles (shown in Fig. 28) (11) reed (12) dents in reed (13) beater (shown in Fig. 28) (14) cloth stick (15) breast beam (16) cloth beam apron (17) cloth beam (18) ratchet, front of loom (shown in Fig. 28) (19) sticks for padding. Drawing, Don Wight.*

board, forming a *cross* in the yarns which keeps them in proper sequence. When the warp is wound onto the warp beam, this sequence is maintained by inserting two *lease sticks* (4) through the warp, one at each side of the cross in the yarns. Although the lease sticks are accessories rather than loom parts, they are included here because of the special importance of their function. Without them the warp could not be transferred from the warp winder to the warp beam except as a tangled mass of yarns without order. The lease sticks also relate to the shedding motion, described next, in that they hold the yarns in proper sequence for drawing them through the heddles.

Loom Parts Related to Shedding Motion

The warp yarns come forward from the back beam, through the lease sticks and then are drawn in, or threaded, through the *heddles* (5) which are lengths of string or metal made with an opening, called an *eye* (6) at the center of their length. (See also Fig. 43, page 66.) The heddles are held suspended on a series of frames called *harnesses* (7), which are supported by a superstructure called the *castle* (8). The harnesses are attached to the *lams* (9) which are side-hinged levers lying directly beneath and parallel to the harness frames. In turn, the lams are tied to the *treadles* (10) so that when a treadle is depressed the harness or harnesses connected with it by the lam tie-up are raised or lowered, thereby raising or lowering all the yarns that are threaded through the heddles on those particular harnesses. The heddles in their frames, the lams, the treadles, and their connecting parts comprise the shedding motion of the loom. The *shed*, shown in Fig. 29 on page 39, is the open space between the raised and lowered yarns through which the filling yarns are inserted and passed across the warp.

Loom Parts Related to Beating or Beat-Up Motion

From the heddles, the warp ends are entered in systematic sequence through the *reed* (11), which is a rigid frame made up of two horizontal rods between which are set a series of narrow, vertical, evenly spaced bars.

The slots or spaces between the bars are called *dents* (12). The size of the reed is designated by the number of dents there are to each inch. There may be, for example, only 6 spaces or dents to the inch in which case the reed is called a No. 6 reed. A reed with 10 dents per inch is a No. 10 reed, and so on. Reeds used by hand weavers seldom number fewer than 4 or more than 30 dents per inch, with sizes in the middle range most in use. Since the reed holds the warp yarns apart at a specific distance, it becomes the first factor in controlling the tightness or looseness, called the destiny, or *sett*, of a woven fabric.

The reed is held in a sturdy frame that pivots from either the top or the bottom of the loom. The reed together with this swinging frame is called the *beater* (13). It is used to pack or beat the filling yarns into place as they are put through the sheds of the warp. If the beater is pulled forward lightly against the filling yarns there will be fewer picks per inch in the woven cloth than if the beater is moved forward forcibly, causing the filling yarns to be packed tightly into the warp. The beating of filling yarns into the warp is called the beat-up motion and is the second factor in determining the density of the cloth.

Loom Parts Related to the Take-Up Motion

When all the warp ends have been entered through the reed, they are gathered into groups and tied onto a stick or rod called the *cloth stick* (14). The cloth stick is secured to the *cloth beam* (17) by cords or a piece of canvas called the *cloth beam apron* (16). The yarns, tied to the cloth stick, travel over the *breast beam* (15), then down toward the cloth beam. The breast beam, except for the fact that it is at the front of the loom, is identical with the back beam (3).

These two beams, as already noted, support the warp in its horizontal position on the loom.

As weaving progresses between the heddles and the breast beam, the newly woven web is rolled forward onto the cloth beam. Since the cloth is rolled onto, or taken up by, the beam, this is called the take-up motion. The cloth beam is held stationary by a *ratchet* (18) which can be released whenever it is necessary to turn the beam to take up the woven cloth.

All contemporary hand looms, regardless of type, have the working parts that have been described, and the four loom motions: let-off motion, shedding motion, beating or beat-up motion, and take-up motion. Table looms have the same motions, but the treadles are replaced by hand levers.

For a description of the various types of looms and the characteristics of each, see Appendix A.

Equipment for Warping

A warp can be wound around any three stationary points, such as pegs or stakes, provided these furnish the means for keeping the warp taut, for making the cross in the yarns to keep them in proper sequence.

Warping devices most in use today are the *warping reel* and the *warping board* or frame. Since the warp for Project 3 will be wound on the reel shown in Fig. 32, page 51, the weaver is referred to the Appendix, on page 224, for information on using the warping board.

OTHER ACCESSORIES NEEDED: Other items which facilitate the warping process are shown in Fig. 30: (1) A floor swift or skein holder for holding yarns; (2) a spool rack or creel, for holding spools and tubes of yarn during the winding process, and (3) an umbrella swift for holding and winding yarns. The other items are used in threading, sleying the warp and in bobbin winding.

Preparing the Yarns for Warping

Yarns are put up in various kinds of packages. The most commonly available are the conventional circular skeins, pull skeins, cones, spools, and tubes. In the process of winding the warp, it is important to have the yarns set up so that they can be pulled freely from their packages. The yarns will be easier to handle if they are transferred to a spool or tube for warping.

Circular skeins come tied in one or more places to keep the yarn in order so that it can be unwound without tangling. Before these ties are cut, the skein should be stretched between the weaver's hands and examined carefully to see that all the strands are lying parallel, that is, under the ties, not over them. Any strand of yarn that crosses over a skein tie should be pulled back into place. Then the skein is stretched around the revolving drums of the swift, the skein ties are cut and the yarn is ready to be unwound for the warping.

If balls of yarn are used, they should be placed in a container, such as a cardboard box or a cooking pot, to keep them from rolling away during the winding process. Cones of yarn can be placed on the floor and the warping done directly from the cones. In this case it is best to place them behind the spool rack with the end of the yarn to be wound pulled straight up from the cone and laid over one of the rods in the rack. The rod serves as the direct feeding point from which the yarn is pulled.

FIG. 30. *Accessories used in warping and dressing loom, reading clockwise from lower left: (1) floor swift (2) spool rack, or creel (3) umbrella swift (4) heddle hook (5) lease sticks (6) template (7) spreader, or raddle (8) reed. At center, below creel, hand bobbin winder.*

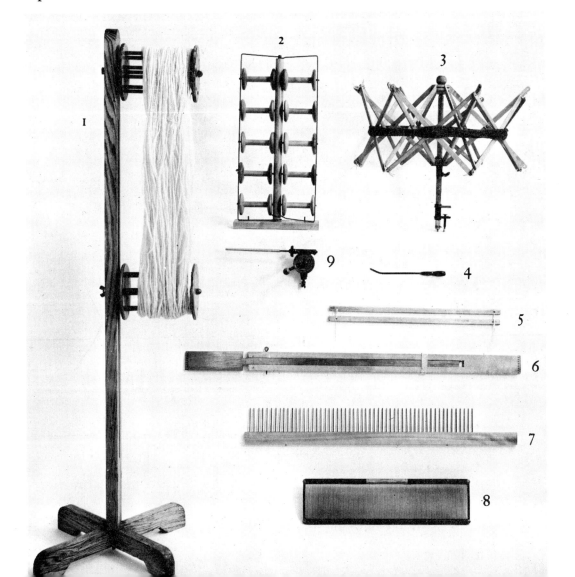

LEARNING TO USE THE LOOM
PROJECT 3

For the purpose of demonstrating loom motions, instructions are given on pages to follow for setting up and weaving a simple striped fabric, in plain weave, suitable for a pillow cover, or a small length of upholstery for chair seat or handbag. Directions for weaving

FIG. 31. *Project 3, material for pillow cover; plain weave, woven on four harnesses on a straight draw, of 8/4 wool; black warp, filling black and magenta; pattern of irregular bandings in black, in magenta, and black and magenta pick-and-pick stripes. Designed by Azalea Thorpe. Photo, Ferdinand Boesch.*

the material on a four-harness setup are accompanied by detailed description of equipment and accessories used, preparation for warping, winding the warp, dressing the loom and tying it up.

Specifications and Calculations for Project 3

Before a warp can be wound, it is necessary to determine the length and width of the fabric to be woven and to calculate the amount of yarn required. As with the outline given for previous projects, the following calculations have been figured on the generous side. They are based on the requirements for a piece of fabric of sufficient size to make a finished pillow cover 15 inches square.

(1) Warp yarn specifications
Fiber: wool   Size: 4/8   Color: black

(2) Calculating width of warp to be set up on the loom:

	Inches
width of finished pillow cover	15.00
allowance for weave-in (or pull-in), 10 per cent	1.50
allowance for shrinkage in finishing, 10 per cent	1.50
allowance for hems, 1 inch each side	2.00
width of warp to be set up on loom	20.00

(3) Calculating length of warp to be wound:

length of fabric to cover both sides of pillow 15 inches square	30.00
allowance for warp take-up, 10 per cent	3.00
allowance for shrinkage in finishing, 20 per cent	6.00
allowance for hems, 1 inch each side	2.00
allowance for loom waste (tying on, etc.)	36.00
allowance for practice and experimentation	36.00
Length of warp to be wound	113.00

Length of warp converted to yards:
113 inches ÷ 36 inches   3 yards 5 inches
(Since the allowances for waste and experimentation are generous and since it is often easier to

work with round figures, a warp length of three yards will be sufficient.)

(4) Calculating the number of warp ends required:
Reed: No. 10   Sett: 1/10 (meaning that one warp end will be entered through each dent of a No. 10 reed, making a warp sett of 10 ends per inch.)
Total number of ends required for fabric 20 inches wide:
10 (ends per inch) × 20 inches   200 warp ends

(5) Calculating the amount of yarn needed for the warp:
200 warp ends × 3 yards (length of each warp end)   600 yards
Since a pound of 4/8 wool yields around 1100 yards, the amount of yarn needed for the warp will be a little over a half-pound.

(6) Calculating the amount of yarn needed for the filling:
Amount of yarn required for one filling pick:
20 inches plus 10 per cent for take-up: 22 inches (The filling yarns, rather than lying flat between the warp yarns, move under and over them so that the length of yarn for each filling pick exceeds the width of the warp. Therefore, this calculation is based on the width of the warp, 20 inches, plus a 10 per cent allowance for the interlacing movement, or take-up, of the yarns.)

Approximate number of filling picks per inch of woven fabric   10
Amount of filling yarn needed to weave one inch of woven fabric: 10 (picks per inch) × 22 inches (amount required for each pick)   220 inches
Filling yarn required for 1 yard (36 inches) of woven fabric: 220 inches × 36 inches
7920 inches
Converted to yards: 7920 inches ÷ 36 inches = 220 yards of filling yarn required to weave one yard of fabric.

As pointed out in Chapter 2, the number of inches of yarn required to weave one inch of fabric is equal to the number of yards of yarn required to weave one yard of fabric. Therefore, calculations involving multiplication by 36 followed by division of the result by 36 may be omitted. For example, in the calculations above, the figure which represents the number of inches of yarn required for one inch of fabric can be directly converted to the number of yards of yarn required for one yard of fabric as follows:

Amount of yarn required to weave one inch of fabric:
10 (picks per inch) × 22 inches (amount required for each pick)   220 inches

Amount of filling yarn needed for one yard of woven fabric   220 yards

Amount of filling yarn needed to weave 3 yards of fabric:

220 yards (required for one yard of fabric) × 3
                                                          660 yards

Since the cloth will shrink both when the loom tension is released and in the finishing, the number of picks per inch will be greater in the finished fabric than in the fabric on the loom. This is true especially of wool because of its elasticity and its tendency to shrink.

For Project 3, a striped effect in two colors is suggested, using 4/8 wool for both warp and filling. As shown in Fig. 119, interesting stripes can be woven with one filling yarn the same color as the warp and another in a contrasting color.

When but two colors are used in striping, the emphasis can properly be placed on spatial variation. The simplest solution to striping is a regular alternation of two colors used in equal dimensions. (See Roman stripe, Fig. 117, page 186.) The pattern becomes more interesting and complex with the introduction of additional variations. Any number of bands may be varied both in width and in sequence according to the whim and ingenuity of the weaver.

The colors used and their arrangement are left to the taste and preference of the individual.

WINDING THE WARP

Having prepared the yarns for the winding, the weaver will need to have at hand a pair of scissors and some stout cord, preferably in a color that contrasts with the warp yarn.

The Measuring Cord

Cut a piece of cord about half a yard longer than the warp is to be. For this project, which requires a 3-yard warp, a length of cord 3-1/2 to 3-3/4 yards will be enough. This is a measuring cord which serves as a guide in winding the warp to its required length.

Tie one end of the cord securely to the peg at the top of the reel. Revolve the reel to the left with the left hand and, with the right hand, guide the cord diagonally down around the reel to the lease pegs at the bottom. The angle of the cord on the reel may have to be adjusted so that it will reach the bottom pegs, with enough left to tie to the last pegs, and perhaps a small amount left over. If there is more than half a yard of cord left over, it means that the warp will be less than three yards long. If the surplus amounts to only a few inches it will create no serious problem, but if greater than that, an adjustment should be made in the angle of the cord and the number of times it circuits the reel. Or, it may be necessary to unscrew the two wing nuts that hold the peg bar in place and move the bar to that section of the winder which will accommodate the length of warp wanted.

When the cord has been adjusted to the correct length on the reel, carry it under the first peg at the bottom of the reel, over the center one, and then tie it securely to the last peg, making sure that it is pulled taut around the reel. Cut away any excess cord after it has been tied.

Tie the end of the black 4/8 wool to the peg at the top of the reel where the measuring cord is tied. Stand facing the reel, with the spool rack at the right. Hold the warp yarn in the right hand between thumb and forefinger so that the tension of the yarn can be felt and controlled as it is being wound onto the reel. Revolve the reel to the left with the left hand and wind the warp yarn around the reel, following the measuring cord to the bottom pegs. Continue to follow the course of the measuring cord carrying the warp yarn under the first peg at the bottom of the reel and over the second one. Then carry the yarn under, around, and over the end peg.

The warp yarn now is in position to be wound to the top of the reel, and the direction of the winding will, of course, be reversed, with the yarn being carried toward the left and the reel revolved to the right. Now, carry the yarn under both the second (center) peg and the first one, and follow the measuring cord to the top of the reel and, again, reverse the direction of winding by carrying the yarn around the top peg on which the warp was started. (It makes no difference whether the yarn goes over and under or under and over this peg.)

Two warp ends are now on the reel. Warp end No. 1 was wound by going from the top to the bottom of the reel; warp end No. 2 was wound when the direction of winding was reversed and the yarn was carried from the bottom of the reel to the top. Each time the yarn makes this complete circuit, top to bottom to top, two warp ends have been put onto the reel; the odd-numbered ends always begin at the top and end at the bottom of the reel and are wound in exactly the same way as end No. 1—under the first peg, over the second one, under and around the third peg; the even-numbered ends always begin at the bottom and end at the top of the reel and are wound in the same direction as end No. 2—over the third peg and under both the second and first pegs.

Whether a warping board or a warping reel is used, the winding should be done as smoothly and evenly as possible. In either case, the yarns should not be wound on top of one another. The correct way is to wind so that each new length of yarn, as the circuit is made, lies closely alongside the previous one. This method should be followed throughout the winding.

The Warp-Counting Cord

When ten ends, for the first inch of the warp, have been wound, secure the yarn temporarily at the top of the reel by winding it several times around the top peg. Cut a 36-inch length of cord in a color contrasting with that of the warp. Loop it around the yarns between the first peg and the center one at the bottom of the reel, and cross the cord ends to encircle the ten warp ends. As each successive group of ten warp ends is wound, mark it by crossing the cord ends to encircle the yarns.

This is a counting cord which helps in keeping count of the warp yarns as they are wound, and in separating the groups as required for spreading the warp later.

Marking the Center of Warp

When half the total number of warp ends is wound—in this case 100—cut a short length of cord and tie it around all the warp ends at a point between the center peg and the last one at the bottom of the reel. This tie, marking the center of the warp, relates to subsequent instructions for dressing the loom.

Continue the winding until the total of 200 warp ends has been wound onto the reel. The last warp yarn will end at the top of the reel. Cut this yarn, allowing enough excess to tie it to the top peg.

Then cut from the reel the measuring cord used to measure the length of the warp. Leave in place, temporarily, the cord that marks the center of the warp, and also the counting cord at the bottom of the reel. The excess length of this cord is tied up in a large looped bowknot.

The Lease Cords

As long as the warp remains on the reel, the all-important cross of the yarns is held by the pegs. Something, therefore, must be substituted for the pegs so that the cross will be retained during the process of transferring the warp from the reel to the loom. For this purpose cut several lengths of cord about 1 foot long. These are called *lease cords* and are used to tie the yarns in place at each side of the cross. *(Note:* All ties needed in weaving should be bow ties [or bowknots or slipknots] unless otherwise noted, else the weaver will find himself spending an unnecessary amount of time undoing knots.)

Run the forefinger alongside the center peg at the bottom of the reel; lift, slightly, all the yarns that lie on top of the peg and tie them together with one of the cord ties. In the same way, tie another length of cord around all the yarns that lie under the center peg. Now run the forefinger down through the warp at the point where it is marked by the center cord which divides the warp in half. Slide the outer half of the warp along the last peg to separate it slightly from the inside half. Slip a lease cord in between the upper and lower layers of the outside group of yarns and tie the cord at the point where the yarns go around the last peg. Tie the inside half of the warp in the same way. Then remove the cord that marked the center of the warp during the winding process. There are now four lease cords at the bottom of the warp, as well as the counting cord. Since the purpose of the lease ties at the cross of the yarns is merely to keep the groups separated, the bowknot should be firmly tied, but the cord itself need not be drawn tightly around the yarns.

Other Warp Ties, Called Chokes

The next series of ties, made in the body of the warp, are called *chokes*. These, too, should be bowknots, but the cords will need to be pulled around the warp yarns as tightly as possible since their purpose is to hold the yarns, when taken off the reel, in the same relative longitudinal position to one another as they had while on the reel.

The most important choke tie is the first one. It should be especially firm and should be about 36 inches from the cross end of the warp. The number of chokes depends upon the kind of warp being wound, its length, and the skill of the weaver. On floor reels, which usually have a span of 27 or 36 inches between the arms, chokes are generally made in every space. The last choke should be near the top end of the warp. Fig. 32

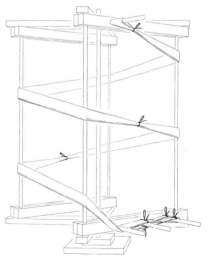

FIG. 32. *A warp wound on floor reel, showing peg and choke ties in place. Drawing, Don Wight.*

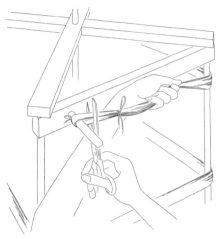

FIG. 33. *In the removing of warp from reel, it is grasped firmly with one hand and cut with scissors in the other hand, as close as possible to top peg. Drawing, Don Wight.*

shows a warp on a reel with choke ties, plus peg ties, in place.

Removing the Warp from the Reel

With all the ties in place, the warp is ready to be taken off the reel. The warp must be kept under tension while being removed, and to offset the pull required to keep it taut during this process, the weaver will need to brace the reel with a knee or a shoulder.

As shown in Fig. 33, the warp is grasped firmly with the right hand at a point halfway between the top peg and the first arm of the reel to the right of the peg. In this position, and with an elbow or shoulder braced against the reel, the warp is cut with scissors as close as possible to the top peg.

As it is being unwound from the reel, make a series of slipknots in the warp at regular intervals approximately one yard apart. A general rule to follow in placing the knots is that the first one be made about half a yard from the cut end of the warp at the top of the reel, and the last one about one yard away from the cross at the lower pegs on the reel. The steps involved in the process of making these slipknots are shown in Figs. 34-40. Fig. 40 shows a section of the warp as it appears with the knots in place. These knots keep the yarns from tangling and make the warp easier to handle. They are easily released later with a mere pull on the warp.

The same routine is followed for removing the warp from the warping frame, or board, as from the reel. When the warp has been removed from reel or board, it is laid aside carefully while the loom is being prepared for the process of dressing.

DRESSING THE LOOM

The term "dressing the loom" means, literally, putting the warp on the loom. The five steps in the process are: (1) winding the warp onto the warp beam; (2) drawing the warp ends through the heddles; (3) entering the warp ends into the reed, called sleying; (4) tying the

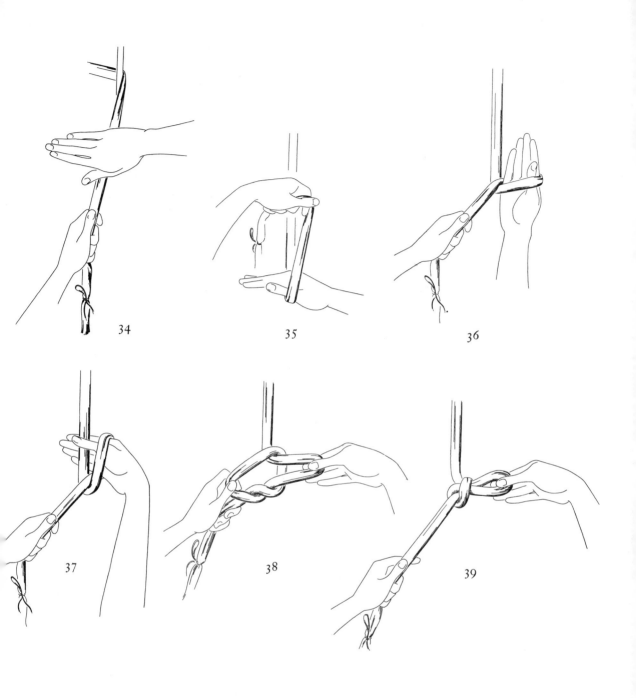

34

35

36

37

38

39

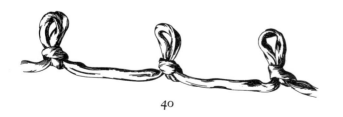

40

warp to the cloth stick, and (5) putting in the heading, adjusting tension and checking for errors.

The several tools and accessories used in connection with this process should be assembled first. (Some are shown in Fig. 30.) They are as follows:

(1) The reed; for this project, 10 reed.

(2) Two lease sticks several inches longer than the width of the warp, each with a hole at each end.

(3) A spreader, or raddle, to keep the warp spread to its proper width while it is being beamed. Raddles consist of a length of wood set with wooden pegs or steel pins at regular intervals, usually an inch apart, and a slotted length of wood that fits in place on top of the pegs or pins after the warp yarns have been put into the spaces between them. An adequate substitute for the manufactured device can be made quite simply by driving headed nails at 1-inch intervals into a slat of wood, 1 inch by 2 inches, so that the nailheads extend about an inch and a half above the surface of one side of the slat.

(4) Two lary sticks which must be several inches longer than the depth of the loom from the back beam to the breast beam and strong enough to bear, without bending, the weight of the lease sticks and the spreader which will rest on them during the spreading and beaming processes. These can be made of pine strips an inch wide by an inch thick, sanded smooth.

(5) A low stool for the weaver to sit on while drawing the warp ends through the heddles, a process which is made easier by having the center of the heddles at eye level.

(6) A draw hook (see Fig. 43.) for drawing the warp ends through the heddle eyes

(7) A pair of scissors

(8) Material for padding—or, rather, "layering"—the warp beam. This can be done with smooth, flat sticks about one inch wide by a quarter-inch thick, and at least 2 to 4 inches longer than the width of

the warp. But the easiest material to use is heavy wrapping paper, or better still, lightweight corrugated paper cut somewhat wider than the width of the warp and in whatever length is available or convenient to handle. There is no disadvantage in using several short lengths of paper and considerable disadvantage in trying to tussle with a length of paper so long as to be clumsy. The weaver should have a supply of both sticks and paper because these materials are in use, one way or another, whenever a warp is put on the loom. (See Fig. 29, item 19.)

Preparing the Loom for Beaming

Remove the beater frame from the front of the loom if it is removable. If not, remove the reed and the bar above it and lay these out of the way. Drop the castle if that is convenient. If not, divide the heddles equally, sliding half of them to the right side and half to the left side of each harness, thereby clearing a space of at least 20 inches through the center of the harnesses. Lay the warp through this space so that the uncut end, where the cross in the yarns is tied, hangs toward the back of the loom and the cut end hangs over and in front of the breast beam.

At the back of the loom, release the ratchet that controls the warp beam and pull the warp stick upward until the stick has been pulled over the back beam and 3 or 4 inches beyond it. Make a pencil mark at the center nail in the stick and two additional marks indicating a distance of 10 inches to the right of the center mark and 10 inches to the left of it. The two outside marks show the position which the 20-inch warp will occupy when it is centered on the stick. Masking tape may be used for this purpose if preferred.

Reaching forward toward the harnesses, pull the uncut end of the warp toward the back of the loom until it reaches the warp stick. Using the lease cord nearest the loop end of the warp as a guide, separate the upper and lower layers of the yarn and slip the stick through half of the warp, then through the center apron cord and, finally, through the remaining half of the warp.

Now slip the two end apron cords over the ends of the warp stick, allowing any other cords that may be on the apron to hang free for the moment. The warp stick now holds the same position in the warp as was occupied by the last peg at the bottom of the warping reel.

Lay one lary stick at the right side of the loom so that it rests on the back beam and the breast beam, spanning the distance between the two; lay the other lary stick in the same position at the left side of the loom. If the width of the warp equals, or is close to, the weaving width of the loom, the lary sticks are usually placed between the harness frames and the castle upright. If the width of the warp is appreciably narrower than the weaving capacity of the loom, a space for the lary sticks can be made between the heddles that were pushed to the sides of the harnesses. Tie each lary stick to the breast beam with a piece of cord. In Fig. 41, this cord is shown close to the left hand of the person holding the warp at the front of the loom.

FIG.41. *The beaming process showing the holder at front of loom, the winder at back of loom. Note cord which ties the lary stick to breast beam at left of holder's hand. Drawing, Don Wight.*

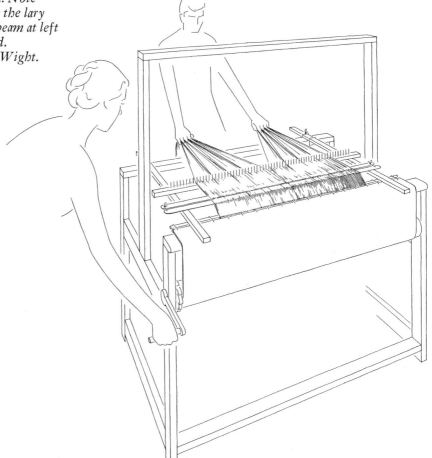

At the front of the loom pull the warp forward firmly so that the weight of it, hanging over the breast beam, pulls against the warp stick. This causes some tensioning of the yarns and makes the warp easier to handle. Again going to the back of the loom, insert one of the lease sticks through the cross so that it lies alongside and slightly forward of the warp stick, in the same tied opening of the warp. Separate the upper and lower layers of the cross where the second set of ties was made and slip the second lease stick through this opening. Immediately tie the lease sticks together so that the warp cannot slip off the ends during the beaming process. It is common practice to leave up to 6 inches of play between the lease sticks so that they can be manipulated independently during the beaming process.

Before removing any of the ties, check the warp carefully to make certain that it is properly set up on the loom. If the warp was wound and tied correctly, and if all other instructions were followed as given, one of the lease sticks will be lying parallel to, and just in front of, the warp stick, through the same opening of the warp. The second lease stick will be lying parallel to the first one but through the warp opening on the other side of the crossed yarns. The lease sticks lying as they do at each side of the cross will hold each warp end in correct sequence. Now remove the four cord ties that were used to secure the cross in the yarns, but leave in the warp-counting cord.

Spreading the Warp

The warp must now be spread out so that it can be rolled onto the warp beam at the specified width of 20 inches. Since the warp ends are to be set 10 ends per inch in the reed, 10 warp ends must be in each of 20 spaces between nails. Make a pencil mark at the center nail or peg in the spreader, and two additional marks indicating the tenth nail (10 inches) to the right of the center mark, and the tenth nail (10 inches) to the left of it.

The bowknot in the counting cord is now untied and the excess length is spread across the 20 warp groups. Now raise the warp slightly, and slip the spreader underneath it. Place the spreader, peg-side up, on the lary sticks between the lease sticks and the harnesses. See that the center of the spreader is aligned with the center of the loom. At this point, hold the warp taut with one hand while moving the lease sticks as close as possible to the back of the loom, and move the spreader to a position a few inches forward of the lease sticks.

Standing at the back of the loom, reach in front of both the lease sticks and the spreader and grasp the left half of the warp firmly with the left hand, stretching it taut against the warp stick which holds it. This tautness will make it easy to pick out the warp ends in their proper order. Working from the left edge of the warp toward the center, pick out the first 10 warp ends encircled by the counting cord and place them in the first space to the right of the pencil mark at the left side of the spreader. Pick out the next 10 ends in the same way and place them in the second space to the right.

Continue this process until all the warp ends in the left half of the warp have been distributed across the left half of the spreader—10 to each space. Now follow the same procedure for the right half of the warp, working from the center to the right selvage. Then, holding the warp taut, take out the counting cord.

When the spreading has been completed, the warp should occupy 10 spaces to the left and 10 spaces to the right of the center of the spreader, a total of 20 spaces approximating the 20-inch width required.

Cut a piece of cord about 30 inches long and tie one end of it to the first nail outside the warp yarns at the left side of the warp. Pull the cord taut and circle it clockwise around the next nail to the right, and to each successive nail until all the nails have been encircled. Tie the cord to the last nail outside the right edge of the warp. All across the warp, push the cord down so that it lies close to the warp yarns at the base of the spreader. This will prevent the yarns from being pulled out of the spreader while the warp is being beamed.

THE BEAMING PROCESS

Of all the procedures in dressing the loom, beaming is the least mechanical and the most subject to the subtleties of manual control. Method and manner are important in order to make beaming as simple as possible for a smooth tight beam of yarn which will make the weaving easier later on. Because excessive handling of the yarns tends to get them out of sequence and to make them fuzzy, beaming should be done simply and quickly, with a sure but light hand.

The beaming process is greatly facilitated if one can enlist a helper to hold the warp taut at the front of the loom while it is being wound onto the beam, as shown in Fig. 41. The helper, called the holder, usually takes care of the tasks to be done at the front of the loom, such as straightening the warp yarns, holding them taut, and keeping the tension of the warp even while it is being beamed.

As the warp is moved from the front of the loom toward the warp beam, the holder will need to pull out the slipknots made when the warp was taken off the reel, and remove the warp ties made while the warp was on the winder. This will free the warp ends so that they can be straightened and will spread out to the required width.

If the cord ties, made in the body of the warp when it was on the winder, were tied tightly around the warp yarns, they should now be holding the yarns in the same lengthwise position, relatively, as they held on the reel. And if the tension of the yarns was kept uniform during the winding, the warp should require only minimum adjustments during the beaming process. In straightening the warp yarns, preparatory to beaming them, the warp should always be held just below a choke tie so that the relative lengthwise position of the yarns will not be disturbed. The choke ties and the slipknots keep the warp yarns from tangling and neither should be removed beyond the point where the warp, hanging over the front of the loom, clears the floor. They should be removed, however, before they pass the breast beam.

Before removing the first choke, the tie closest to the spreader, grasp the warp at the point just below it and shake the warp several times, using a forward, jerking motion. Do this carefully and deliberately several times. Pull the warp taut to determine whether any yarns are tangled or unduly slack. (Any slack end inevitably will have its corresponding tight end on the other side of the loop.) If necessary, the shaking should be repeated.

Remove all cord ties and slipknots from the length of warp that lies between the spreader and the floor. This allows the holder to grasp the warp well in front of the breast beam and leaves no ties close to the spreader. The warp now is divided so that half of it is held in the right hand, the other half in the left hand.

The holder should stand as far from the breast beam as possible, with feet apart, and should lean back slightly, taking a stance which allows the weight of his body to pull against the warp.

When the warp has been shaken and is being held under tension, the winder—attending to the tasks that must be performed at the back of the loom—begins to revolve the warp beam by turning the crank handle provided for this purpose. The beam should be wound slowly and evenly to help maintain even tension of the warp. The winder will need to keep a constant check on tension. He does this by running the flat of his hand across the top of the warp in the area between the back beam and the warp beam. The holder will need to give particular attention to the selvages of the warp; these should be kept as taut as the rest of the warp.

As the warp is rolled onto the warp beam, the lease sticks and spreader will move with it. The winder will need to watch these and periodically push them forward. The lease stick closest to the spreader can almost always be moved easily; the lease stick closest to the back of the loom cannot be pushed forward as easily because it lies behind the cross in the yarns. If the yarns become tangled in any way at the cross, it will be necessary to straighten them out before the lease stick can be pushed forward; forcing the stick forward is likely to cause yarn breakage. When tangled yarns reach the cross they will lock the lease stick in. These must be untangled by the winder; not until these have been smoothed out can the lease stick be moved forward. Usually warp ends that have been tangled will be slack when untangled. This slack, or excess warp, belongs on the beam; therefore, the excess should be pulled back by the winder. Much of this trouble can be avoided if the holder will shake the warp while the spreader and lease sticks are being pushed forward.

Padding for the Warp

As the warp is wound onto the warp beam, a separation of some kind must be provided between the layers of yarn to ensure that the yarns build up evenly. This padding, or layering, material must be wider than the warp but not as wide as the warp beam. When the warp stick with the warp looped around it has reached the warp beam, it is time to insert padding between the warp yarns and the beam. (See Fig. 29, item 19.)

Padding material may be flat sticks, heavy wrapping paper, or lightweight corrugated paper, which is best. If sticks are chosen, insert one or two at a time, laying them flat on the warp beam at the point where the warp is in position to be taken onto the beam. Revolve the warp beam slightly so that the warp yarns, held at tension by the holder, bind the sticks to the beam and prevent them from slipping out of position. Continue adding sticks, one or two at a time, laying them flat with edges abutting, until the beam has made a complete revolution and is covered with sticks bound to it by a layer of warp yarns. Secure this first roll of sticks to the beam by encircling both ends with a firmly tied length of cord. While the first round of sticks is being inserted, it is important that the holder keep the warp taut. Should he relax his hold, the sticks will slide under each other or slip out of the warp roll. If this should occur, remove the sticks, release the warp beam ratchet, allowing the warp to be pulled forward, and begin inserting the sticks again at the point where the warp is ready to be taken onto the beam.

On subsequent revolutions of the warp beam, the sticks should be inserted as is necessary to keep the layers of warp yarn separated. Two sticks per revolution is usually enough; sometimes only one will be needed.

If wrapping or corrugated paper is used it, too, must be wider than the warp but not as wide as the beam. When the warp is in position to be taken onto the beam, pull one end of the paper underneath, up, and around the beam until it is caught and held in place by the tension of the warp yarns on the beam. Be sure that the paper is given a straight start on the beam, otherwise it will wind on at an angle causing the warp yarns to fall off at one end. If this should happen, unroll the warp and start anew. When the first length of padding has been taken onto the beam, insert another length immediately following the first and continue the procedure until the beaming is complete.

When the cut end of the warp is even with or slightly past the breast beam, the beaming process has been completed. Using the center mark on the spreader as a guide, divide the yarns into two equal sections—the right half and the left half of the warp. Divide each section into several smaller groups of yarn and make a slipknot close to the end of each group. Remove the guard cord from the nails of the spreader and tilt the spreader, nail side down, in order to free the warp yarns, and slide it out at one side of the warp. Push the lease sticks as close as possible to the harnesses and adjust the lary sticks to a position which will allow the lease sticks to rest on them at a level slightly lower than the eye of the heddles. Or the lease sticks may be suspended by cords from the castle above, at this level. In this case, the lary sticks are removed from the loom.

THREADING THE HEDDLES

The next step in dressing the loom is called drawing-in or threading, the process of putting each of the warp ends through the eye of a heddle on one of the harnesses. The warp ends are drawn in on the harnesses in a specific sequence, according to the requirements of the weave. The threading is done with the aid of a long, slender implement with a hooked end called a threading hook or a draw hook. See Fig. 30, item 4, and Fig. 43 (page 66).

To thread the heddles, sit on a low chair or stool as close to the harnesses as is comfortable. From this position, the eyes of the heddles will be approximately at eye level and in clear view, as will the lease sticks holding the yarns in the crossed position which indicates the order for picking up and threading the warp ends. It is an advantage to have a loom which has either a removable breast beam or one which can be released and dropped to the floor so that it is out of the way while the threading is done. Otherwise, it may be possible to slide a low stool inside the loom, into the space between the breast beam and the harnesses.

The warp will be threaded in two sections: first, working from the center of the warp to the right edge; then, from the center to the left edge. The heddles are counted and then equally distributed on the harnesses, each harness with half of its total heddle load on the right side and half on the left side of the harness. If this plan is held to, it will be unnecessary to count heddles or to redistribute them when subsequent warps are put on the loom. Another advantage in the center-to-side method of threading is that if a project requires fewer heddles than the total number available on the harnesses and if the draw is balanced—meaning that each harness will carry the same number of yarns—the unused heddles will remain equally distributed at each side of the harnesses rather than all bunched at one side. An imbalance in the distribution of heddles is undesirable because it disturbs the balance of the harnesses and may cause undue friction of the yarns that lie next to the unused heddles, making it necessary to remove some of the heddles.

Whenever it is necessary to remove heddles from the harnesses, a length of cord or wire should be threaded through both the top and bottom openings of the heddles, where they are attached to the heddle bars of the harnesses. If cord is used, it sould be tied securely before the heddles are removed; if wire, the ends of it should be twisted together before removing the heddles. It should be noted that most metal heddles rest on the harnesses with the heddle eyes at an angle. Tying the heddles as described will keep all of them facing at the same angle and make it easier to replace them on the harnesses when needed. To add heddles to a harness, slip the number needed—in a group—onto the heddle bars and then remove the ties. Make certain that the group of heddles is put on at the same angle as those already on the harness.

Before beginning the threading process, see that the warp yarns extend from the warp beam in sufficient length to hang 10 to 12 inches in front of the harnesses. This is to prevent their slipping or being pulled out of the heddle eyes once they have been drawn through.

Numbering the Harnesses

Each harness is given a number according to its position in the loom. Some weavers number the harnesses from the back to the front of the loom; others prefer to begin the number sequence at the front of the loom so that the harness which is closest to the front is harness No. 1; this is followed by harnesses Nos. 2 and 3, and, finally, 4, which is closest to the back of a four-harness loom. This is the numbering sequence which will be used here.

The warp ends will be threaded through the heddles in a *straight draw* from left to right; this means that in working from left to right the first warp end will be drawn through a heddle on harness No. 1, the second warp end through a heddle on harness No. 2, the third warp end through a heddle on harness No. 3, and the fourth warp end through a heddle on harness No. 4. The next four warp ends will be drawn, similarly, one end through a heddle on each of the four harnesses in the sequence just described. This procedure must be repeated until all the warp ends have been drawn through the heddles. This sequence of drawing-in is sometimes called a right-hand twill threading, a term derived from the fact that the sequence of each of the threaded heddles forms a diagonal line similar to that in a twill-woven cloth.

Threading the Right-Hand Half of the Warp

The right-hand half of the warp will be threaded through the heddles grouped at the right-hand end of the harnesses. The chance of errors in threading will be reduced if the weaver will slide the first available heddle on each of the four harnesses from the side towards the center of each harness. (See Fig. 42.) Untie the slipknot in the first group of yarns on the left side of the right-hand half of the warp. Pull these yarns through to the front of the harnesses and place them so that they lie over the lower frames of the harnesses and between the four heddles just moved to the center of the harnesses and those grouped at the right-hand end of the harnesses. Hanging in this position, the yarns separate the four heddles, ready to be threaded, from the other heddles.

Since the correct sequence of the warp ends is indicated at the point where they cross between the two lease sticks, it is from the area just in front of the lease sticks that each warp end should be picked up for threading. Reach through the harnesses toward the lease and, beginning at the left side of the group of yarns just untied, pick up the first warp end which is not crossed in by any other warp end and which, therefore, can be moved to the left freely without interfering with any other warp end. Slide this yarn to the left of the four heddles that are in position for threading. Insert the draw hook through the eye of the heddle on harness No. 1 and pull this warp end through, as shown in Fig. 43. See that the remaining heddles (on

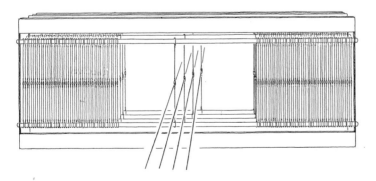

FIG. 42. *Before threading heddles, the weaver slides the first available heddle on each of the four harnesses from the side toward the center of each harness. Drawing, Don Wight.*

harnesses 2, 3, and 4) are kept to the right of this warp end. Pick up the next free warp end, slide it to the left of the three empty heddles, and draw it through the heddle on harness 2. Pick up the next warp end, slide it to the left of the two empty heddles and draw it through the heddle on harness 3. Pick up the fourth warp end in sequence, slide it into position and draw it through the heddle on harness 4. This completes the threading of the first four warp ends.

The second four-end unit is threaded in the same manner as the first one. Select the first heddle available at the right-hand end of each of the four harnesses and slide them slightly to the left. Reach through the harnesses to the right of these heddles and, circling the hand behind and to the left of them, pick up the group of yarns hanging loose over the lower bars of the harnesses. Lay the yarns over the harness bars to the right of the heddles and slide the heddles to the center of the loom. Select the next four warp ends in sequence and draw them on harnesses 1, 2, 3, and 4, in exactly the same way as the first warp ends were drawn. Continue this procedure, untying the slipknots from groups of yarns as needed, until all the warp ends in the right-hand half of the warp have been drawn through the heddles.

As the threading progresses, it is advisable to check for errors. In a simple draw such as this one, four units at a time can be checked. Hold the yarns taut with one hand and check for correct sequence with the side of the draw hook or index finger. When checked, each group of four units, totaling sixteen ends, should be tied in a slipknot to prevent their being pulled out of the heddles accidentally.

FIG. 43. *Threading the heddles; inserting the draw hook through the eye of the heddle on harness No. 1 to pull the warp end through. Drawing, Don Wight.*

Threading the Left-Hand Half of the Warp

The left-hand half of the warp will be threaded from right to left—opposite to the direction in which the right-hand half was threaded. Therefore, in order to retain a right-angled draw throughout the warp, the left-hand half must be drawn-in on the harnesses in the sequence of 4, 3, 2, 1. In every other respect the threading of the left-hand half of the warp follows the same procedure as that for the right-hand half.

Select the first heddle available at the left-hand end of each of the four harnesses and slide them to the center of the loom. To thread the first four-end unit in the left-hand half of the warp, draw the warp end which is first in sequence through the heddle on harness 4, keeping this heddle to the right of the three empty ones on harnesses 3, 2, and 1. Draw the next warp end through the heddle on harness 3, keeping this heddle to the right of the two empty heddles on harnesses 2 and 1. Draw the third warp end through the heddle on harness 2, keeping it to the right of the remaining heddle on harness 1. Draw the last end of the unit through the heddle on harness 1; this heddle will be at the extreme left of the group of four threaded heddles.

After completing the threading of this unit, compare it with the threading of the units in the right-hand half of the warp. If correct, the draw will be the same in both sections of the warp—beginning on the left with harness 1, and ending on the right with harness 4.

INCOMPLETE THREADING UNITS: In a warp totaling 200 ends, as specified for this project, each half section has 100 ends which divide evenly into 25 threading units of 4 ends each.

If the specifications were changed, however, in order to make the cloth narrower or wider and if the change should result in a warp with half sections comprised of ends in a number not divisible by four, the last group of ends at each edge of the warp would be fewer than the four required to complete the threading sequence.

In this particular project, the incomplete threading units would be unimportant; should they occur, simply follow the threading procedure as given for as many ends as are available. For example, if there are only two ends left in the last group at the right edge of the warp, they would be drawn in sequence on harnesses 1 and 2; at the left edge of the warp the two remaining ends would be drawn in sequence on harnesses 4 and 3.

THE SLEYING PROCESS

The next step in dressing the loom is entering the warp ends into the reed. This procedure is called sleying, illustrated in Fig. 44, which shows a warp with the right-hand half sleyed and the left-hand half in the process of being sleyed. The order in which the ends must be picked up and sleyed is the same as that in which they were drawn through the heddles.

If the breast beam has been removed, replace it in the front of the loom. The lary sticks should be placed so that all the threaded heddles lie between them, with one end of each stick resting on the breast beam, the other on the back beam so that they span the depth of the loom. Any unused heddles should be pushed aside so that they lie outside the sticks toward the ends of the harnesses.

FIG. 44. *Sleying the warp, or entering warp ends through the reed. The right-hand half of the warp has been sleyed, the left-hand half is in process of being sleyed. Drawing, Don Wight.*

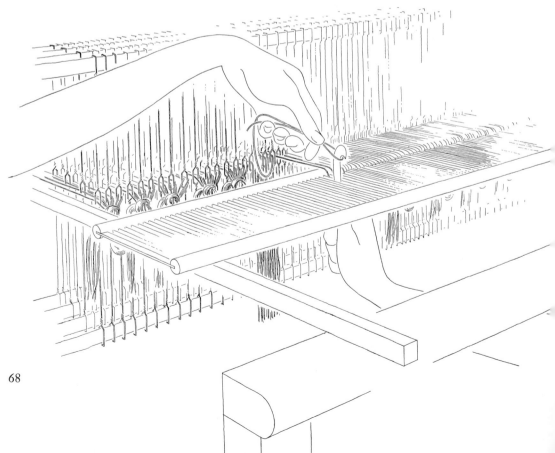

Lay the reed in front of the heddles, flat side down, across the width of the loom so that the reed is supported at each end by the lary sticks. If the sticks are too far apart to support the reed, push the threaded heddles toward the center of the loom and move the sticks closer together. When the sticks are in the correct position, lash them to the breast beam and the back beam with pieces of stout cord. Measure the width of the reed with a tape measure and mark its center by entering a 4- or 5-inch length of fine, colored yarn through the center dent of the reed, tying it tightly around one of the horizontal cross pieces. Clip off the ends of the yarn marker close to the knot. Once the reed has been measured and marked in this way, it will not need to be marked again for future projects.

As noted, the warp ends will be sleyed in the same sequence in which they were threaded: first, working from left to right on the right-hand half of the warp, and then working from right to left on the left-hand section. Beginning at the inside of the right-hand half of the warp, untie the slipknot in the first group of yarns. Let the loose warp ends hang down from the heddles in front of the harnesses, as shown just to the left of the weaver's hand in Fig. 44.

The first warp end at the left-hand side of the group of yarns just untied is the end which was drawn through the first heddle on harness 1 when the right-hand section of the warp was threaded. Move this heddle toward the center of the harness so that the yarn can be picked up and held in position over the center dent of the reed. Insert the sley hook from the underside of the reed through the center dent and catch the yarn in the hook. Pull the yarn down through the dent so that it hangs underneath the reed. The next warp end in sequence was drawn through the first heddle on harness 2; move this heddle and warp end toward the center of the harness, in position to be entered with the hook into the dent at the immediate right of the center dent. The next warp end in sequence was drawn through the first heddle on harness 3; move this heddle so that the yarn is over the empty dent at the immediate right of the last dent entered. The next warp end, drawn through the first heddle on harness 4, is entered through the empty dent immediately to the right of the last entered dent. This completes the sleying of the first group of four warp ends.

To continue the sleying, begin again with the warp end in the first heddle on harness 1 and draw it through the empty dent immediately to the right of the last entered dent. Pick up each subsequent warp end in sequence and sley it in the same way, moving one dent to the right each time.

When the first group of sixteen warp ends has been entered, tie the ends together in a slipknot at the underside of the reed. As the sleying progresses, tie all subsequent groups of ends in the same way. This will prevent the yarns from being pulled out of the dents inadvertently. Continue sleying the right-hand half of the warp until all the warp ends in this section have been entered into the reed.

To begin sleying the left-hand half of the warp, untie the first group of yarns at the right-hand side of the section. The first warp end at the right-hand side of this group is the end which was drawn through the first heddle on harness 4, when the left-hand half of the warp was threaded. Move this heddle toward the center of the harness; pick up the warp end and enter it through the empty dent which is immediately to the left of the marked center dent, where the sleying of the right-hand half of the warp was started. With the sley hook, pull this yarn through the dent to the underside of the reed.

Pick up the next warp end, drawn on harness 3, and enter it through the empty dent immediately to the left of the last entered dent. Sley, in sequence, the warp ends drawn on harnesses 2 and 1, moving one dent to the left each time. Continue until all ends in the left-hand half of the warp have been entered through the reed. As the sleying progresses, group the warp ends and tie them with a slipknot at the underside of the reed, as was done in the right-hand half of the warp.

When the sleying has been completed and all the warp ends have been tied into groups with a slipknot, slide the reed off the supporting lary sticks and lower the reed so that it hangs by the knotted warp ends. Untie the lary sticks and remove them from the loom. If the beater frame was removed from the loom, replace it. The horizontal bar at the top of the beater frame is adjustable so that it can be raised or lowered to accommodate the height of the reed. Usually this bar is held in position by wing nuts; loosen these and raise the bar high enough to allow the reed to be set inside the frame. As the reed is placed in the groove in the lower part of the beater frame, check to see that no warp ends are caught between the reed and the frame. Support the reed at one side so it will remain upright and lower the top bar of the frame until the reed is secure in the grooves of the top and bottom bars. If the reed is off-center, jar it with the hand until it slides into proper position. Then secure the top bar of the beater frame to the side pieces of the frame by tightening the wing nuts at each end of the bar.

THE TYING-ON PROCESS

Note: Before the warp is tied onto the cloth bar, the threading and sleying of warp ends should be carefully checked to see that no errors have been made. If there should be an error, it will be far easier to correct it before tying on the warp than after. It is safe to say that every weaver, sooner or later, is confronted by errors made in threading and sleying a warp. It was in order to minimize the incidence of errors, for example, that precautionary measures were suggested in the threading process—the grouping of heddles to correspond with the number of ends in the threading unit, and the separation of the unit heddles from the others on the harness. (See Fig. 42.) For detailed instruction in correcting errors, turn to Appendix D.

Before attempting to tie the warp onto the cloth stick, refer to Figs. 45-52, a step-by-step illustration of how the tie-on knot is made; also to Fig. 53, which shows a section of a warp tied onto the cloth stick. (*Note:* In Fig. 53, the tie-on has been started at right edge, working toward center; not from center, working alternately, to right and left.)

To prepare for tying on, release the ratchet that holds the cloth beam stationary and pull the cloth stick out in front of the loom, then up and over the breast beam until the stick is 3 or 4 inches beyond the inner edge of the breast beam.

In most looms there is a beam between the cloth beam and the breast beam which supports the apron, keeping it high enough to allow the weaver knee room. Make certain that the apron is pulled behind and over this beam before it goes over the breast beam. As a rule, this supporting beam is removable so that if the warp apron should be pulled from the cloth beam directly to the

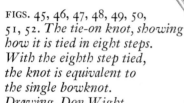

FIGS. 45, 46, 47, 48, 49, 50, 51, 52. *The tie-on knot, showing how it is tied in eight steps. With the eighth step tied, the knot is equivalent to the single bowknot. Drawing, Don Wight.*

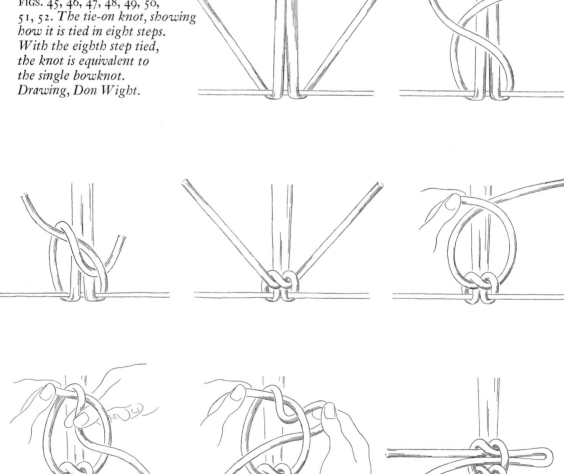

breast beam, without being carried over the supporting beam, it is unnecessary to untie the warp to correct the error. Simply remove the supporting beam from the loom, release the cloth beam ratchet, and pull the cloth apron forward until it is slack. Then insert the supporting beam in front of the apron.

The first warp ends to be tied onto the cloth stick are those at the very center of the warp. This tie is made first so that the cloth stick will be balanced and held parallel to the breast beam. As shown in Fig. 53, the warp ends are tied around the cloth stick in groups of equal size, except the selvage groups which usually are smaller.

For this project, ten ends will be used for each group except the two selvage groups which will have five ends each. Remove the slipknots from the right center and the left center of the warp. Working from center to right, pick up five ends from the right center group; let the remaining ends hang loose in front of the harnesses. Working from center to left, pick up five ends from the left center group of yarns. Gather the ten ends into a group and, using the right and left hands alternately, work the yarns forward until all of them are at the same tension when the group is pulled taut.

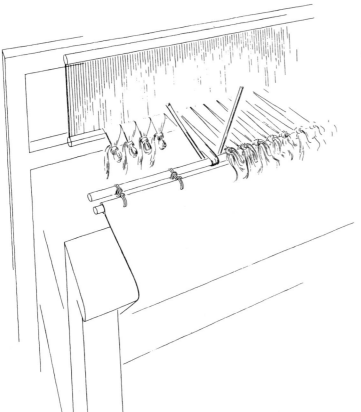

FIG. 53. *Tying the warp onto the cloth stick has been partially completed; warp ends are tied in groups of equal size using the knot described in Figs. 45-52. At this point only the first four steps of the knot are used. Drawing, Don Wight.*

Reach to the reed and divide the tie into two sections, each having five ends in sequence. Pull the two groups forward, keeping them at equal tension, and tie them around the center of the cloth stick, leaving a tail of yarns about 6 inches long. Complete only the first half of the knot shown in Figs. 45-48. The final knot, shown in the last four steps, Figs. 49-52, is not tied until all the warp groups have been secured to the cloth stick by the first half of the knot.

In tying on, the yarns should be kept as smooth and straight as possible so as to avoid the problems caused by twisted or tangled yarns. All subsequent warp ties are made alternately, to the right and to the left of the yarns already tied on. Therefore, the second group of yarns to be tied is comprised of the ten ends to the right of the center tie. Pick up these ends, working the yarns forward until they are even and taut; pull them straight forward from the reed and tie them onto the cloth stick. To make the third tie, repeat the process with the ten ends to the left of the center tie. Continue with this right-left alternation until all the groups of yarns have been thus secured to the cloth stick. The last two groups to be tied will be those at the selvages.

The tie-on knot—sometimes called the girth hitch—is completed as shown in Figs. 49-52. This is the equivalent of the single bowknot which is shown, also, as it looks on the loom in Fig. 23, page 31. Since it frequently is necessary to untie knots in order to make adjustments in tension, or to correct errors, the single bowknot is preferred here.

Again, the group of yarns at the center of the warp is tied first and all subsequent ties are made alternately to the right and to the left of the groups previously tied. Before starting with a tie, take up the slack that will have developed in the yarns since the first half of the tie-on knots was made. Grasp both sections of the tie, one in each hand, and pull them up firmly until the warp yarns are taut. The illustrations show the yarns in a slack position in order to indicate clearly the direction they take. After tightening the initial knot, however, do not allow the yarns to slacken. Try to maintain tension while the single bowknots are being completed.

These knots must be tied firmly enough to withstand warp tension while weaving is in progress.

When tying is finished, once more test the tension of the warp, both between the cloth stick and the reed, and at the back of the loom. Any variations in tension should be equalized by untying, retensioning, and then retying the yarns affected. The next step is to check the heddle bars at the top and bottom of the harnesses to see that they are securely fastened into the spring locks or hooks on the harness frames.

Gating the Loom

Before making the *tie-up* which will affect the sheds for the insertion of the filling, the harnesses must be adjusted so that they will be evenly balanced and will all hang at the same level and at the correct height. This is called *gating the loom.*

Begin at the top of the loom, with the uppermost cords which control pairs of harnesses. See that these cords are adjusted so that the harness rollers—horses, or pulleys—from which the harnesses are directly suspended, are hanging evenly and at the same height. Next, adjust the cords which are circled around these rollers to which the harnesses are attached so that all of the harnesses are hanging evenly and at the same height.

The correct height for the harnesses is determined by the point at which the warp yarns must intersect the reed in order to attain a full open shed. On a jack loom, the eyes of the heddles should be in line with a point barely above the bottom of the reed. With the heddle eyes in this position, the warp yarns that are to be raised can be lifted for the entire height of the reed, thus creating the widest possible opening between the upper and lower yarns of the shed. On a counterbalanced loom, the eyes of the heddles should be in line with the center point between the top and bottom of the reed. With the warp yarns intersecting the reed at this point, the rising yarns will move the same distance from the center to the top of the reed as the sinking yarns will move from the center to the bottom of the reed, thus creating the widest possible shed. Adjust the cords as necessary to hold the harnesses at the correct height,

75

then tie all of them together with a length of heavy cord bound tightly around their top frames at each end. This will prevent the harnesses from moving out of position while the tie-up between them, the lams, and the treadles is being made.

THE TIE-UP

On a foot-power loom the sheds are made by means of treadles to which the harnesses are connected. The tie-up is the order in which the lams are tied to the treadles. This order must be such that it will raise and lower the harnesses as required to produce a particular weave, in this case plain weave.

Since the instructions that follow are for a project woven on a *counterbalanced loom*, it is important to keep clearly in mind the rules which govern the raising and lowering of warp ends: when a treadle on a counterbalanced loom is depressed, the lams tied to that treadle will lower the corresponding harnesses, thus lowering the warp ends threaded on those harnesses. The harnesses which are not tied to that treadle will be raised by the counterbalance cords at the top of the loom, thus raising the warp ends threaded on those harnesses.

The action of a *jack loom* is different from that of a counterbalanced loom. Therefore, if the project is to be woven on a jack loom, it is important to keep clearly in mind the following rule which governs the raising and lowering of warp ends: when a treadle on a jack loom is depressed, the harnesses controlled by the lams which are depressed by that treadle will be raised, thus raising the warp ends threaded on those harnesses. The harnesses *not* controlled by those lams will remain in position, as will the warp ends threaded on those harnesses. (For further information on jack looms, turn to page 219.)

In planning the tie-up for plain weave, keep in mind the sequence in which the warp ends were drawn in on the harnesses. The threading unit consisted of four warp ends drawn from left to right with the first end on harness 1, the second on harness 2, the third on harness 3, and the fourth on harness 4. Since every four-end unit was threaded in this sequence, the warp ends in every unit throughout the warp will rise and sink according to the order planned for the warp ends in a single four-end unit. The first filling pick will interlace *under* the warp ends drawn on harness 1, *over* the ends on harness 2, *under* the ends on harness 3, and *over* the last ends of the unit on harness 4.

Therefore, for the first filling pick, harnesses 1 and 3 must be raised, thereby raising the yarns drawn on them so that the filling pick will lie *under* these yarns. At the same time, harnesses 2 and 4 will be lowered, thereby lowering the yarns drawn on them so that the filling pick will lie *over* these yarns. Since tying a lam to a treadle on a counterbalanced loom causes the corresponding harness to be lowered, the interlacing of the first filling pick requires that lams 2 and 4 be tied to the first treadle. When this treadle is depressed, harnesses 1 and 3 will be raised by the counterbalance motion. No tie-up is required on this first treadle for harnesses 1 and 3.

The second filling pick interlaces in the sequence opposite to that of the first pick. This second pick will interlace *over* the warp ends drawn on harness 1, *under* the ends on harness 2, *over* the ends on harness 3, and *under* the ends on harness 4. Therefore, for the second filling pick, harnesses 1 and 3 must be lowered so that the filling pick will lie *over* the yarns drawn on these harnesses. At the same time, harnesses 2 and 4 will be raised so that the second filling pick will lie *under* the yarns drawn on these harnesses.

The interlacing of the second pick requires that lams controlling harnesses 1 and 3 be tied to a second treadle; no tie-up for harnesses 2 and 4 is required on this treadle. Plain weave repeats on the alternation of these two filling picks. When the lams have been tied to the treadles, as described above, the tie-up is complete. A detailed, step-by-step description of the process follows.

The Lams

As already indicated, the *lams* consist of a series of bars lying underneath and parallel to the harnesses, controlling their movement. The lams on a *counterbalance loom* are connected at the *bottom* of the harness frames. When a treadle attached to the lams is depressed, it lowers the corresponding harnesses. The counterbalance mechanism at the top of the loom causes all the harnesses, not attached to that treadle, to rise. The lams on a *jack loom* are tied to cords which connect with jacks, or pulleys, at the top of the loom connected, in turn, with the *top* of the harness frames. Thus, when the treadle is depressed, the lams attached to that treadle are lowered but, because the cord runs to the jack at the top of the loom, and down to the top of the harness, that harness is raised. In either case, each lam is tied permanently to its corresponding harness and is numbered accordingly:

Harness 1 is tied to lam 1 which is closest to the front of the loom; harness 2 is tied to lam 2; harness 3 is tied

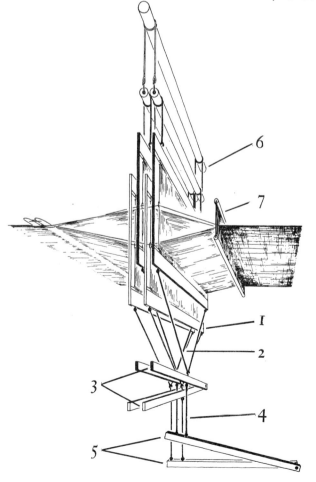

FIG. 54. *Diagram of loom showing parts involved in shedding motion and the tie-up:* (1) *lower edges of harnesses* (2) *lam cords* (3) *lams* (4) *treadle cords* (5) *treadles* (6) *rollers, above harnesses* (7) *reed. Drawing, Don Wight.*

to lam 3; and harness 4 is tied to lam 4 which is closest to the back of the loom.

All ties must be made so that the cords, or connecters, form a straight vertical line. To this end, the connecters on the lams are located directly above the corresponding connecting points on the treadles. (See Fig. 55.) This permanent connection between lam and harness assures an even, level pressure on the harness so that it rises or sinks in a level position irrespective of the position of the treadle used to activate it.

Connecting Points

A connecting point may be a hole or a screw-eye through which to pass a cord that connects a lam to a treadle, or it may be a metal connecter of some kind. Each lam has connecting points equal in number to the treadles on the loom. If the loom has six treadles, as do most four-harness looms, each lam will have six connecting points—one positioned directly above each treadle. Since there are four lams, there will be a total of four connecting points above each treadle, to be used for tie-ups on that treadle only. In turn, each treadle has four connecting points which correspond in position with those on the lams.

The four connecting points on each treadle are numbered 1 through 4, from front to back. Connecting point 1 is the tie-up position for lam 1 (which, as noted, controls harness 1). This is followed by connecting points 2 and 3, which are the tie-up positions for lam 2 and lam 3 respectively. Connecting point 4, closest to the back of the loom, is the tie-up position for lam 4.

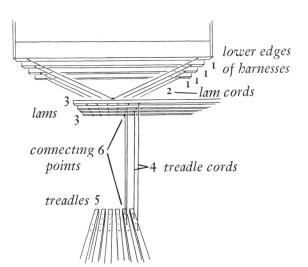

FIG. 55. *Connecting points and cords used in tie-up of loom: (1) lower edges of harnesses (2) lam cords (3) lams (4) treadle cords (5) treadles (6-6) holes in harnesses bottoms and lams for connecting points. Drawing, Don Wight.*

The treadles on a loom may be numbered in any sequence desired; from left to right or vice versa. All the treadles may be given permanent numbers or they may be numbered according to only those treadles needed to produce a weave. In the instructions given here for a counterbalanced, six-treadle loom, the four treadles on the right will remain unnumbered. The tie-up for plain weave will be made on the treadles at the left of the loom and these will be numbered 1 and 2, from left to right.

The connecting points on the lams also will be numbered from left to right to correspond with the numbering of the treadles. The four connecting points on the lams above treadle 1 are lam tie-up position No. 1, and are used for the tie-up on that treadle only. The four connecting points on the lams above treadle 2 are lam tie-up position No. 2, and are used for tie-ups on that treadle only.

Note: A single treadle can have tied to it as many lams as are required to produce the weave planned, except that all the lams on the loom cannot be tied to a single treadle. To do so would mean that all the harnesses were tied to move in the same direction and, therefore, a shed in the warp ends could not be made. A single lam can be tied to as many treadles as are required to produce the interlacing planned, except that a single lam cannot be tied to every treadle. To do so would result in the warp ends on that harness being moved, always, in the same direction no matter which treadle was depressed. Hence, on a counterbalanced loom, these warp ends always would be lowered, never interlacing with the filling picks.

Tie-Up Cords

Some looms are equipped with metal tie-up connecters which never need to be adjusted in length. Others, however, have ties made of a continuous length of cord with snap hooks (dog-leash type) at both ends so that the cords can easily be snapped into place on screw-eyes. Or, on treadle and lam there may be only one hook at the end of the lam cord and one at the end of the treadle cord; in this case, the two cords are snapped into position on lam and treadle and then tied together with a snitch knot shown in Fig. 56. It is easier to make tie-up changes when snap hooks are used rather than plain cord. If the loom is not equipped with this kind of connecter, it is simple enough to buy the screw-eyes and snap hooks at a hardware store and make the cords. The tie-up connections also can be made of lengths of chain with snap hooks attached to the ends; these do not stretch with use but are rather noisy.

If cords without snap hooks are used, they are threaded through the lam and treadle connecting points and tied together with a snitch knot. The treadle cord, usually shorter than the lam cord, is made by doubling a length of very stout cord to form a loop and tying the two free ends into an overhand knot. The knot must be firm enough to hold under tension and, if the connecting point is a drilled hole, the knot must be large enough not to slip through the hole when the cord is pulled taut by a depressed treadle. The loop end of this cord is pulled up through the connecting hole, from beneath the treadle, with a crochet hook or a looped length of wire. If the connecting point is a screw-eye, the loop end of the cord is pulled through the eye from one side to the other, and then is drawn through the knotted end of the cord to form a loop around the screw-eye.

The lam cords are made of two separate lengths of cord laid parallel and then knotted at one end, leaving the opposite ends free. The free ends of the cord are threaded through the hole from the top side of the lam to the underside, so that the free ends hang down toward the looped end of the treadle cord. If the connecting point is a screw-eye, the lam cord may be made by doubling a length of cord and looping it through the screw-eye. When a harness must be tied to a treadle, the loop in the treadle cord is folded down on that cord to form a double P, as shown in Fig. 56. The free ends of the lam cord are slipped through the double loop which then is tightened into a knot.

The ties must be adjusted so that all the treadles are held at the same height. This is done by holding the lam

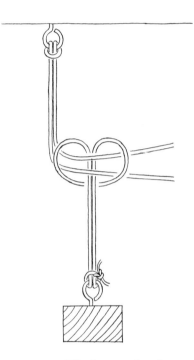

FIG. 56. *The lam cord and the treadle cord are set into position and then tied together with snitch knot shown here. Drawing, Don Wight.*

cord taut and slipping the loop knot of the treadle up or down, as is necessary. When all the treadles in use are at an even height, the free ends of each lam cord are tied into a single knot and pulled snug against the tightened loop knot of the treadle cord. This prevents the loop from slipping down when the cord is pulled taut by a depressed treadle.

To tie up for plain weave, used for this project, the first pick requires that harness 2 and harness 4 be tied to a treadle. The alternate pick requires that harness 1 and harness 3 be tied to another treadle.

In making this tie-up, work from the back to the front of each treadle so as to avoid reaching behind one tie-up to make another. To make the tie-up for the interlacing of the first pick on treadle 1, pick up the cord on lam 4 (position 1), and tie it to the cord on treadle 1 (position 4). Then, tie the cord on lam 2 (position 1), to the cord on treadle 1 (position 2). This completes the tie-up for the first filling pick of the weave.

To make the tie-up for the interlacing of the second pick on treadle 2, connect lam 3 (position 2), to treadle 2 (position 3). Then, connect lam 1 (position 2), to treadle 2 (position 1). This completes the tie-up for plain weave.

Untie the cords holding the harnesses in place and check the tie-up by depressing the treadles in sequence. When treadle 1 is depressed, harnesses Nos. 1 and 3 should be raised; when treadle 2 is depressed, harnesses Nos. 2 and 4 should be raised.

BOBBIN WINDING AND EQUIPMENT

The filling yarns for the project will have to be reeled from their packages—skeins, cones, or tubes—and wound onto bobbin quills. Bobbins can be wound directly from any of these packages, although it is more difficult to wind directly from a skein than from the others. If skeins are used, the beginner is advised to transfer the yarns from skeins to cardboard spools, available from suppliers of weaving equipment; or to make balls of yarn from which to wind the bobbins. For this purpose he will almost certainly need a skein holder. (See Fig. 30, Nos. 1 or 3.) Also, for the yarns on cones or tubes it is desirable to have a spool rack to hold them during the reeling.

A bobbin winder is a necessity. For the hand weaver, the choice lies between one that is electrically driven and one that is operated by hand. The hand-operated bobbin winder is relatively inexpensive, but it is slower in operation than an electric machine. And also, since one hand must be used to hold the yarn while the other hand rotates the shaft which propels the spindle, it may be somewhat difficult to start the winding and to keep it under control. Anyone who expects to engage in weaving, even to a moderate extent, should investigate the advantages of an electric bobbin winder with a rheostat foot control. The model shown in Fig. 57 has, instead of a spindle, an adjustable stock which can be moved so that a bobbin quill is held firmly between it and the drive stock.

Bobbin quills are made of various materials such as wood, plastic, and hard cardboard, all of which are satisfactory. However, hard cardboard quills have the advantage of being easily cut to the length of the shuttle well, and they are inexpensive enough to buy in good supply.

On spindle winders, hand-operated or electric, quills are often made of circular or elliptical shaped pieces of heavy brown wrapping paper. These are started on the spindle along with the yarn, and the quill shape is held by the yarn as it builds up on the paper.

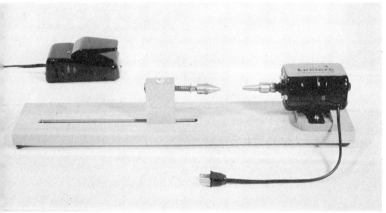

FIG. 57. *Electric bobbin winder. Adjustable stock, left; drive stock, right (attached to motor); rheostat foot control, above left. From Nilus Leclerc, Inc., Quebec. Photo, Ferdinand Boesch.*

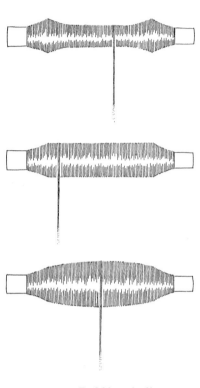

FIG. 58. *Bobbin winding, with three stages in the process shown. Drawing, Don Wight.*

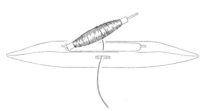

FIG. 59. *Bobbin with yarn end threaded through shuttle eye being inserted into well of shuttle. Drawing, Don Wight.*

WINDING A BOBBIN

Before beginning to wind a bobbin, study Fig. 58, which shows a bobbin in three stages of winding. Good bobbin winding is a matter of practice. The tension of the yarn as it winds onto the bobbin quill is controlled by pressure of the fingers. The yarn should not be held so tightly that it cuts through and dislodges yarn that is already on the quill. Neither should the yarn be held so loosely as to result in a spongy bobbin. The yarn should be allowed to run easily between the fingers with just enough pressure applied to produce a bobbin which is evenly wound and firm to touch. Take care to see that the yarn is kept far enough away from the ends of the quill so as not to slip off while being passed through the warp shed.

In starting a bobbin, do not tie the yarn to the quill but, instead, anchor the yarn by winding it several times around the quill at the center. Place the quill in position on the bobbin winder and, immediately, guide the yarn toward one end of the quill. Move the yarn back and forth in that area of the quill until a small, firm mound of yarn has been formed. Then guide the yarn to the other end of the quill and make a similar build-up of yarn. Guide the yarn back and forth across the quill, never going beyond the peaks of the mounds of yarn at the ends of the quill. The yarn should be kept in motion and guided rhythmically from side to side; it should not be held still in any one place so that the yarn piles up in the center parts of the quill. Gauge the size of the bobbin so that it will fit into the well of the shuttle without dragging on the sides of the well. Several bobbins of each filling yarn required should be made at one time, both for the sake of practice and to cut down the number of stops to make bobbins.

TO START WEAVING

When the bobbins have been wound and the weaving is to be started, see that the lease sticks are pushed back as far as possible from the harnesses so that they will not interfere with the shedding of the warp yarns.

Either keep the sticks just in front of the back beam or loosen the warp enough to let them be pulled over the back beam and down to the area just above the warp beam. Tie the sticks together with a short length of cord threaded through the holes at the ends of the sticks to prevent their falling out of the warp when it is moved forward. The lease sticks will need to be pulled back periodically because they will ride forward as the warp is let off the beam.

Many weavers remove the lease sticks once the weaving has been started; others prefer leaving them in place throughout the weaving to preserve the order of the yarns. This is often an advantage as when, for example, it is necessary to correct an error in yarn sequence or trace a broken end.

WEAVING THE HEADING

The heading is the beginning of a length of cloth. A few inches of heading are woven in order (1) to spread the warp ends and pull them into alignment with their parallel position in the reed, and (2), to facilitate the detection of any errors in the interlacing sequence made in the threading or in the sleying. For this purpose, the filling yarn for the heading should be bulkier than the warp yarn and of a color in strong contrast with it. Since black yarn has been used for the warp in this project, a heavy white or other light colored yarn should be used for the filling. White roving is ideal for this dual purpose. Thread the end of the bobbin yarn through the opening in the side wall of a shuttle, slip the bobbin onto the shuttle rod and secure it in the shuttle. (If roving is used, it will be easy to handle if it is wound on a long stick shuttle, shown in Fig. 60, No. 8.)

To begin weaving, depress treadle 1 and, with one hand, throw the shuttle through the open shed; with the other hand, catch the shuttle as it leaves the shed at the opposite edge of the warp. As treadle 1 is released and the first shed closes, pull the beater forward against the filling pick just entered through the warp. Meanwhile, depress treadle 2 and throw the shuttle through

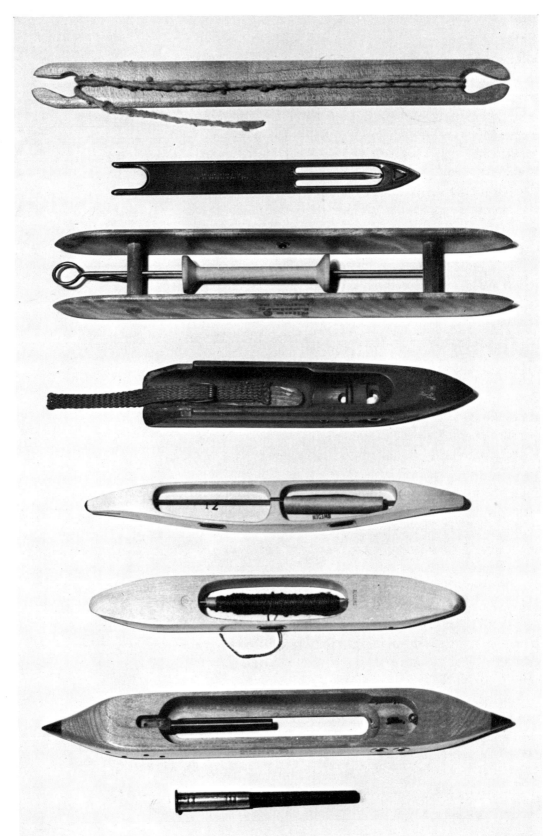

the second shed, catching it as it leaves the shed at the edge of the warp where it first was entered.

Release the treadle and, at the same time, pull the beater forward to pack in the second filling pick. Continue this procedure until two or three inches of heading have been woven and the warp yarns run in a straight line from the reed to the fell of the cloth.

Before proceeding further, make a careful check to see that all the warp yarns are interlacing through the filling in the sequence required for plain weave. Any yarn which is interlacing out of sequence must be traced from its position at the fell of the cloth back through the reed and the heddles to find the cause of the incorrect interlacing and to determine what must be done to correct it. (See Appendix D, page 233, on Correction of Errors.) Also, if the tension is unequal in any area of the warp, it is likly to show up as the heading is woven. If an area at the fell of the cloth curves toward the breast beam, the warp yarns are too taut. In either case, the groups of yarns affected should be untied and retied in proper adjustment to the rest of the warp.

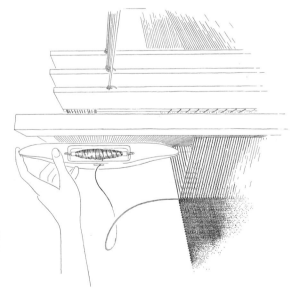

FIG. 60. *Seven kinds of shuttle and a bobbin, beginning at top:* (1) *long stick shuttle* (2) *stick shuttle* (3) *throw shuttle with spool* (4) *homemade half shuttle* (5) *boat shuttle with two bobbin wells* (6) *boat shuttle with single well* (7) *shuttle for over-end bobbin* (8) *bobbin.*

FIG. 61. *Weaving of the pillow cover can begin as soon as the heading is woven and the interlacing sequence and warp tension checked. Drawing, Don Wight.*

When the heading has been woven, the interlacing sequence checked, and the tension of the warp equalized, the pillow cover proper can be started. However, the beginner should plan on using at least a half yard of the warp for practice. It is better to do this with a single shuttle rather than the two needed for a striped effect. If the same yarn is used as was used for the warp, the result will be a fabric of solid color which, if it is suitably woven, can be used to make the back of the pillow cover, using stripes only on the front.

Secure the bobbin of filling yarn in the shuttle and proceed with the weaving in the same way as for the heading. Remember that filling picks should never begin or end in the center of the warp, but always at the selvages. The tail end of a yarn, whether at the start of a new bobbin or at the end of a depleted one, should be wound once around the last warp end at the selvage and tucked back into the shed, so that for a distance of five or six warp ends at the edge of the warp it lies as an extra yarn alongside the filling pick. Pull the tucked-in end of the yarn up between two warp ends and close the shed. Leave this end of filling yarn projecting from the surface of the cloth until several subsequent picks have been beaten into place; then cut it as close as possible to the web, leaving the surface clean.

The second shuttle, carrying the yarn to be used for the striping, can be started as soon as a sufficient length of cloth has been woven in solid color to cover the back of the pillow. This will require approximately half a yard on the loom. If the pillow cover is to be striped on both back and front, the second shuttle can be started whenever the weaver chooses to do so.

The two shuttles are alternated in whatever sequence will give the desired effect. The striping may be worked out on paper with crayons or colored pencils, or even with strips of pasted colored paper. Or, it can be worked out on the loom as the weaving progresses. If a plan is made on paper, it should serve only as a guide since color arrangement very often takes on an appearance in the woven cloth quite different from that on paper. A weaver should always feel free to make changes as he works.

When a stripe has been woven to the width desired, the filling yarn should be cut, wound once around the last warp end at the selvage, and tucked back into the shed alongside the last filling pick inserted. The contrasting stripe should be started in the same way, with the filling yarn tucked into the warp. If the stripes are quite narrow, the yarn can be carried over from one stripe to another instead of being cut and tucked in. In this case, when the stripe has been woven to the desired width, lay the shuttle on the web while the alternate shuttle is being used.

As the weaving builds toward the reed, the tension of the warp will need to be released so that the newly woven cloth can be taken on to the cloth beam while the warp beam lets off a new length of warp. This should be done at regular intervals. Otherwise, there will be a change in the appearance of the fabric due to the angle of the reed when it pivots too far in either direction from its upright position. Not more than three or four inches of fabric should be woven without letting off the warp and taking up the cloth; and, accordingly, about the same amount of weaving should be done between each adjustment.

To adjust the warp, rest the beater against the fell and depress the brake treadle to release the warp beam. Roll the cloth beam forward until the beater is about an inch from the breast beam, with the warp taut. If too much of the warp is let off so that the beater hits the breast beam, it will be necessary to go to the back of the loom and wind the excess back onto the warp beam.

WEAVING RHYTHMICALLY

The skilled weaver works rhythmically whether he is winding a warp, dressing the loom, or weaving the cloth. It is more important for the beginner to concentrate on developing rhythm at his work than to be unduly concerned with such matters as maintaining a perfect pick count or making impeccable selvages. Accurate pick count and good selvages will inevitably be the result when the motions of throwing the shuttle, beating the filling, and changing sheds are well coordinated and performed rhythmically.

There should be no need to stop and adjust filling yarns in order to produce good selvages, provided the yarns at the edges of the warp are at correct tension. Also, well-wound bobbins are an important factor in this respect since any interference with the even unreeling of the yarn from the bobbin will affect the weaving.

The Beat-Up

The tension of the filling yarn is affected by the timing of the beat. If the filling is beaten before the shed is closed, or just as it is being closed, the amount of filling yarn needed to cross the warp yarns without pulling them in will be drawn from the shuttle into the shed—provided an excess length of yarn is allowed to hang loose between the shuttle and the edge of the warp. If, on the other hand, the shed is changed before the beat is made, the filling yarn will be locked into place by the crossed warp yarns before it can move through the warp in sufficient length to prevent the cloth from pulling in. This should be avoided since it causes breakage of the warp yarns at the selvages.

The Pick Count

The number of filling picks per inch of woven fabric, called the *pick count*, will depend upon how the beater is used against the filling yarns. The weight of the beater itself makes it unnecessary to exert great force in the forward pull of the beater. In fact, the term "beating" is apt to be misleading. The beater should be pulled forward with only sufficient force to ease the filling yarn into place. With practice, one develops a sense of beating which is largely tactile. Packing twenty picks into an inch of warp has a different "feel" from packing in only ten; the weaver soon becomes aware of the particular sensation that produces a specific pick count. This is affected, of course, by the materials used, the sett of the warp, and the construction of the cloth.

Rugs or other fabrics of considerable density often require a sturdy loom and a forcible, sometimes a double, beat-up. In weaving sheer fabrics, on the other hand, it may be necessary to beat on a closed shed in order to gain better control in spacing the filling yarns. In this case, one light beat should be made before changing the shed and, for accurate placement of the pick, a second beat after the shed has been changed.

BROKEN WARP ENDS: Broken ends usually can be avoided by seeing that the warp is wound, beamed and tied on the loom at proper tension; also by seeing that the cloth is not allowed to pull in to any great extent. There is an implement, called a *template*, or *temple*, designed to keep the warp from being pulled in too much. (See Fig. 30, No. 6.) The template may be inserted near the fell of the cloth as soon as a few inches have been woven. As the weaving builds up, the template is moved forward and reinserted at the fell of the cloth.

It is essential, of course, to use good-quality yarns which have enough tensile strength and abrasion resistance to withstand ordinary loom motions. If breakage does occur, it should be corrected at once. First, remove the broken yarn from the reed and the heddle. Pull the broken end at the front of the loom toward the breast beam. Pull the end at the back of the loom out of the lease sticks and let it hang from the warp beam. Wind a bobbin of warp yarn and thread the end of the yarn through the lease sticks.

Then enter it through the empty heddle and dent. Insert a common pin into the woven cloth a few inches from the fell. Anchor the new warp yarn by winding the end of it in figure-eight fashion several times around the pin, as shown in Fig. 62. Tie the bobbin yarn in a loop or secure it with a rubber band so that the bobbin will hang free from the back beam without unwinding. The weight of the bobbin should be sufficient to tension the yarn.

When enough weaving has been done so that the original end will reach from the back of the loom to a point beyond the fell of the cloth, it can be replaced in the warp. Cut the bobbin yarn an inch or two beyond the fell and remove it from the reed and the heddle. Pull the original yarn forward and thread it

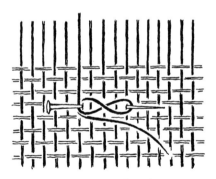

FIG. 62. *Diagram showing how to mend broken warp ends. Drawing, Don Wight.*

91

through the heddle and the reed. Move the pin to within an inch or two of the fell and anchor the yarn as previously described.

Measuring the Woven Cloth

When the woven cloth extends below the breast beam and before it is taken onto the cloth beam, measure the woven length with a tape measure and pin the tape in place close to one edge of the cloth. As the weaving progresses and newly woven cloth is taken onto the cloth beam, the pinned tape will move along with the cloth toward the beam. As this occurs, pull the tape measure up toward the fell of the cloth and repin it, thus keeping a running count of the yardage woven. When the tape has been repinned, remove the pin which was placed first, and which now holds the tape in place, close to the cloth beam, so that neither the pin nor the tape measure will be taken onto the beam with the cloth.

When the woven cloth has reached the cloth beam, the beam should be padded just as the warp beam was padded when the warp yarns were beamed, with heavy brown paper, lightweight corrugated paper, or sticks, as described on pages 60-61. See also Fig. 29, No. 19.

Continue weaving until the measured yardage is sufficient for the pillow cover. If there should remain an additional length of warp on the beam, it need not be wasted. Use it for experimental work or make fabric for a handbag or some other item requiring only a short length of material.

Weaving can be continued until the end of the warp is so close to the heddles that the yarns will no longer separate to form a shed; or, until the warp apron or cords have been let out to their full length and can be rolled no further forward.

Cutting Off

When the weaving is completed, release the fabric from tension by releasing the ratchet on the cloth beam. With scissors, cut through the warp yarns at a point which is several inches beyond the last filling pick. For example, this may be just in front of the heddles or just behind them. The fringe of warp ends left on the fabric will prevent the filling yarns from raveling. When the fabric has been cut free from the warp beam, disengage the ratchet on the cloth beam and pull the fabric forward to unroll it from the cloth beam. When the cloth rod has been pulled free from the cloth beam, cut the warp yarns between the tie-on knots and the heading of the cloth. Put in a row of machine stitching at each end of the cloth. Then cut off the excess length of the warp, leaving only a short fringe about a quarter-inch to a half-inch in length.

Wherever the cloth is to be cut to separate the pillow covering from the rest of the fabric that has been woven, put in two rows of machine stitching approximately half an inch apart, and cut the cloth between these rows of stitching. The stitching will prevent the filling yarns from raveling during the finishing process.

THE FINISHING PROCESS

Finishing hand-woven cloth may involve nothing more than steam pressing; by this process the least percentage of shrinkage will occur. Although this is the quickest and easiest method of finishing cloth, it has the disadvantage of not shrinking the fabric fully so that further shrinkage will occur when the finished item—in this case the pillow cover—is dry-cleaned or laundered. Subsequent shrinkage can be avoided by having the cloth commercially dry-cleaned and steam-pressed before the pillow cover is made up.

Many weavers prefer to use washing as the finishing process; a pillow cover made of fabric so treated could be either dry-cleaned or washed without incurring any additional shrinkage.

To wash newly loomed fabric, use warm water and mild soap. Agitate the fabric gently: over-agitation causes a thickening of the fabric, called felting. Rinse the fabric thoroughly in water of about the same temperature as that in which it was washed. Then squeeze out as much of the excess moisture as possible and blot-dry the fabric between towels or some other absorbent material. Air-dry the material and then steam-press it, or have it commerically steam-pressed.

If the washing is done by machine, set the controls for delicate fabric. Shorten all the cycles, if possible, to avoid felting of the fabric. It is not advisable to machine-dry the cloth unless the door of the dryer can be left open while the machine is in operation, or there are controls which can be set to insure cool drying. Since the tumbling action of drying machines tends to cause fuzzing in wool fabric, it is advisable to leave the material in the machine only long enough for partial drying. The fabric then should be air-dried and, finally, steam-pressed.

For larger projects, and for apparel fabric in general, having the fabric pressed on the steam table of a dry cleaning shop will produce a professional job. A light pressing or sponging is used on most hand-woven fabrics except linens. Tweeds and other wool fabrics for tailoring are first scoured and then sent out to be London-shrunk, a process which insures against any further shrinkage.

Scouring, which is done with laundry soap—not harsh detergents—removes soil, starches, and grease from the yarns. The process also gives loft to the fabric and meshes the fibers. Drape and hand become softer, and raveling is reduced.

CHAPTER FOUR

Drafting

Drafting is a system of notation which depicts the construction or weave of a cloth and the mechanics of producing it. Although simpler, a draft for a woven fabric is written in much the same way as a musical score, by the use of symbols. And just as the symbols of music must be learned in order to understand their relationship to the sounds they represent, so the symbol language of weaving must be learned in order to understand its relationship to the construction and design it represents in woven cloth.

The system used for notating music is pretty universally understood. But symbols for weaving vary by geographical areas and by eras. This can be confusing to beginners and to veterans alike when they encounter a new set of symbols or a different system. Even an experienced weaver is obliged to deduce the correlation between a new set of symbols and that to which he is accustomed. Fortunately, a thorough understanding of one system of notation serves as a guide for deciphering others. The system of drafting described here is one so widely used today that, despite numerous variations, it comes close to being standard.

Most weavers learn easily enough how to write drafts based on given information and, also, how to read and interpret drafts when they are given in full. But there is often a tendency to learn these "loom setups" by rote, a practice which is in no way the equivalent of knowing how to plot original drafts, or even to plot comprehensive drafts when the available information is incomplete.

The only requirement for gaining facility in plotting drafts is an understanding of the relationship between the required drafts and the motions of the loom. The problem of plotting the threading and tie-up drafts when the weave draft alone is known involves a step-by-step procedure: the weave draft is used as the basis for plotting the threading draft. These two drafts in turn are used as the basis for plotting a tie-up draft.

Drafts are written on squared or cross-sectioned paper, which is available in various sizes to the inch. For example, 4 by 4 paper has 4 vertical and 4 horizontal rows of squares per inch; 8 by 8 paper has 8 vertical and 8 horizontal rows of squares per inch. Squared paper, which has each square inch bounded by heavy lines, is easiest to work with.

COMPREHENSIVE DRAFT

A comprehensive draft for a woven fabric consists of three parts: the draw-in or threading draft; the weave draft, sometimes called the design draft, and the tie-up draft, related to the treadling sequence. The three drafts seen in Fig. 63, Nos. D-1, D-2, and D-3, comprise the comprehensive draft for plain weave on four harnesses, as described in Chapter 3. The order of the harnesses and heddles used, in relation to the warp ends threaded through them, creates the threading draft, No. D-1. The warp ends interlaced with the filling picks produce a pattern which, when charted, is the weave draft, No. D-2; a graph of the ties between lams and treadles, required to produce the weave, is the tie-up draft, No. D-3.

The threading draft is complete when it shows how all the warp ends in one threading unit or repeat are drawn on the harnesses. The weave draft is complete when it shows how all the warp ends in one threading unit, or threading repeat, interlace with all the picks in one filling repeat of the weave. A tie-up draft is complete when it shows all the ties between the lams and treadles that are required to raise and lower all the harnesses used, in the sequence which will produce the weave.

Nos. D-4, D-5, and D-6 in Fig. 63 will help the weaver to visualize the relationship of the parts of the loom to the drafts, to be explained here in detail.

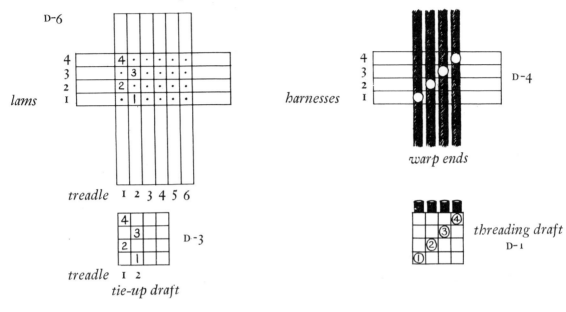

lams

treadle 1 2 3 4 5 6

D-3

treadle 1 2
tie-up draft

harnesses

D-4

warp ends

threading draft
D-1

filling picks
D-5

weave draft
D-2

FIG. 63. *Comprehensive draft
for plain weave on a straight draw.*

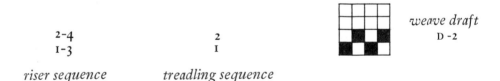

2-4	2
1-3	1
riser sequence	*treadling sequence*

THREADING DRAFT FOR A STRAIGHT DRAW

The threading draft shows the sequence in which the warp ends are drawn in on the harnesses. The threading draft is plotted to show one repeat of the threading sequence. In Project 3, the warp ends were drawn in a straight draw, from left to right, on four harnesses, as shown in Fig. 42, page 65.

The horizontals in No. D-4 indicate a top view of harnesses numbered 1, 2, 3, and 4 from the front to the back of the loom. The verticals intersecting the harnesses represent the warp ends for one threading unit; the circles might be thought of as heddle eyes. The number within the circle is the harness number. Thus, the first end on the left is shown entered through a heddle eye on harness 1. The second end is entered on harness 2, the third on harness 3, the fourth on harness 4.

The harnesses and the warp ends threaded through the heddles on these harnesses create the threading draft in No. D-1. Each horizontal row of squares on the draft represents one harness. The row of squares at the bottom of the draft represents harness No. 1 which is closest to the front of the loom; the next two rows represent harnesses 2 and 3 respectively; the top row of squares represents harness No. 4, which is closest to the back of the loom.

Each vertical row of squares represents one warp end.. A circled numeral indicates that a warp end is drawn through a heddle eye on that harness. See again Fig. 42, which gives a graphic representation of this process. (Circled numerals are used in threading drafts to indicate the number of the harness on which an end is entered. This is done so that the beginning weaver may distinguish clearly between threading drafts and weave drafts, which have blacked-in squares, and from the tie-up drafts which are indicated by treadle numbers, uncircled.)

No. D-1 shows that the first warp end, at the left of the warp, was drawn on harness 1. This is indicated on the threading draft, No. D-1 by the circled numeral 1, written in the square which represents the first warp end drawn on harness 1. The circled numerals 2, 3, and 4 show that the second, third, and fourth warp ends were drawn on harnesses 2, 3, and 4, respectively. No. D-1 shows how all the warp ends in the threading unit were drawn on the harnesses and, therefore, is the complete threading draft for a straight draw on four harnesses. This is, of course, the threading draft for Project 3.

Using Four Harness Rather Than Two

The minimum number of harnesses required to produce a weave cannot be fewer than the number of warp ends which have a different order of interlacing in the weave draft. All warp ends which have the same order of interlacing may be drawn on the same harness. A separate harness is required for each warp end which has a different order of interlacing from any other warp end.

It becomes apparent, therefore, in weave draft No. D-2, that four harnesses are not required for plain weave, since the first and third ends interlace in the same order, and the second and fourth ends also interlace in the same order.

In Fig. 64, No. D-7, a column representing the weaves on the woven strip in Figs. 71 and 72, pages 116 and 117, shows examples of weaves, other than plain weave (No. 1) having ends which interlace in only two ways. These weaves, Nos. 2, 3, and 4 also could be woven on a two-harness threading. The threading would show two ends entered in separate heddles on harness 1, and the next two ends entered in separate heddles on harness 2. (They also could be entered as two ends through the same heddle eye, but the ends then would have a tendency to twist.)

It often is advisable, however, to use more than the minimum number of harnesses required, as in the case of the four-harness plain weave specified for Project 3. By distributing the warp ends on four harnesses, each harness is less crowded and the ends are subjected to less friction than if they had been drawn on two harnesses only. Also, the counterbalanced loom performs best with an even distribution of ends on all the harnesses.

Furthermore, greatly increased flexibility of weave is, perhaps, the most important reason for using four harnesses. The two-harness threading allows for the alternation of harnesses only; the sole variation possible is the weaving of additional picks through one or both of the sheds, as in basket weave, No. 4 in Fig. 71. Other weaves, including Nos. 5 through 9 on the strip, are but a few of the variations which can be woven on the basic four-harness straight draw.

FIG. 64. *Comprehensive draft for basic weaves and derivatives for four harnesses on a straight draw. (See Figs. 71 and 72, pages 116-117, which correspond to these weaves.)*

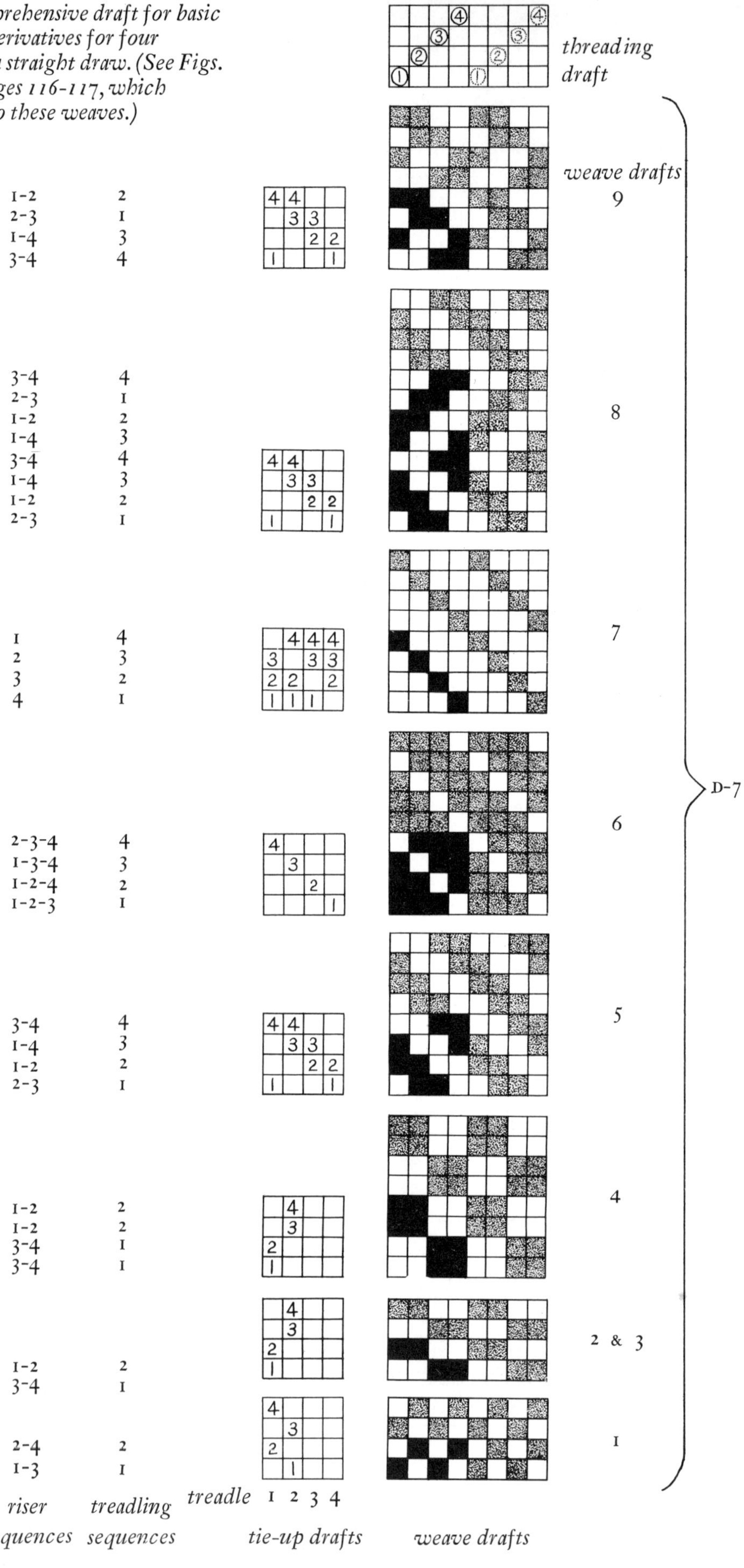

threading draft

weave drafts

9

8

7

6

5

4

2 & 3

I

D-7

riser sequences	treadling sequences	treadle 1 2 3 4
		tie-up drafts

weave drafts

The weave draft shows how the warp and filling yarns interlace. The interlacing order of all the yarns in a weave, up to the point where that order of interlacing is repeated, is one unit of the weave called the repeat. A weave draft must show the interlacing of all the warp ends and filling picks in the repeat.

Each vertical row of squares on a weave draft represents one warp end while each horizontal row of squares represents one filling pick. The notation of the interlacing involves the use of only two symbols: a filled-in square and a blank square. A filled-in square represents a *warp end* raised and, therefore, interlaced *over* a filling pick. A *blank square* represents a *warp end lowered* and, therefore, interlaced under a filling pick.

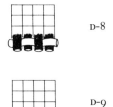

D-8

Beginning at the left side of the warp, the first filling pick interlaces under the first warp end, over the second end, under the third end, and over the fourth end of the four-end threading unit, shown in Fig. 65, No. D-8.

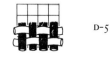

D-9

The first filling pick is represented by the first row of squares at the bottom of the weave draft and the interlacing is written on that row of the draft as shown in Fig. 65, No. D-9. The filled-in squares show that warp ends 1 and 3 are raised and, therefore, they interlace over the first filling pick. The blank squares show that warp ends 2 and 4 are lowered and, therefore, interlace under the first filling pick.

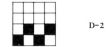

D-5

The second filling pick interlaces in alternate order to that of the first pick: over the first warp end, under the second, over the third, and under the fourth end, as shown in No. D-5 of Figs. 63 and 65. This pick is represented by the second horizontal row of squares from the bottom of the weave draft and the interlacing is written in that row of the draft as shown in No. D-2 of Figs. 63 and 65. The blank squares show that warp ends 1 and 3 are lowered and, therefore, lie under the second filling pick. The filled-in squares show that warp ends 2 and 4 are raised and, therefore, lie over the second filling pick.

D-2

FIG. 65.

No. D-2 shows how all the warp ends in the four-end threading unit interlace with the two-pick filling repeat of plain weave. This, therefore, is the complete weave draft for plain weave when the warp ends are drawn-in on a straight draw, from left to right on four harnesses, as shown in Fig. 63, No. D-1.

THE TIE-UP DRAFT

The tie-up draft, Fig. 63, No. D-3, shows the ties of the lams to the treadles. A tie-up draft must show all the connections between the lams and the treadles that are required to raise and lower the harnesses and, thereby, the warp ends drawn on them, in the sequence that will produce the weave. Remember that each lam must be tied to at least one of the treadles but that the same lam cannot be tied to every treadle. Nor can every lam be tied to any one treadle.

In plotting the tie-up for a weave, the action of the loom must be considered. For a counterbalanced loom, the tie-up draft will be based on the fact that those lams which are to *lower* harnesses must be *tied* to a treadle; and those harnesses which are to be raised must not have their lams tied to that treadle.

To understand the tie-up draft, think of the numbers as ties from the lams to the treadles. As explained in Chapter 3, each lam has a hole or a hook relating to a hole or a hook on each treadle. The lams are situated directly above the treadles, so that a bird's-eye view shows how they are superimposed. (See Fig. 63, No. D-6.)

When a harness is to be raised and, therefore, not connected with a treadle, no notation is made on the tie-up draft. When a harness is to be lowered, its lam must be tied to a treadle. This is indicated by writing the harness number in the square which represents the tie from lam to treadle.

Here again numbers have been chosen as symbols because they show clearly, and at a glance, the sequence of the harness tie-up required on each treadle.

Two treadles were used to produce plain weave in Project 3. They were designated treadles 1 and 2, at the left of the group of treadles. In order to raise harnesses 1 and 3 on the first filling pick, lams 2 and 4 were tied to their corresponding tie-up positions on treadle 1, as shown in Fig. 63, No. D-3, by the numerals 2 and 4. On the second filling pick, lams Nos. 1 and 3 were tied to their corresponding tie-up positions on treadle 2, as shown in No. D-3, by the numerals 1 and 3.

The complete draft for this tie-up, No. D-3, shows all the connections between lams and treadles that are required to raise and lower all the harnesses used to produce plain weave.

THE TREADLING SEQUENCE

Treadling sequences and riser sequences are given here in vertical columns reading from the bottom up, although they may appear in the text running horizontally from left to right, as 1-2, 3-4. In the treadling sequences in Figs. 64 and 66 the first number at the bottom of the column indicates the treadle to be depressed when the first pick is inserted through the warp. The number next above indicates the treadle to be depressed when the second pick is inserted, and so on to the top of the column. This constitutes one repeat of the weave; the sequence is then repeated, from bottom to top, throughout the weaving. In weaving the fabric for Project 3, the first filling pick was inserted through the shed made by depressing treadle 1, causing harnesses 1 and 3 to rise. The second filling pick was inserted through the shed made by depressing treadle 2, causing harnesses 2 and 4 to rise. With the threading and tie-up sequence described, the treadling sequence is 1, 2, because the treadles were so designated.

This tie-up for plain weave on two treadles only is, of course, limited to the alternation of the two treadles. The only variation possible would be the insertion of more than one pick through the same shed.

Any tie-up for four treadles, however, allows a good deal of variation in the treadling sequence. Weaves 5, 8, and 9, in Fig. 64, all are accomplished with the same tie-up; only the treadling sequences make the different patterns.

The Repeat

The weaver now has had the opportunity of visualizing a comprehensive weave draft, with the tie-up and the treadling sequence required to produce plain weave, its variations as well as several twills, on a straight draw. Before continuing with an explanation of riser sequences it may be helpful to show more than one unit, or repeat, of the weave draft in order to get a clear picture of the total pattern of the cloth.

The dark squares in the weave drafts shown in Fig. 64 (a column of weaves corresponding to the woven strip in Figs. 71 and 72, pages 116 and 117) indicate the warp ends raised for one repeat of the weave. The shadowed squares in the drafts show the second repeat both vertically and horizontally. The second repeat is identical to the first, that is, the first warp end of the second repeat is raised in the same sequence as the first warp end of the weave draft because that end is entered on the same harness and, therefore, must interlace with the filling in the same order. The second end of the shadowed repeat interlaces in the same way as did the second end of the weave draft because it is drawn on the second harness, and so on.

In the vertical repeat also, the treadling sequence must be identical with the first throughout the weaving. The treadles must be depressed in the sequence given as "treadling sequence" reading, from the bottom of the column of figures, upward. If the tie-up uses but two treadles, as for plain weave, and the treadling is shown as treadle 1 for the first pick, and treadle 2 for the second pick, the third pick will be identical to the first pick, the fourth the same as the second. Therefore, these two picks constitute the second repeat of the treadling sequence and of the design.

THE RISER SEQUENCE

The riser sequence is a listing of harness numbers indicating the "risers," or raised harnesses, for each pick, in the sequence required to produce the weave.

Riser sequences, not treadlings, are given as directions in Chapter 5 on weaves. This system has the advantage of applying to every kind of loom, whereas treadlings differ with specific types of looms and tie-up drafts. Table looms have no treadles and, therefore, no tie-up of combinations of harnesses is possible.

It is easier, also, to see the direct relationship between the raised harnesses and the weave formation than it is the twice-removed connection between treadle and weave. Further, the raised harnesses can be clearly observed by the weaver as he works at the loom.

Riser sequences for the weaves are given at the far left of the weave drafts in Fig. 64, No. D-7. These are the weaves that appear on the woven sample strip in Figs. 71 and 72, pages 116 and 117.

THREADING DRAFT FOR POINTED DRAW

To illustrate further the relationship of the weave in the cloth with the drawing-in of the warp, a one-line pointed draw, or herringbone, draft is shown at top of Fig. 66, No. D-10. (This column corresponds to the woven strip in Fig. 75, page 119.)

The pointed draw is but one of many threadings which can give variety of pattern. Unlike the four-end threading unit of the straight draw, the pointed draw has a six-end threading unit or repeat. The first four ends of the six-end repeat are entered exactly as were the four ends of the straight draw: the first end is entered on harness 1, the second on harness 2, the third and fourth on harnesses 3 and 4. The fifth end of the unit is entered on harness 3, the sixth on harness 2. The first end of the second repeat will be on harness 1 as shown in the shadowed draft in Fig. 66. The pattern of the repeated draft is a zigzag from harness 1 to harness 4, back to harness 1 and so on across the warp. This creates *a point* in the draft at harness 4, and again at harness 1. Therefore, it is called a pointed draw.

The primary difference between the patterns created on this draw and on the straight draw is that the pointed threading develops symmetrical motifs in the pattern whereas the straight draw, or twill threading, will often develop weaves with a diagonal direction.

In the pointed draw, as explained, the repeat consists of six ends. One end of the six is on harness 1, one end on harness 4. Harnesses 2 and 3 each has two ends entered on it. These harnesses, then, control twice as many ends as harnesses 1 and 4.

Compare the drafts in the columns Fig. 64, No. D-7, and Fig. 66, No. D-10. Note that when any one harness is raised, if the warp end is entered in a straight

FIG. 66. *Comprehensive draft for pointed draw.*

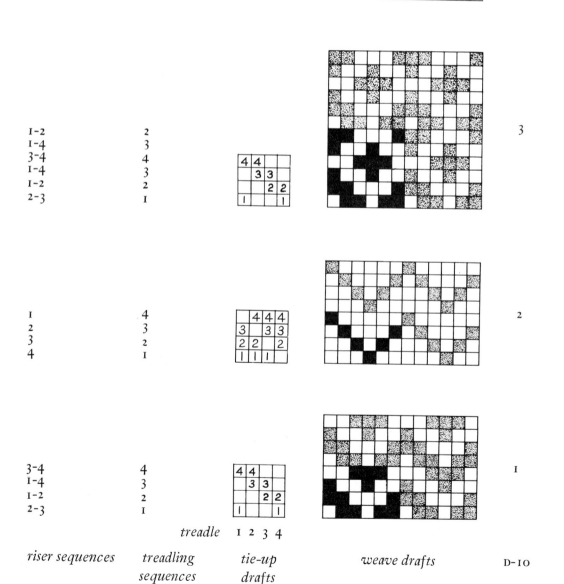

threading draft

3

2

1

| riser sequences | treadling sequences | tie-up drafts | weave drafts | D-10 |

draw, every fourth end across the width of the warp
will be raised. If the warp end is entered in a pointed
draw, when harness 1 is raised, every sixth end will
be raised because only one end of the six-end unit is
on that harness. The filling will lie under the end on
harness 1, and over the ends on harnesses 2, 3, 4, 3,
and 2, respectively. When harness 2 is raised, the filling
will lie over the end on harness 1, under the end on
harness 2, over the three ends drawn on harnesses 3, 4,
and 3, and under the last end of the repeat which also
is drawn on harness 2. Raising harness 3 will again raise
two ends of the repeat. The filling will lie over the
end on harnesses 1 and 2, under an end on harness 3,
over the end on harness 4, and under the other end
which is drawn on harness 3. Raising harness 4 will
again raise every sixth end in the warp. The filling
will lie over the five ends on harnesses 3, 2, 1, 2, and
3, respectively, and under the end on harness 4.

This threading, and a variation of it, a 3-line pointed
draw, were used to create the weaves in the sample
strip, Fig. 75, page 119.

In Fig. 64, No. D-7, the column of weave drafts is
related to the straight draw threading draft at the top;
the column Fig. 66, No. D-10, relates to the pointed
draw threading at the top of that column. The tie-up
draft, the treadling and riser sequences are shown at
the left of each weave draft. (Note that 1 and 2 in No.
D-10 have exactly the same tie-up, treadling and riser
sequence as 5 and 7 in Fig. 64, No. D-7.) With the
exception of plain weave 1 in No. D-7, which can be
done on any threading with alternate ends on odd-
and even-numbered harnesses, none of the weaves in
No. D-7 can be accomplished on the other threading,
No. D-10, or vice versa.

The Direct Tie-Up

There is a simple and at the same time flexible tie-up
that a beginner can use to advantage. It is a *direct
tie-up*, to be used for experimental weaving, trying
out combinations of weaves, or for the weaver who is
undecided about a design. It involves the use of four

or more treadles. In this arrangement one harness only is controlled by each treadle. The lam for harness 1 is tied to treadle 1, lam 2 is tied to treadle 2, lam 3 to treadle 3, and lam 4 to treadle 4.

The tie-up for weave 6 in the column No. D-7 is an example of the direct tie-up. Also weave 5 could be produced on this tie-up by depressing two treadles at once in this sequence: 1-4, 1-2, 2-3, 3-4. Plain weave, 1, could be done by treadling 2-4, 1-3. In fact, all the weaves in the sample strip of basic weaves, Figs. 71 and 72, pages 116 and 117, could be produced on a direct tie-up of four harnesses with multiple treadling.

Most hand looms have more treadles than harnesses —four-harness looms usually have six treadles. Four of the treadles can be used as shown above for the direct tie-up; the two additional treadles might be tied to produce a plain weave. The treadles can be depressed one, or two, or three at a time as necessary.

Again it should be said that the direct tie-up is for experimental weaving only. Once a weave has been developed, and is to be reproduced in any quantity, the weave should be drafted and the loom retied to produce that specific weave in the most efficient manner.

As a general rule, one treadle only at a time should be used to open each shed once the design has been determined. Treadling several treadles at once can be awkward. Furthermore, it often invites mistakes. The time spent under the loom tying the treadles properly for the intended weave can save time in the production of fabric.

CHAPTER FIVE

Weaves

Weaves in themselves are simple. They are limited in variety and logical in formation, and most of them can be woven on a simple four-harness loom. A new weaver, confronted by a multiplicity of weaving directions and drafts, may well experience moments of discouragement or confusion but, given a little time, he will discover that the complexities of weaving are more apparent than real. Once he has mastered the warping process and the dressing of the loom, and has begun actual weaving, he will find its challenge both stimulating and rewarding.

The endless variety of woven cloth arises not from the weaves themselves but through the nearly limitless combination of weaves, with different kinds of yarns, changes in sett, in scale, and in color. Each of these factors multiplies the almost infinite possibilities for variety and invention.

BASIC WEAVES AND THEIR DERIVATIVES

Some weaves are called basic weaves; each one of these follows a specific system of interlacing. Other weaves are called derivative weaves because they are formed by some modification of the interlacing order of the basic weave. These derivative weaves, even though their order of interlacing is altered, are based on the same principle of interlacing as the basic weave from which they derive.

In the view of most authorities on weaving there are three systems, or classes, of basic weaves. These are:

Plain weave, based on two harnesses

Twill weave, based on three, four, or more harnesses

Satin weave, based on five or more harnesses

Some weavers consider satin to be an extension of twill weave; like twill, satin may be either warp-face or filling-face. However, because of the multiple harnesses required for weaving satin, and because of the very fine yarns used, satin is not an elementary technique for hand weavers and is not developed in this book.

PLAIN WEAVE

In plain weave, as shown in Chapter 1, the filling is interlaced through the warp in the order of 1/1— over one—under one—with this order alternating on each successive pick. See Figs. 5, page 2, and 67.

Plain weave is shown in the woven sample strip, Fig. 71, No. 1, at the lower edge. Figs. 71 and 72 show the basic weaves and their derivatives described in this chapter.

Plain weave is the simplest of the basic weaves. It is the universal weave known to weavers everywhere. A very high proportion of all weaving is done in plain weave.

To the beginner, plain weave is indispensable as a simple means of studying and understanding the operation of his loom. It is essential that the weaver comprehend the *why* of every single action of the loom, especially if he is ever to originate weaving of his own.

Plain weave is the basic construction for brocades, for double cloth, for tapestry, pile weaves, and others.

STABILITY OF PLAIN WEAVE: It is important to remember that, for comparable weight of yarn and number of ends and picks, plain weave is the tightest and strongest of all constructions. It is especially desirable for a cloth in which stability is imperative, as in suitings and upholstery. One would have to use heavier yarns or closer sett for the same degree of stability in a twill.

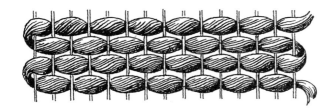

FIG. 67. *Diagram of plain weave, filling faced, on a sparse warp. Drawing, Don Wight.*

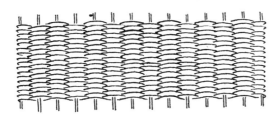

FIG. 68. *Diagram of plain weave, filling face, with tight beat-up. Drawing, Don Wight.*

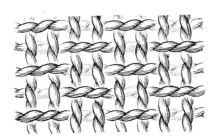

FIG. 69. *Diagram of rib weave. Drawing, Don Wight.*

Rib Weave, a Derivative Weave

Rib weave is a derivative or extension of plain weave. (See Fig. 69.) The extension may be either horizontal or vertical. The 1/1 plain-weave order of interlacing can be extended *horizontally* so that it becomes a 2/2 order of interlacing—over two—under two—with the order of interlacing alternating on *each successive pick;* the construction then becomes a filling-face rib. (See Fig. 68.) If the 1/1 plain-weave order of interlacing is extended *vertically*, so that warp ends interlace alternately over and under groups of filling picks, but with the order alternated *every second pick*, forming a *horizontal rib*, the construction becomes a warp-face rib weave.

A filling-face cloth, it should be explained, is one in which the filling yarns predominate over the warp ends. If the filling yarn has sufficient body, and is beaten in closely, it will cover the warp completely; if tightly packed on a loose sett, the surface becomes hard and smooth, with unique opportunities for small patterns created from pick-and-pick alternations.

Conversely, in a warp-face cloth, the warp yarns outnumber the filling yarns, tending to conceal them. In such case, very often heavier yarns are used for the warp than for the filling. Or, perhaps the filling will be interlaced to float under more yarns than it floats over. (A float is a warp yarn which extends over or under two or more successive filling picks; or a filling yarn which extends over or under two or more successive warp ends.)

FIG. 70. *Diagram of basket weave. Drawing, Don Wight.*

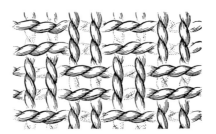

Basket Weave, a Derivative Weave

Another important plain-weave derivative is basket weave. If the 1/1 order of plain weave is extended both lengthwise and crosswise, so that there is a 2/2 order of interlacing, and if this order is alternated on *every sec-*

ond pick, the construction is called basket weave. This is a derivative weave because the 2/2 order of interlacing and the 2/2 order of alternation are extensions of plain weave. (See Fig. 70.) Basket weave also is shown in Fig. 71, No. 4, above rib weaves.

In basket weave the yarn groupings need not be a regular 2/2 or 4/4; they could as well be irregular extensions such as 2/4/4/, or with a random repeat of 3/2/4/4/4/2/4, and so on. Nor need the yarns be always identical; they may be mixed, as in the Metsovaara-Nystrom fabric in Fig. 111, page 179.

Basket weave, and variations thereof, can be woven in several ways: For the warp, groups of yarns can be drawn through single heddles; two yarns, instead of one, could be drawn through each heddle so that two yarns would rise when a harness is raised. Or the warp yarns may be drawn on the harnesses in a straight draw, as 1, 2, 3, 4 and two adjoining harnesses raised alternately. These could be risers 1 and 2 followed by 3 and 4; or risers 2 and 3 followed by 4 and 1.

Or the warp may be drawn on the harness sequence of 2, 3, 1, 4 in which case risers 2 and 3 would be followed by 1 and 4; or risers 3 and 1 by 4 and 2. In these examples, the multiple interlacing of warp ends results because two ends in succession were raised while two were lowered.

The multiple interlacing of the filling yarns can be achieved by passing a bobbin wound with a single yarn twice, or more, through each shed; or by using a bobbin on which two or more yarns are wound together. Thus a group of yarns enters each shed when the shuttle is shot through.

TWILL WEAVE

A twill weave is produced when the filling and warp are interlaced in such a way that the points of intersection move one warp end to the right (or to the left) on each successive pick. The movement of the points of intersection forms a diagonal line characteristic of all twill weaves.

Next to plain weave, twill is the most important construction or interlacing. It has been used all over the world since earliest times. It is an appropriate choice for many fibers, yarns and cloth weights. While twill may have more resiliency and better draping qualities than plain weave, it also may stretch more. Whereas plain weave and its derivatives require but two harnesses, twill weave requires a minimum of three, usually four, and sometimes more. There are simple twills woven on straight draws on three to eight harnesses, and fancy twills requiring six or more harnesses.

Three Important Twills

In weaving twill, the warp yarns may be drawn through the harnesses in a straight draw, either from right to left or from left to right. On a four-harness straight draw threading, three important twills can be woven. These are:

A 2/2 twill, a 1/3 twill and a 3/1 twill. These are shown on the sample strip of basic weaves and their derivatives in Fig. 71, No. 5, and in Fig. 72, Nos. 6 and 7.

Of these three, the most common is the 2/2 twill in which both warp and weft interlace over two-under two, in a diagonal progression. The cloth is the same on the face and the back. This 2/2 twill has maximum strength and body.

In a 1/3 twill, the filling goes over three ends and under one end in a diagonal progression. The warp goes under three picks and over one. This becomes a filling-face twill; if the warp and filling are of different yarns or colors, the fabric will be different on face and back.

In a 3/1 twill, the filling goes over one end and under three ends, also in a diagonal progression. This becomes a warp-face twill and is used chiefly on striped warps, or in combination with a 1/3 twill to form a damasklike pattern. Again, if the warp and filling are in contrasting colors or fibers, the fabric will have a different face and back.

A 3/1 twill allows for packing in more filling than

does a 2/2 twill, or than plain weave. A classic example of this is blue denim, which has a blue filling face on a white warp. In denim, the filling covers the warp —a convenience when it is necessary to develop several colorings from a common warp. One could conceivably weave a black, red, green, and yellow denim on the same white warp used for blue denim.

Twill Variations

A right-hand twill is any twill with the diagonal rising from left to right; a left-hand twill rises from right to left. The difference between them is unimportant except when they are used together. The simplest combination of these is a reversed twill in which one treadles a left-hand twill for a number of picks, then treadles the same number of picks for a right-hand twill. The effect is of a horizontal herringbone, as in No. 8, in Fig. 72.

BROKEN TWILL: Broken twill refers specifically to twill treadlings in which the diagonal progression is interrupted or proceeds out of sequence. A typical treadling for a broken twill is: 1-2, 2-3, 4-1, 3-4. This is used, not to change the construction, but to disguise or vary the diagonal.

SUMMARY OF BASIC WEAVES AND THEIR DERIVATIVES THREADED ON A STRAIGHT DRAW

The woven strip in Figs. 71 and 72 gives a sampling of the basic weaves and derivatives described in this chapter. The strip, threaded on a straight draw, was woven on four harnesses of 8/4 worsted with black warp set twelve to the inch, and white filling. Riser sequences are given below. Read from the bottom upward, Fig. 71 at No. 1.

3-4
1-4
1-2
5. 2/2 left-hand twill weave 2-3

1-2
1-2
3-4
4. basket weave 3-4

1-2
2. and 3. rib weave 3-4
(No. 3 has tight beat-up)

2-4
1. plain weave 1-3

FIGS. 71 and 72. *The sample woven strip shows basic weaves and their derivatives, threaded on a straight draw. Photos, Ferdinand Boesch.*

1-2
2-3
1-4
9. broken twill 3-4

3-4   3-4
1-4   2-3
1-2   1-2
8. 2/2 reverse twill 2-3   and reverse 1-4

1
2
3
7. 3/1 left-hand twill 4

2-3-4
1-3-4
1-2-4
6. 1/3 left-hand twill 1-2-3

TWILL WEAVE ON A POINTED DRAW THREADING

A derivative or extension of twill weave is herringbone weave. Its distinguishing mark is the vertical succession of diagonals, alternating in direction like repeated V's to form the herringbone, named for the skeleton of the fish. The pattern, sometimes called chevron, is accentuated when the warp contrasts with the filling in color or in texture.

The herringbone V can be extended and enlarged simply by increasing the length of the threading repeat—that is, the threading can be repeated from right to left for any desired distance before reversing. In this way up to half the width of the fabric could be in one direction, and half in the reverse direction to form a giant V that extends from selvage to selvage. Or, a direction can be reversed at random.

Unlike the twill weaves shown in Figs. 71 and 72. which are threaded on a straight draw, herringbone requires a pointed draw threading, shown in Chapter 4. Fig. 75 gives a sample strip of herringbone weave with variations. The warp on the left side of the sample is threaded on a single-line pointed draw, Fig. 73 below:

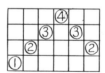

FIG. 73.

The warp on the right side of the blanket is threaded on a three-line pointed draw (not shown in Chapter 4).

FIG. 74.

Reading upwards from the bottom; the riser sequences for the left half of the herringbone sample, Fig. 75:

4. The samples on the top row (not shown in Chapter 4) are woven as drawn in on the three-line pointed draw at the right side of the blanket. Therefore the riser sequence is:

4. First,		Then,	
4		1	
3	three times	2	three times
2		3	
1		4	

A goose-eye pattern occurs in the sample at top.

3. Samples in the third row are woven on the same principle as drawn in, on the one-line pointed draw at the left side of the blanket. Here the bird's-eye pattern formed on the left is scarcely discernible. Riser sequence follows.

$$
\begin{array}{c}
1-2 \\
1-4 \\
3-4 \\
1-4 \\
1-2 \\
3.\ 2-3
\end{array}
$$

2. In the next row, a warp-faced herringbone has riser sequence as follows:

$$
\begin{array}{c}
1 \\
2 \\
3 \\
2.\ 4
\end{array}
$$

1. The balanced, or 2/2, riser sequence for the filling on the first sample row is

$$
\begin{array}{c}
3-4 \\
1-4 \\
1-2 \\
1.\ 2-3
\end{array}
$$

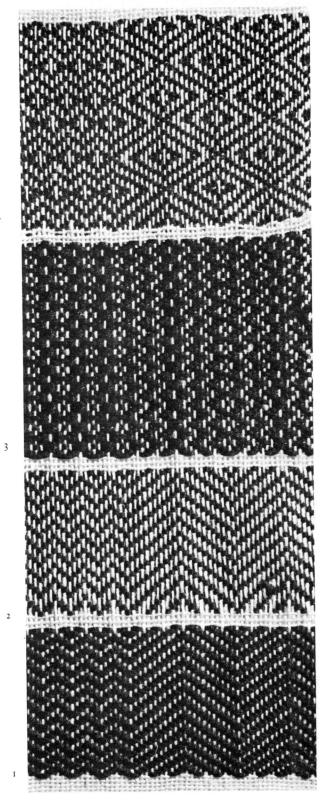

FIG. 75. *Sample strip of herringbone weave and variations threaded on a pointed draw. Text explains threadings for right and left side of each row together with riser sequences. Woven by Fan Mason.*

BASIC WEAVES AND THEIR COMBINATIONS

A broad range of basic weaves, and their derivatives, can be developed on a straight draw. The nine variations of these in Fig. 76, devised by Wendell Riggs, are woven on four harnesses with the same white warp. These examples might be considered as an extension of the sample strip, Figs. 71 and 72, demonstrating basic weaves and derivatives. Read the samples beginning at top, from right to left as numbered.

Indicated below are the riser sequences, or the order in which the harnesses are raised to weave these samples. Read horizontally.

(1) Simple filling brocade with underfloats on plain weave ground. (Because the brocade yarn is dark blue, it does not show clearly beside the black filling picks.)
Black 1-3, blue 3, black 2-4, blue 1.

(2) Combined plain weave and basket weave. (All plain-weave picks have been doubled on the bobbin.)
Black 1-2, 3-4 (basket); white 1-3, 2-4 (plain); black 3-4; white 1-2, 3-4 (basket); black 1-3, 2-4 (plain); white 3-4 (basket).

(3) Combination of rib weave and plain weave.
Black 1-3, 2-4 (plain)—(five times); black 2-3-4, white 1 (rib)—(four times); black 2-3-4.

(4) Plain weave with filling floats.
White 1-3, 2-4, 1-3; black 2 (float on face); white 1-3-4, black 1-2-3, white 1-3-4 (floats on back); black 2 (float on face).

(5) 3/1 filling-faced rib weave.
White 1-2-3, 4.

(6) All plain weave with random insertion of black and white picks.
Black 1-3; white 2-4; black 1-3; white 2-4; black 1-3; white 2-4, 1-3; black 2-4; etc.

(7) Miniature spot weave with underfloats (a brocade).
White 1-3, 2-4; 1-3, 2-4; black 4; white 1-3, 2-4; 1-3, 2-4; black 2.

(8) A broken twill. Combination of plain weave and rib weave.

Black 1-3, 2-4, 1-2, 3-4, 1-2.

(9) Various line stripes on a plain weave ground.

White 1-3, 2-4, 1-3; black 3-4, 1-2; white 1-3, 2-4, 1-3, 2-4; white 1-3; black 3; white 2-4. 1-3 (eight times); black 1, white 2-4, 1-3, 2-4, 1-3; black 2-4, 2-4.

FIG. 76. *Basic weaves and their derivatives, some in combination, are developed on a straight draw by Wendell Riggs. These nine samples may be considered an extension of sample strip, Figs. 71 and 72. Text gives riser sequences. Read from right to left, top row, as numbered. Photo, Ferdinand Boesch.*

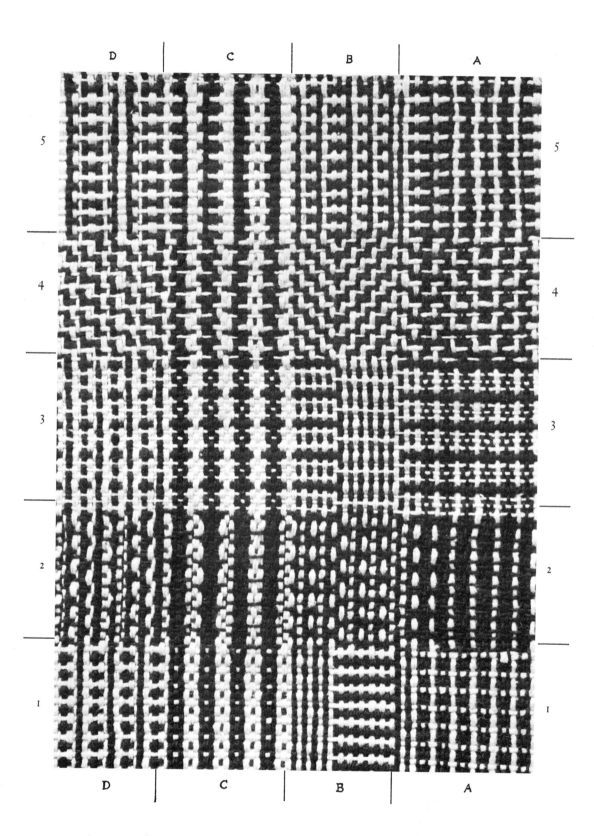

TEXTURE PATTERNS DERIVED FROM YARN SEQUENCE

Patterns, textural or otherwise, may also derive from changes in yarn sequence across a warp which alternates straight draw threadings with pointed draws. These are especially effective and instructive when simple yarns are used, as in the section of a black-and-white blanket, Fig. 77.

Carpet warp—8/4 cotton and 4/4 cotton in both black and white—is used in this sample, showing pattern variations through alternating or contrasting yarn sequences in warp or filling, or in both. All are woven in basic weaves on either pointed draw or straight draw threadings.

Warp Setup for Sample Blanket

A. Beginning at right below, Section A, the first warp section is threaded on a straight draw with three ends of black 8/4 and with every fourth end of white 4/4, as indicated by parentheses:

$$(4)$$
$$3$$
$$2$$
$$1$$

B. The next warp section, to the left of A, is threaded on a 3-line pointed draw, all in 8/4 (carpet warp), doubled:

(4-4)		(4-4)		(4-4)			4-4	
3-3		3-3		3-3			(3-3)	
(2-2)		(2-2)		(2-2)		2-2	2-2	
1-1		1-1		1-1		1-1		(1-1)

Note: Numerals in parentheses indicate black. At the point of the draw white changes from even- to odd-numbered harnesses, producing a vertical rib instead of a horizontal one.

FIG. 77. *The pattern blanket shown here alternates straight draw threadings with pointed draws across the warp. It demonstrates how change of sequence in contrasting yarns varies pattern. The text explains the texture of selected sections, or squares, all in basic weaves. Sample woven by Fan Mason. Photo, Ferdinand Boesch.*

C. The next warp threading, section C, to the left of B, is a single line pointed draw, using 8/4 in both black and white, with all warp ends doubled, as follows:

$$(4-4)$$
$$(3-3) \qquad\qquad (3-3)$$
$$2-2 \qquad\qquad 2-2$$
$$1-1$$

This produces a stripe which is centered on the point of the draw. (Ends in parentheses are black.)

D. The last threading section on the left is threaded on a straight draw, with three white 8/4 ends and one black 4/4; the second and third white ends are threaded in one heddle. Parentheses indicate black:

$$4 \qquad\qquad 4-4 \qquad\qquad (4)$$
$$(3) \qquad\qquad 3 \qquad\qquad 3-3$$
$$2-2 \qquad\qquad (2) \qquad\qquad 2$$
$$1 \qquad\qquad 1-1 \qquad\qquad (1)$$

Note: Because the three-heddle yarn sequence and the four-heddle harness sequence are not related, the repeat is lengthened to twelve heddles. Observe the diagonal progression of doubled ends and of black ends which shows up on the threading draft and in the 2/2 twill of square D4.

Sequence of Filling Yarns

The yarn and riser sequence for the bands of filling is indicated below.

Band 1: White (4/4) 1-3; black (4/4) 2-4.
Notice in square B1 the effective pattern resulting from white filling under white warp and black filling under black warp.

Band 2. In Band 2, next above, the filling is black 8/4; the riser sequence is: 1-2, 2-3, 3-4, 1-4, 3-4, 2-3. Square A in this band is effective because the single white yarn contrasts vividly with an all-black ground.

Band 3. In Band 3, the filling is white 8/4 and black 4/4. The riser sequence is as follows: White (8/4) 1-3, 2-4, 1-3; black (4/4) 2-4.

Band 4. In the fourth band the riser sequence is: White (4/4) 1-2; black (8/4) 2-3; white (4/4) 3-4; black (8/4) 1-4.

This is the riser sequence for a 2/2 or balanced twill. The twill shows up on square D4; also, because of the pointed draw of warp section B, a large-scale herringbone is discernible in square B4.

Band 5. In the top, or fifth band, the riser sequence is: Black (4/4) 1-2; white (4/4) 3-4.

By and large, the pattern of Band 5 is a version of Band 1, but larger in scale, because the warp ends are paired and the filling is 4/4 instead of 8/4 yarn.

BROCADE

From past tradition, the word brocade connotes luxurious, richly colored, complex stuffs woven from fine silk yarns. Actually, brocading is one of the easiest devices for decorating fabrics. Simple brocade can be woven on three or four harnesses.

Brocade is, in effect, an imitation of embroidery. It has often been developed as such and is of the nature of embroidery in that the decorative brocading yarns are extraneous to the cloth construction. As with embroidery, all the brocade yarns can be pulled out of the fabric—traditionally in plain weave—and leave it intact.

Introducing a Third Element

Weaving, of course, produces a typical, two-element fabric composed of warp and weft yarns. There are single-element fabrics such as knitting, crocheting, and bobbin lace. With brocading, on its two-element plain weave ground, a third element is introduced. This element is composed of supplementary yarn or yarns which are non-essential to the two-element ground cloth.

Other techniques may have three or more elements. Pile fabrics, for example, whether warp piles like velvet and terry cloth, or filling piles which are hand-knotted, have a third element which is the pile yarn. Double cloth, with two warps and two fillings, has four elements. A brocaded double cloth would have five elements, and so on.

BROCADES: THREE TECHNIQUES

The three important kinds of brocade are warp brocade, filling brocade and laid-in, or discontinuous, brocade. These techniques in both England and America are sometimes referred to as "overshot" patterns; in all three, the brocading element is extraneous to the base cloth. Laid-in, common to many historical periods, is a discontinuous brocade in that the supplementary brocading yarn does not run from selvage to selvage. *Dukagang*, the Swedish term for this, is but a provincial variation of discontinuous brocade.

Warp Brocade

A warp brocade is the simplest to plan and weave. For a four-harness loom, it consists of a simple plain-weave ground running the width of the web on harnesses one and two. The brocading element is a supplementary warp threaded on harnesses three or four, or on both. Very simply, a block of supplementary warp ends on the third harness could produce a warp stripe or an interrupted warp stripe may become a rectangle. A second brocade block, threaded on a fourth harness, can be brought up independently of the first to produce alternate squares; or to work in relation to block one to form simple figures such as a cross, a hollow square, a T, an L, an H, and most other alphabet shapes.

FIG. 78. *Diagram of a two-block, four-harness warp brocade. The long bands are floats. Drawing, Don Wight.*

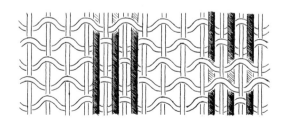

As a rule the brocading yarn is heavier than the ground cloth yarn, and usually it is so soft that it can be squeezed between the ends and picks of the plain woven web. When it is thus squeezed, there can be little slippage of the brocade floats. Usually, but not always, the brocade yarn contrasts with the ground in color or texture, or in both.

There is always at least one end of basic warp between each end of brocading warp. In sleying, the basic cloth ends are pulled through independently of the brocade ends. If the basic or ground cloth is sleyed fifteen ends to the inch there will be one basic end in every dent of a fifteen-dent reed. The brocading ends, wherever they occur, will fall in the same dent as a basic end.

Filling Brocade

A filling brocade may be either continuous, with the brocade shuttle weaving from selvage to selvage, or it may be discontinuous; in this case the brocade yarn is woven back and forth only across a motif. With continuous-filling brocade, as with warp brocade, the ground cloth is almost invariably in plain weave. Traditionally, the warp is simple and in one yarn. Between each pattern pick there must be a plain-weave pick. These plain-weave picks are on alternate sheds to form a true plain woven ground, and are quite independent of the pattern picks.

As already noted, the classic overshot weaves familiar in hand weaving milieus are all continuous filling brocades. These patterns exhaust the structural variations of the technique, but the weaver today still has

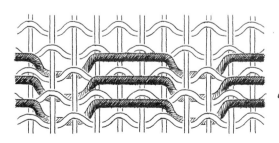

FIG. 79. *Diagram of filling brocade shows interlacing of warp and filling yarns with brocade yarn floating over and under ground cloth. Drawing, Don Wight.*

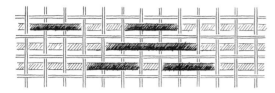

FIG. 80. *Diagram shows the interlacing of yarns in a continuous-filling brocade. Drawing, Don Wight.*

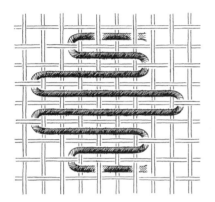

FIG. 81. *Diagram of discontinuous brocade in which brocade filling yarn floats over ground cloth. Drawing, Don Wight.*

FIG. 82. *Diagram of discontinuous-filling brocade with bang-tail ends left untrimmed. The supplementary wefts are laid in the same shed as the basic filling. Useful as a rug technique. Drawing, Don Wight.*

a broad range of new patterns to work out in the sequence and combination of simple motifs—such as the diagonals, circles, and checkerboards.

In designing a simple filling brocade for four harnesses, the basic tenet is that a plain-weave ground cloth be maintained. Therefore the threading sequence must insure a cloth that is plain woven. The simplest way to be assured of this is *always* to thread from an odd-numbered harness to an even-numbered one, even when making the transition between threading blocks. In general, threading is done in blocks using three harnesses, one of which acts as a tie-down. (A tie-down secures a float to the cloth.)

Discountinuous Brocade, and Free Weaving Techniques

Discontinuous, or laid-in, brocade introduces the free-weaving techniques. Others to follow are the gauzy, lacy weaves, referred to sometimes as finger weaving. Up to this point all the weaves and patterns described have been loom-controlled. Loom-controlled means that the weave is formed through the interaction of the harnesses. Loom-controlled weaves may be as simple as plain weave and others already demonstrated, or they may be extremely complex.

In any case, loom-controlled weaves always have a filling which runs from selvage to selvage directly, in one continuous shed. This may not be the case with free weaving, in which the pattern yarn is introduced and controlled by the weaver's fingers.

Since the weaver is not limited by the geometry of harness-manipulated patterns, the greatest freedom is in order. He should take effective advantage of this new latitude, introducing freely drawn shapes and

FIG. 83. *Large varicolored dots ornament a sheer casement of broad, skip-dented bands. The discontinuous-filling brocade yarn for dots is inserted in a 1/3 filling-face twill arrangement. An Alexander Girard design for Herman Miller.*

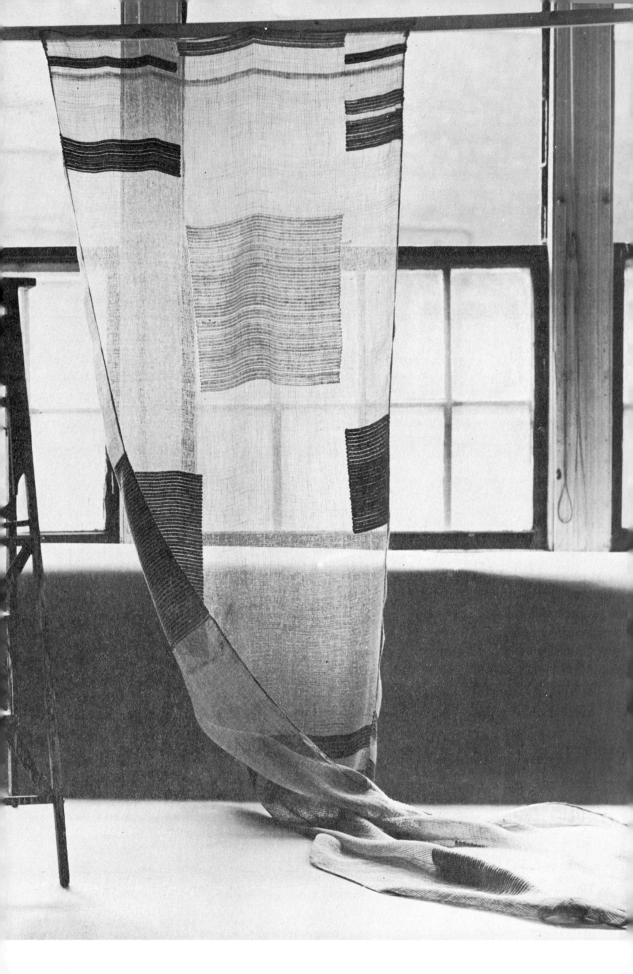

curves, without repeat if he prefers, and forms not feasible with loom-controlled techniques.

While discontinuous or laid-in brocade is a simple, primitive process, it is also time-consuming. It should therefore be used sparingly, for detail or accent. It may be used effectively in combination with loom-controlled techniques such as striping, or as a small decoration with a plaid, as a border or a spot motif.

Laid-In Brocade: A Procedure

The woven sample, Fig. 85, can best demonstrate the procedure for weaving discontinuous brocade. A few simple motifs are suggested for following the elementary steps. Practicing the different techniques will give the weaver wider scope in designing later on; with this actual experience, he can better grasp the relationship between yarn, sett, and technique. He will be prepared for more advanced work in manipulating yarn, shapes, and colors.

Laid-In on a Plain-Weave Shed

The warp is set up on four harnesses. The ground cloth is plain woven of a size 14/2 boiled linen, balanced in warp and weft. The brocading yarn is black cotton floss, a softer and slightly heavier yarn than that used for the ground cloth.

(1) The diamond at the lower left side of the sample provides an easy example of laid-in, on a plain-weave interlacing. First a heading of one inch, twenty picks or so, is done in plain weave. Then, with the next shot of basic filling and in the same open shed, a short length or ball of brocade yarn is laid in, covering one warp end only, about one inch from the left selvage.

FIG. 84. *A discontinuous brocade of chenille yarns on a sheer hemp ground. The denser brocade areas are laid in freely on two loom-controlled threading blocks. Designer, Jack Lenor Larsen. Photo, David Vestal.*

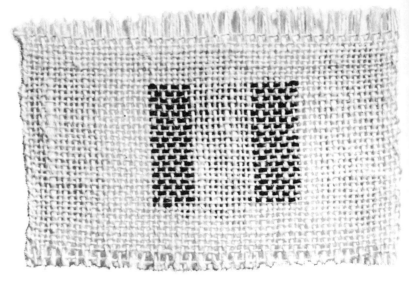

FIG. 85. *Samples show discontinuous brocade, or laid-in motifs, with cotton floss in black and two colors on ground cloth of boiled linen yarn. Photos, Ferdinand Boesch.*

FIG. 86. *Reverse side of discontinuous brocade samples, showing the floats. Woven by Fan Mason. Photo, Ferdinand Boesch.*

This is the lower point of the diamond. The shed is changed and the filling beaten up. On the return ground pick, the brocading yarn is laid in to cover three warp ends—over one, under one, over one, under one, over one. These are centered directly over the first covered warp end. On each succeeding pick of basic filling, for eight or ten picks, the figure is widened by covering an additional warp end at each side with the brocading yarn. At this point the figure will resemble an inverted triangle. The weaving then is continued back and forth, but decreasing the width of the brocaded figure with each shot by one warp end at each side until the tip of the diamond is reached and the figure completed.

The tension of the brocade yarn should be watched, especially where it loops back into the web: it should be kept even and consistent but never taut. (*Note:* If a pattern requires dense coverage, the brocade yarn will be laid in with the filling pick in every shed; but if the pattern is sparse, or if the ground cloth picks are tightly packed, two or more base cloth picks may be woven between brocade picks.)

It can be seen from the reverse side of the sample, in Fig. 86, that the brocading yarn in the diamond figures is carried from one pick to the next under the warp for concealment.

(2) The diamond at the lower right of the sample is woven in the same way as the first—and at the same time—but with a difference in the brocading yarn. Here two finer yarns, one black and one turquoise, are carried as one in the brocading element. The additional color adds sparkle to the motif.

(3) Again, the central diamond figure is woven in the same way, but "striped," that is, the brocading yarn in the lower half is turquoise, in the upper half it is black.

Laid-In on a 3/1 Shed

Not all discontinuous brocade picks are laid in on a plain-weave shed. Frequently a 3/1 shed is used in order to get most of the brocading on the surface. In

Fig. 83, a Girard design, a true 3/1 twill is superimposed on a plain-weave base. An alternative to this is the Swedish dukagang technique in which only the first harness of a straight-draw threading is used as a tie-down.

(4) In the letter F on the sample, for instance, the brocading yarn (the same black cotton floss, but doubled) is not inserted in the same shed as the ground cloth pick. In this case, the bottom row is laid in, starting from the left, and floats above the basic plain-weave cloth on an over three—under one interlacing. The basic filling is woven as usual on a riser sequence of 1-3; 2-4. To begin the motif, harness 1 alone is raised and the brocading yarn laid in. Then 1 and 3 are raised, and the brocading yarn is returned. Then a basic filling pick is woven with harnesses 2 and 4 raised. A repeat of the riser sequence begins as the brocading yarn is entered with harness 1 raised again.

(5) The letter O is done in the same way as F. The brocading yarn is floated on the surface of the cloth, except for the empty center of the O, where it underfloats.

(6) In the "matches" motif, at the top of the sample, double floss brocading yarn in gold is used for the match head, black for the matchstick. The matchstick weft itself has a short underfloat, the head a very long one, as shown on the reverse side of the sample, Fig. 86.

Cut-Float or Bang-Tail Motif

The figure at the top, a cut-float or bang-tail motif, returns to the plain-weave shed for the brocading as in the diamond shapes. The two long rectangles or bands of plain woven brocade are separated by an overfloat that was cut after the figure was completed. In this overfloat, the brocade yarn is simply carried across the face of the cloth from one band to the other. A bang-tail effect can also be done on continuous brocade—any filling or warp float can be cut after weaving provided the float yarn is well anchored to the ground cloth.

MOCK DOUBLE CLOTH

The best way to describe the woven samples in Fig. 87 is to call them mock double cloth. A true double cloth has two warps and two fillings. The cloth under discussion has one warp and two fillings—a construction sometimes classed with double cloth. The second filling is a true filling, not a brocading element. The visual effect is rather like tapestry.

The warp is black, 10/2 cotton, the filling a soft worsted that packs in well. Here, the filling is packed down around the spots eccentrically, that is, off the usual horizontal direction of filling, thus modifying the pattern.

The threading draft for Block A is 1-2, 1-2; for Block B it is 3-4, 3-4. (*Note:* The threading is the same as for the Marie Howell grouped casement in Fig. 116, page 184.)

Blocks A and B in the patterns at left in Fig. 87 are regular in size (Nos. 1, 2, 3, and 4); those on the right (Nos. 5, 6, and 7) are irregular in size.

In any given pattern block, only one filling at a time is engaged in the warp; the other filling floats underneath. (Note the down-turned corner of sample 4.) If a figure of more than three or four picks were desired, it would be necessary to weave ground filling between and under the figure.

The principle of the riser sequence is as follows: Plain-weave ground: 1-3, 2-4. Pattern Block A: 1-2-3; 1-2-4. Pattern Block B: 1-2-3; 2-3-4. The filling for pattern blocks contrasts with the ground. Any number of colors may be used.

(1) In the first sample, No. 1 at lower left of Fig. 87, both Blocks A and B have been used for patterns in an irregular sequence of sizes. Care has been taken to balance the blocks in order to maintain tension. Reading horizontally, the riser sequence is as follows:

Gray ground 1-3, 2-4, 1-3; white 1-2-3; gray 2-4, 1-3, 2-4, 1-3; white 1-3-4, 2-3-4, 1-3-4, 2-3-4; gray 2-4, 1-3, 2-4, 1-3; white 1-2-3, 1-2-4, 1-3; gray 2-4, 1-3; white 1-2-4; etc.

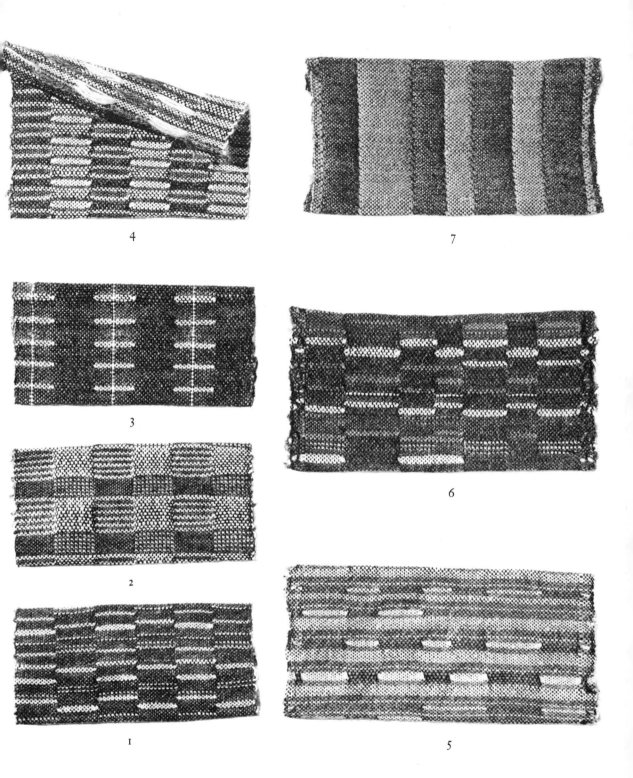

4

7

3

6

2

1

5

FIG. 87. *Mock double cloth, not a brocading technique, but similar in effect as it is to tapestry. Seven examples, using filling underfloats between pattern areas. Note down-turned corner of No. 4. Woven by Fan Mason.*

(2) In No. 2, filling picks of white and gray are alternated in the gray bands of Block B, giving a checked effect. Riser sequence follows:

Gray 1-3, 2-4, white 1-2-3 (five times); gray 1-3, 2-4; white 1-3, 2-4, gray 1-3-4, 2-3-4 (five times); white 1-3, 2-4.

(3) A single white warp end has been tied in to form a line stripe on a gray stripe centered on Block A. Ten picks of gray ground in plain weave are followed by: White 1-3-4, 2-3-4, 1-3-4.

(4) A positive-negative alternation is created by white spots on a gray stripe, in contrast with gray spots on a white stripe. The riser sequence is:

Gray 1-3, 2-4; white 1-2-3, 1-2-4, 1-2-3, 1-2-4; gray 1-3, 2-4; white 1-2, 2-4; gray 1-2-4, 2-3-4, 1-3-4, 2-3-4; white 1-3, 2-4.

(5) In Nos. 5, 6, and 7, the spacing of the stripes is random. Threading blocks, irregular in size, have replaced the regular, even blocks of the first four samples. In No. 5, the pattern is one of white spots and white horizontal lines on gray ground which is broken by wide white stripes. The weave is the same as in No. 4, with random repeat.

(6) In No. 6, a third filling color has been added to vary the pattern of No. 1. The weave is the same.

(7) In No. 7 the pattern of vertical stripes is made by weaving Blocks A and B, alternately, without plain weave ground. The effect is slightly three-dimensional, or sculptured, because the underfloats exert a tension that pulls the cloth in at the selvages. The riser sequence is as follows:

Gray 1-3-4, 2-3-4; white 1-2-3, 1-2-4.

To summarize the methods used to vary these designs: In No. 1, the size of the figures is varied, and random spacing is used. In 2, weft striping and other yarn sequence effects combine with the weave to form a block pattern. In 3, the warp has been striped; in 4, both the ground and the figures have been striped. In Nos. 5, 6, and 7, the threading block proportions have been varied. White motifs on gray ground, gray motifs on white ground form positive-negative stripes in No. 5; and in No. 6, there is an additional filling color. No. 7 has been woven on opposites.

FREE-WOVEN LACY WEAVES

Another free-weaving technique is used to create open, lacy patterns which include gauze, leno, Spanish lace, and variations of these. The open spaces are created by deflecting warp ends in various ways by hand, either by crossing them in pairs, or in groups, or by twisting or wrapping them between bands or areas of plain weave. See Fig. 89.

While most of these methods can be done with the fingers, some are easier to do with the help of a crochet hook or a flat, pointed stick called a pick-up stick.

These techniques may be combined; they also permit of numerous elaborations, as in the frequency with which crossings or wrappings are done and in the number of warps which are crossed or wrapped, as seen in Fig. 89.

Effects thus created may be traditional, formal, and more or less mechanical. The traditional yarn is a round, plied line linen, in one color. Used in this way, the lenos in particular are most attractive for handkerchiefs, fine table linens and babies' things. Since the lace technique is a slow one, it should be reserved for fine quality yarns and the lace figures should remain the dominant decorative device.

If, on the other hand, such finger weaving is interpreted more freely, any yarn and combination of colors can be used. The freer, modern versions are seen principally in decorative panels. If the piece is loose and gauzy, the weaving goes much faster than in closer versions, but may be fragile to a fault.

Weaving time for finger laces is determined by the scale of the ground cloth and the amount of lace within it. If the scale is large enough, lacy weaves may even be considered for curtain material, as in the Kay Sekimachi piece, an example of large-scale wrapping, Fig. 90. See also Fig. 91.

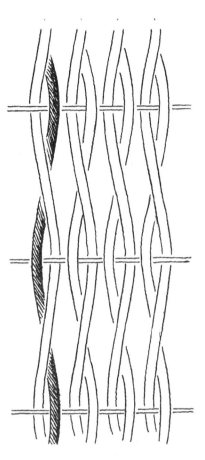

FIG. 88. *An example of warp twining in the group of gauze weaves. Drawing, Don Wight.*

139

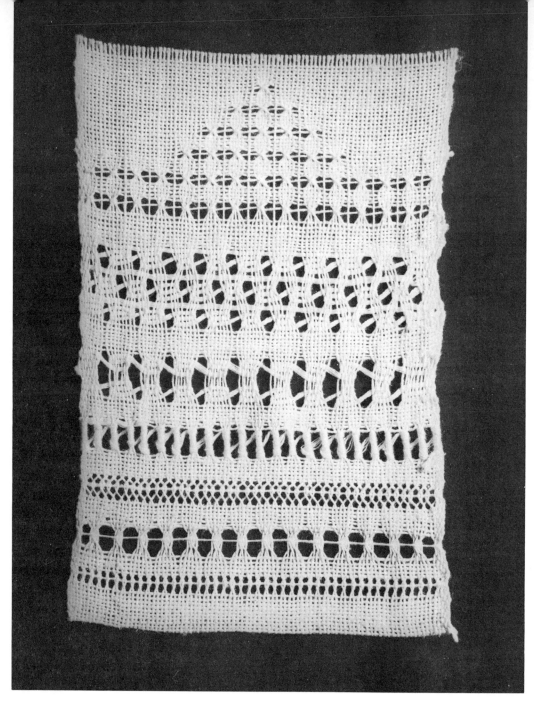

FIG. 89. *Leno and other lacy open weaves. Reading from bottom upward: three versions of leno; next above, a row of warp-wrapping; then two rows of Spanish lace; last, above, an open weave somewhat resembling leno, woven as a triangular inset.*

FIG. 90. *Casement with interesting silhouette, developed in weft wrapping techniques, a fine example of contemporary freedom in applying a conventional technique. Designer, Kay Sekimachi.*

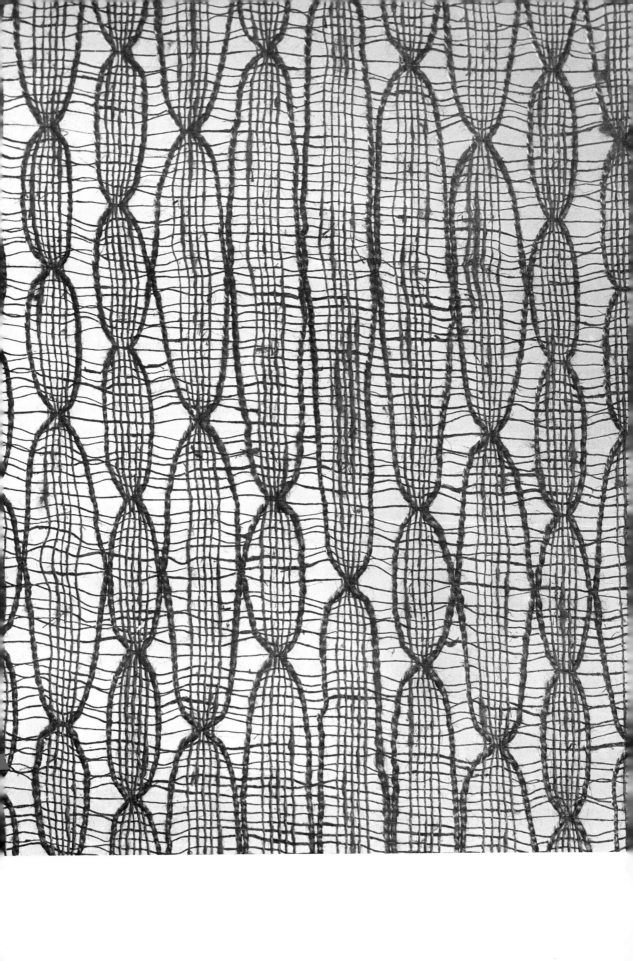

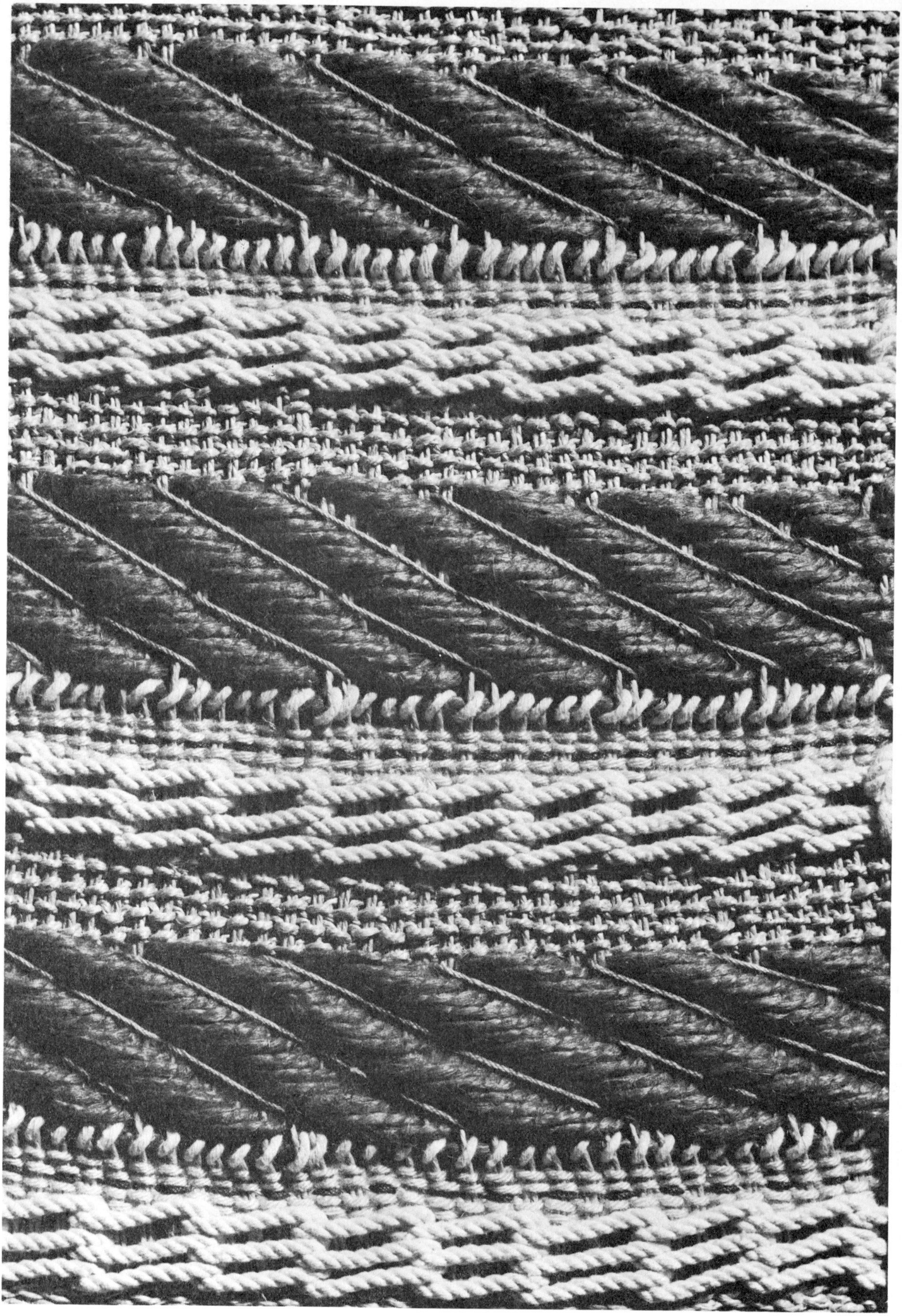

Leno

In Fig. 89 the three bottom rows of the woven sample are versions of leno. In the first row of single leno, the warp crossings are done in simple pairs. This means, of course, that the warp has been planned with an even number of ends. The procedure is as follows:

(1) On two harnesses, set up a warp of plied linen yarn with an even number of ends. Weave a narrow heading of plain weave, ending with the bobbin at the right-hand selvage. Lay the bobbin down, beat the fabric and change the shed. Using the pick-up stick, place it to the left of the second warp end, which is raised. Lower the stick at an angle so that it goes over, and to the right of, the first warp end, which is lowered. Turn the stick to the left so that it catches the lowered warp end and brings it up to the left of the second (and raised) warp end.

Next slide the stick to the left so that it goes over the fourth warp end, which is raised. Again, lower the stick at an angle, and to the left of this warp end, so that it goes over and to the right of the third warp end, which is lowered. Turn the stick to the left as with the first crossing so that it catches the lowered warp end and brings it up to the left of the fourth (and raised) warp end.

Continue thus across the warp until all the warp ends are crossed in pairs. Then the stick is turned on edge to make a space for the bobbin to pass through the shed.

As already explained, this process can be done with the fingers, or a crochet hook. If the pick-up stick is preferred, it should be made several inches longer than

FIG. 91. *Filling bands of open-weave, free techniques in an experimental composition done on a weaving frame; combines two kinds of wrapping and twining, with bars of twill and plain weave on paired warp ends; in jute, hemp wrapping cord, cotton twine, and fishline. Designer, Jerome Yatsunoff. Photo, Ferdinand Boesch.*

the width of the warp so that it can easily hold the crossed warps across the width of the web, and a little beyond.

At this point, the stick is withdrawn slowly and the weft is beaten into place carefully. Change the shed and beat again. There should now be an openwork band measuring about three-eighths of an inch. Another band of plain weave can be woven next, as in the sample, Fig. 89, or the leno can be continued.

(2) Next above the single leno is a 3/3 leno. The crossings are made in the same way as in Leno No. 1 except that three ends (upper layer) are crossed over three ends (lower layer) right across the warp. Again, as in No. 1, the pick-up stick is turned on edge to form a shed through which the single weft is passed. As in all versions of leno, the weft bisects the open spaces made by the crossings as evenly as possible, leaving equal open spaces on each side of it.

(3) In the third example of leno, sometimes called Mexican lace, the pick-up stick is manipulated so that the warp ends cross three times. The uneven order in which the ends are started results in the triple twist of the lace; the leno weft is inserted in the central crossing. The first end crosses the fourth, the third end crosses the sixth, the fifth end crosses the eighth, the seventh end crosses the tenth, the ninth end crosses the twelfth, and so on across the warp.

Warp Wrapping

(4) In the fourth row, after another band of plain weave, is an example of warp wrapping. For this a soft, five-strand supplementary weft of embroidery floss was chosen and wound into a ball or on a bobbin. On a closed shed, beginning at lower edge of the selvage at right, begin to coil this weft tightly around the first four ends. Care must be taken to do this evenly, maintaining an even tension, winding in a spiraling but almost horizontal direction.

When a height of about half an inch has been reached, the weft is brought down to the base of the next four ends and again begins the coiling of the soft weft yarn around these. Continue in this way until all groups of four ends across the warp are wound.

Spanish Lace #1

(5) The next example is a version of Spanish lace. The method here is to weave three picks of the supplementary floss back and forth, in an S shape, to form the warp groups, using the harnesses alternately to open the sheds. In the first group, at the right of the sample, eight warp ends are engaged, pulling the warp group together on each return. Then the filling declines diagonally, to engage the next eight ends for three picks. (A comb is substituted for a beater which cannot be used here.)

At the left selvage group, six picks are woven in the same way, and the process reversed across the warp from left to right.

Spanish Lace #2

(6) In this version of Spanish lace, the first three-pick band is woven exactly as it was in No. 5 above. But when the filling is woven, for three picks at the left selvage, it then returns to the right selvage on an open plain-weave shed. The second row is staggered above the first. The three-pick motif is woven through the first four ends, then declines, and continues across the warp engaging ends five through twelve, thirteen through twenty, and so on. The third band is identical with the first.

(7) The lace weave in No. 7 somewhat resembles the 3/3 leno in band 2, but is easier and faster. Also, the pick-up stick is not necessary in weaving it.

On an open plain-weave shed, encircle the first three raised ends with the weft, rather in the manner of backstitching, then the second group of raised ends, and so on across the warp. Beat into place. Although the ends of the lower layer are compressed within the groups, they are not actually engaged by the weft. The second and fourth ends conform to the wrapped group while the sixth end alone remains independent, forming the small cross motif within the open space.

Now weave five picks of plain weave, repeat the

wrapping across the warp, then weave another band of plain weave. Like leno and other finger laces, this technique is used to create an open pattern on a plain woven ground. In this sample, a triangular shape is formed by the successive reduction of wrapped groups at each side, replaced by plain weave.

CHAPTER SIX

Materials

Possibly the greatest difference between the weaving of today and that of the ancients lies in the materials. Primitive weavers relied, for the most part, on one simple yarn, hand spun and usually single ply. Spinners had one or perhaps two fibers to work with— cotton and wool or silk, or linen.

Today there are tens of thousands of yarns, natural and man-made, differing in fiber, twist, size and texture. Apart from the growing variety of synthetic yarns there are a dozen types of wool, eight of silk, and corresponding ranges of cotton and linen. These have been developed through the enlightened cultivation of plant fibers, scientific breeding, and modern processing methods.

With the free interchange provided by today's trade channels from one country and climate to another, various agencies and distributors have made these yarns generally available to hand weavers, most of them obtainable by mail order. Some of these can be bought in small "put-ups"—on spools, bobbins, or by the skein. Frequently these are offered in quarter- or half-pound lots, to be reordered when necessary. This is important in view of the fact that a weaver's studio, however small, needs a profusion of yarns, varied in color, texture, and size. These become the basic vocabulary for articulating design; they are the means by which a weaver determines the color, texture, and the quality of the fabric.

FIBERS, OLD AND NEW

FIG. 92. *An all-white upholstery fabric woven of lustrous yarn for the warp with matte calfhide strips for the filling, a textural play of glossy and dull, white-on-white. Designer, Hella Skowronski.*

To the wealth of natural fibers, and the familiar manmade fibers such as rayon and nylon has been added a range of thermoplastic and glass fibers. In appearance, however, most new fibers contribute little to our broad traditional range of materials. They are not intended to; they are meant to supplement or to blend with natural fibers. A designer's usual preference for natural materials may point to a need for the further "humanizing" of the synthetics.

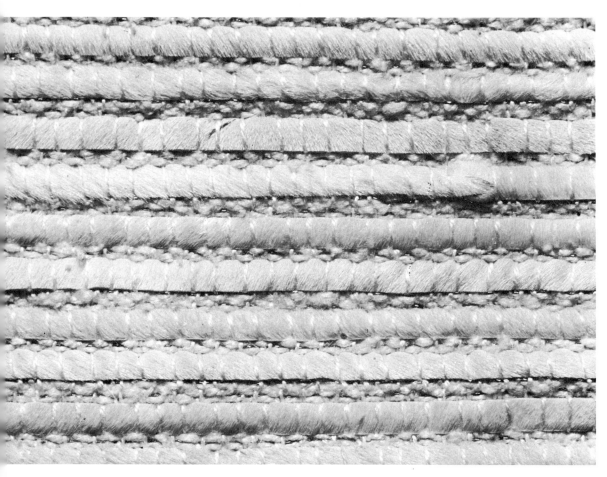

FIG. 93. *An all-paper fiber wall covering, with filling brocade of paper braid on a plain weave ground. American Import Company, New York.*

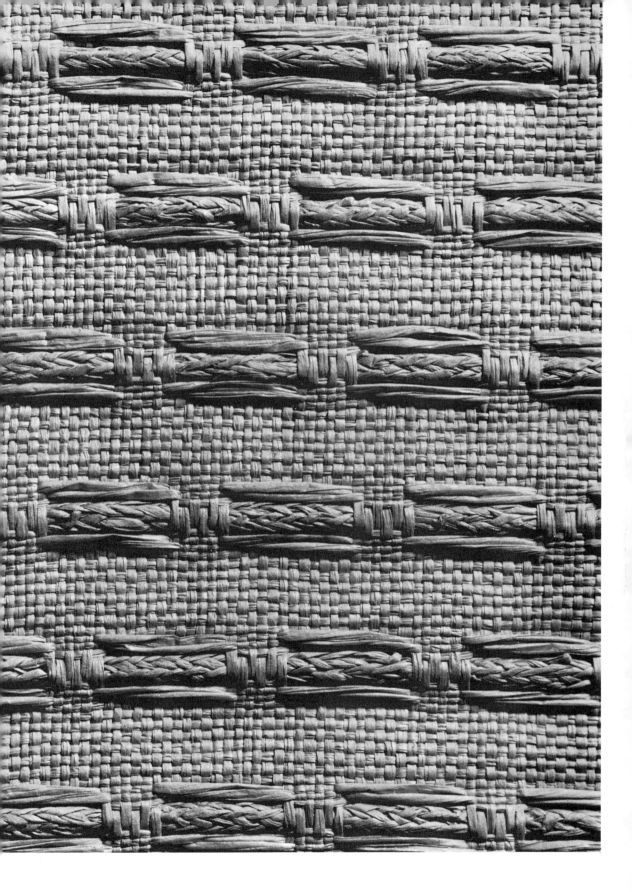

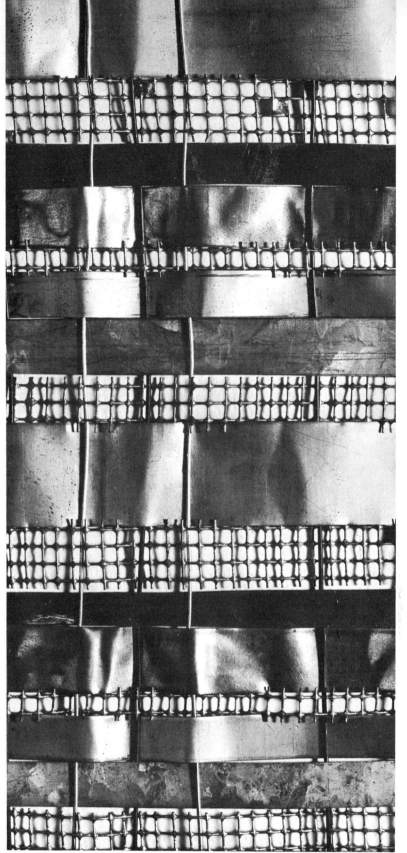

FIG. 94. *Experimental weaving for a screen exploits metallic reflections in copper, steel, and brass tones. The warp alternates dark with light wire ends; the filling, metal strips with wire mesh screening. Designer, George William Fagan.*

FIG. 95. *A smooth, even-surfaced wall covering of paper fiber, raffia, and copper wire in plain weave. The warp alternates copper wire with raffia ends sleyed loosely enough to lie flat; the filling of paper fiber is stiff enough to stay flat, not twist in the weaving. Designer, Marjatta Metsovaara-Nystrom. Photo, Pietinen.*

FIG. 96. *Experimental fabric in exotic materials and colors—reds, orange and magenta feathers—with string, raffia, and cloth strips for filling, on a sparse warp of twine. Designed by Diane Glen and woven on a frame loom. Photo, Ferdinand Boesch.*

FIG. 97. *Contrast of fine and heavy, hard and soft yarns, with eiderdown, cotton roving, cotton string and hemp for the filling. These natural fibers fall within a close range of color values, providing unity to a twill weave fabric of exaggerated texture. One of Dorothy Liebes' hunky weaves, originally in the Collection of the Museum of Modern Art, New York.*

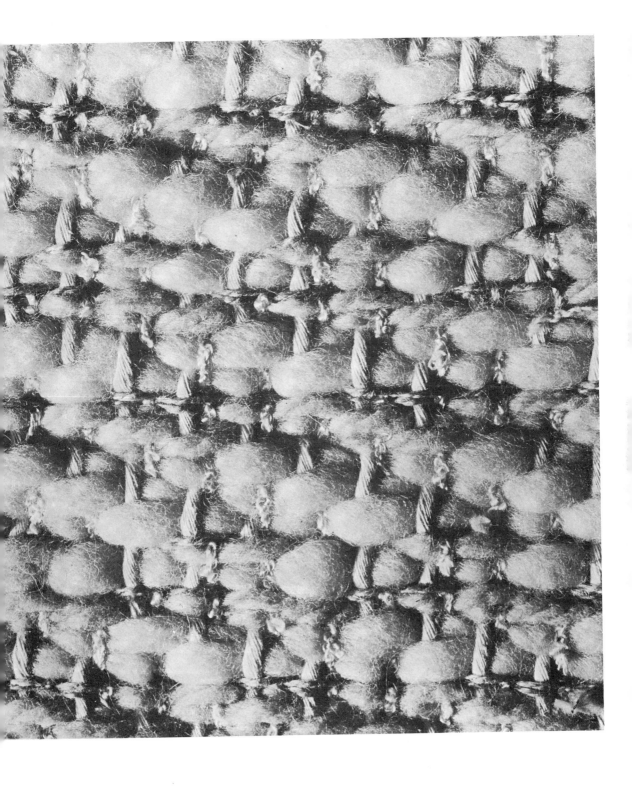

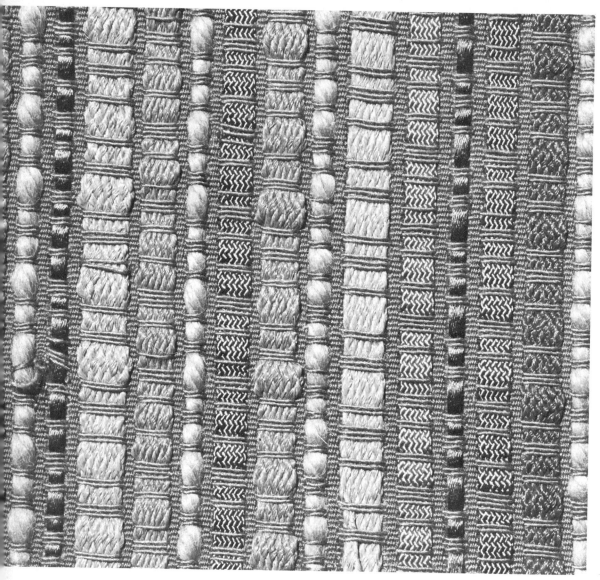

FIG. 98. *Heavy yarns and braids in jewel tones alternate with tight bands of cotton to form a warp, on a ground cloth of plain woven nylon. A Larsen Design Studio upholstery. Photo, Ferdinand Boesch.*

FIG. 99. *White felted roving, size of a little finger, plain woven on a tightly twisted black warp gives strong contrast in scale and value. Contemporary Moroccan blanket.*

There are two main fiber classifications: filament and staple. The monofilament yarn is a single, continuous, extruded strand—in simple terms, the strand as the spider makes it. In natural textile fibers there is the single continuous strand of silk as it is unwound from the cocoon. Among the man-made monofilaments are nylon and Saran.

Multifilament yarns are composed of several continuous filaments of silk, rayon, acetate, nylon, Fiberglas, and so on. These yarns generally have only a slight twist. In this category are the multifilament yarns which have been processed to resemble spun yarns. These bulked, lofted, or textured multifilament yarns often are produced under trade names such as Taslan (nylon) or Chromespun (acetate). Some of these are extruded in color, thus eliminating the dyeing process and increasing color-fastness. These are designated as solution-dyed, dope-dyed, or under trade names such as Jetspun.

In the other main classification are the yarns made from staple fibers, shorter-length fibers as opposed to continuous filaments. Staple yarn is made by spinning staple, or lengths of fiber, into a continuous strand of yarn. Staple lengths vary greatly—from as short as an inch in length or less, to as long as twelve inches, and more, in the case of the Angora goat. These variations are described by the terms long-staple fibers and short-staple fibers.

Yarns spun from staple fibers constitute the larger group by far, including all those made from natural fibers (except filament silk), as well as synthetic yarns made by cutting continuous filaments into staple lengths before spinning.

In natural-fiber staple yarns, the length of fiber is a prime quality consideration. Fibers are graded according to length and uniformity. Long-staple linen, cotton, and wool bring premium prices because of their superior luster, strength, and fineness. Long-staple cotton fiber, for instance, is frequently more expensive and more lustrous than short-fiber or noil silk. While linen is known as a luxury fiber with notable strength and luster, many tow linens are as cheap as the lower grades of cotton, and are equally fragile and lusterless. As a general rule, there are greater differences in quality within a fiber classification than there are between the different fibers.

How Natural Fibers Are Graded

COTTON	Long Staple	Short Staple	Waste & Linters
LINEN	Line	Demi-Line	Tow
WOOL	Worsted	Woolen	Noils
SILK	Filament	Spun	Noil

Long linen fiber is called line; an intermediate grade is demi-line, and short linen fiber is tow. The wool of long-haired sheep is long-staple wool; it may be spun into yarn that is wool, or it may be combed, before spinning, so that a yarn smoother than wool, silkier and glossier, results. This kind of yarn is used for fine worsted gabardines. Shorter-haired sheep like the merinos produce a fine quality of wool fiber—up to six inches in length; this usually has more crimp, or waviness, than the longer-haired sheep. A typical cloth example of merino wool is seen in homespun or jersey. Silk fiber is graded in similar fashion, as indicated on the chart.

The metallic yarns and some of the synthetics are fabricated in sheets of film and then slit into fine strips or ribbons. Examples of this process are Rovana (Saran), a flat monofilament, by the Dow Chemical Company, and cellophane.

YARN CONSTRUCTION

In a listing of yarn construction, a single strand or ply of yarn comes first. This single-ply strand is called a single. A single-ply yarn may be regular or slubbed. (The slubs are caused by irregular twisting.) It may have little, or slack, twist; it may have high, or crepe, twist. More usually the twist is something in between these two extremes.

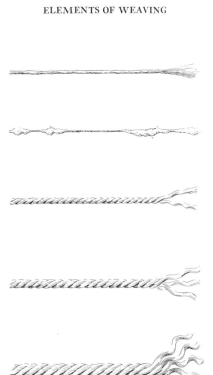

FIG. 100. *Yarn plies, reading from the top, down: single-ply, singly-ply slub, 2-ply, 3-ply, 4-ply. Drawing, Don Wight.*

In plied yarns, two or more singles are twisted together to form a heavier yarn. Plied yarn is stronger and more expensive than the equivalent single-ply yarn. Three or more singles twisted together tightly produce a yarn that in cross-section is cylindrical. Cable-ply is usually eight or more singles twisted together to give a firm, round yarn.

A spiral twist is one in which one or more yarns remain untwisted and form what is called a core, around which another yarn is twisted. Guimpe, for example, has a spiral twist in which the outer yarn winds around the core yarn in an almost horizontal direction. Usually made of metallic or silk fiber, guimpe is one of the more expensive yarns.

Chenille is a woven yarn—a dense filling on a sparse, banded warp which is cut between the warp bands to form a woven fringe. In the washing and finishing process, this double fringe becomes a round yarn. Hand-woven chenilles can be made and used for rug making. These rugs are called chenille, or twice-woven, rugs.

NOVELTY YARNS

Ratiné yarn is one in which a heavy-ply yarn zigzags between two fine binder yarns for a rickrack effect. Similar to ratiné, bouclé is a round nubby yarn of two or more strands, plus binder yarns used to make it rounder. Loop yarn is an exaggerated bouclé with large open loops. A *seed* yarn is a bouclé with occasional knots, or "seeds," caused by a horizontal wrapping around a core. In most novelty yarns, the core yarn comes from the spinning machine at a slower rate of speed than the wrapping yarns, causing these eccentric divergences. All these are available in many varieties.

FIG. 101. *Six examples of novelty yarns. Reading from top to bottom: guimpe, chenille, ratiné, bouclé, loop, and seed yarn. Photo, Ferdinand Boesch.*

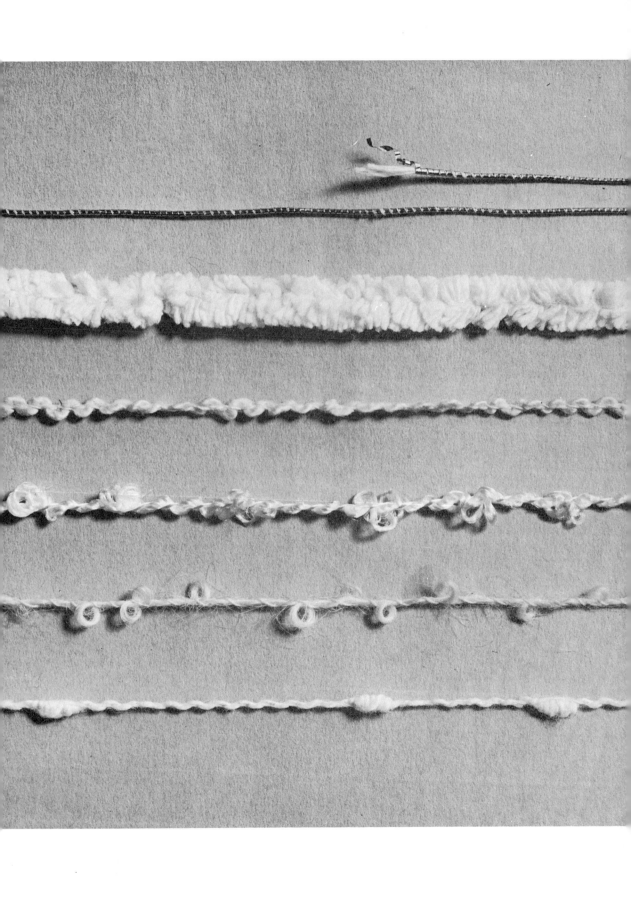

YARN SIZES

There is no limit to the sizes of yarns, particularly for those yarns used on the hand loom. A yarn may be as big around as a finger, or almost invisibly fine. A yarn's size is measured by the number of yards per pound. Some weavers speak in terms of a 900-yard yarn, or a 9000-yard yarn. However, more conventional measuring terms give both the number of plies and the yarn size. For example, in the cotton count system there is 8/2 cotton, or 8's 2-ply. This means that two singles of size 8 cotton yarn are twisted together, or plied; 8/3 means that three singles of size 8 yarn are plied, and so on.

In the cotton count system, a single strand of size 1 cotton has 840 yards per pound. The number of yards per pound of a given yarn is determined by a simple equation: the size number times 840 divided by the number of plies equals the yards per pound.

Wool, worsted, and linen all have their traditional counting systems. Silk and synthetic yarns are measured by deniers, or weight of standard-length skeins. Turn to Appendix C for Yarn Count Systems.

Simple Yarn Tests

Much that a weaver should know about yarns he can learn directly through his fingers. He can develop a sensitivity to the feel of his materials. This practiced sensitivity, coupled with common sense, will enable him to determine the relative strength, elasticity, and resilience of his yarns. For instance, the ability of a yarn to resist breaking—called its tensile strength—is especially important in selecting yarn for a warp.

A primitive, and by no means conclusive, method for determining fiber content is the burning test. The cellulose or vegetable fibers—cotton, linen, and rayon —smell like paper burning. The flame is quick and bright, the ash is soft and flaky.

Silk, wool, and thermoplastic synthetics like nylon and Dacron burn slowly, forming a ball-like ash. The animal fibers, silk and the various types of animal fleece and hair, differ from the others in that they have a smell like burning hair or feathers. The acetates dissolve in acetone (nail polish remover). Laboratory tests, microscopic and chemical, are the only means by which fibers, both natural and man-made, can be isolated and identified when the fiber content of a yarn is mixed.

MATERIALS OTHER THAN YARN

The hand weaver is not limited to using yarns for the filling. Certainly, hand weaving with non-yarn filling such as grasses, bamboo, metal or plastic strips has been a most interesting rediscovery of the twentieth century. Experimentation of this sort is diverting and relaxing; sometimes the results are extraordinary. However, the weaver must never fail to evaluate what he has done from both an aesthetic and a practical viewpoint. If much of such work is neither beautiful nor functional, it is because it was done merely as a stunt, presuming solely on the use of extraneous and unorthodox materials.

If a piece of fabric contains rigid filler, it should be handled wisely and with considered consistency. For example, grasses woven with an otherwise soft web are bound to become broken. Care should be taken to provide a strong and resilient warp which will not break in the beat-up or crush a fragile filling element.

Among other non-yarn fillings is wire, either rigid or malleable. Non-rigid ribbons, strips of fur or cloth can be woven, as well as raffia or leather. Wool roving offers good possibilities for blankets and rugs. Bundles of long pine needles have been used successfully for washable place mats. In fact, almost all materials should be considered as weavable provided the weaver keeps a critical eye on their practicality and effectiveness.

SELECTING YARNS

Most new weavers are unwisely frugal in acquiring yarns. Even less excusable is their rather common practice of hiding them away in closed cartons and bins. They should be exposed to view on shelves or in open bins, at least in sample variety, and preferably by color families. In this way, the weaver leaves himself open to inspiration, consciously and unconsciously, as he moves about the studio.

Some yarns have simple richness in themselves, a positive contribution in fiber, a definitive texture. These yarns, usually simple ones, have character of their own and a certain sensuous appeal. They invite one to feel them, to test their softness, their strength. Whether they are fine or heavy, smooth or rough, these are the yarns that hand weavers should collect.

It is distressing to contemplate the amount of hand weaving done with yarns which are either characterless and mechanical or, on the other hand, ostentatiously important in themselves. These last include many of the novelty twists, often gaudy, extravagant, but cheap in character. This kind of yarn is the yarn maker's, not the weaver's, idea of design, and such material requires great skill in handling. At the very least, these yarns should be used with simple, quality fibers, and with great restraint.

After World War II, it was hard to find any kind of yarn other than string. Hungry for variety, weavers became infatuated with novelty ranges as these became available. Sometimes these yarns, the bouclés and the chenilles, so completely cover the surface of a cloth that one longs to scrape off the "crust" in order to see the structure beneath it.

One thing is certain with such demanding yarn: it's a theme stealer; it becomes the most important thing about the fabric. Its own patterns and color mixtures obscure the integrity of the structure and design of the fabric itself.

In selecting yarns, the hand weaver's prime consideration should be quality and beauty. Hand weaving by its nature predicates a cloth made of yarns which provide substance, character, a measure of personal expression. The process of hand weaving is slow, unmechanized, and personal; the product should express these things. Even a fast weaver can use but a limited amount of yarn, since the appetite of the hand loom is a small one. Therefore that small quantity of yarn should be worth the weaving time and the time it took to shop for it.

The point at issue is that a weaver must learn to value his time, himself and his weaving sufficiently to invest in the right materials. If he settles for cheap yarns and colors he happens to have around, perhaps he had better abandon the project. If a scarf takes approximately fourteen hours to weave, the weaver will shortly begin to realize that he can't possibly *not* afford to use yarns that cost at least two or three dollars, possibly five dollars for fine cashmere yarns. If he sets an hourly rate on his time, and invests a fraction of that amount in yarns, he will be able to work it out at a reasonable profit. Hand weaving is a luxury, and unless the product is luxurious, there is no point in weaving by hand.

It follows, therefore, that the more time-consuming the technique, the more precious the materials. Cerlike tapestry, finger lace, and hand-knotted piles deserve yarns of the finest quality. If the weaver puts in a day's work on a piece of weaving, he must weigh the worth of this time against the cost of the yarn. Again, beauty, character, and durability should be his most important considerations.

CHAPTER SEVEN

An Approach to Design: Texture, Pattern, Color

In weaving, design presents its own special challenge, for it is not essentially a surface matter. Cloth is structural, and the final aesthetic effect involves the entire weaving process from the selection of fiber to the finishing. For a fabric to fit its purpose and, at the same time, to be beautiful requires skillful engineering, technical competence at all stages, as well as taste and the disciplined use of color.

The weaver must understand that the interlacing of warp and weft creates a three-dimensional fabric. Someone has said that weaving is architecture in miniature. This is a sound concept for the weaver who contemplates the designing of textiles. The problems he will face in handling materials are three-dimensional, especially in relation to developing texture and color effects.

Suitability, or fitness, are words which perhaps best pinpoint good design in weaving: the fitness of material to function, the appropriate relationship between fiber and yarn, between yarn, weave, and sett; between construction, finish, and use. The simple, direct fulfillment of functional requirement can often result in superb design.

For practical purposes, it may be best here to break down the analysis of design in weaving into three parts—texture, pattern, and color. This is a fairly arbitrary but useful division.

Examples chosen to illustrate these three aspects of

design will be grouped under these heads. Inevitably, however, since these properties are so closely interrelated, it often will be expedient to explain in the text the several elements that compose the whole, even though the spotlight for the moment may be focused on but one of its components.

TEXTURE

The basis of texture in cloth lies, first, in the fiber and the construction and size of yarns; second, in the weave which includes the manipulation of sett, the grouping of yarns, and the combining of weaves; and, third, in the finishing process.

Texture includes the feel of a cloth as well as its appearance. The texture of a cloth embraces its weight and hand, and the degree of coarseness or fineness of the surface. A textured cloth or yarn is generally considered to be a non-smooth one. Hand weavers sometimes talk of "texture weaving," meaning weaving without definite pattern in which the look of the cloth relies on its surface texture. Descriptions of textural quality tend to fall into opposites: rough or smooth, dull or shiny, soft or hard, coarse or fine. In fact, most textures fall between extremes; a yarn which may look smooth next to a rough one will seem rough next to a very much smoother one.

Developing Texture Through Fiber and Yarn

Yarn fibers in themselves have a broad range of textures, from the short, flat uncombed fibers of cotton and noil silk to the long, fine, glistening fiber of mohair. Twist and yarn construction accentuate or diminish the textural properties of a fiber. Combing, plying, mercerizing can make a dull cotton fiber silky and lustrous; and mohair, if tightly twisted, can be made to look hard and dull. Sometimes yarn is in itself so handsome that weaving it simply, so as to retain its own characteristic texture, is the logical course.

The floor matting in Fig. 102 offers a satisfying textural quality in dramatic scale. In plain weave, it is composed of heavily grouped filling picks, alternating hemp with raffia on a loosely spun and widely spaced warp.

Unusual materials make for distinctive texture in a fine screening, Fig. 103, which has a single yarn of hand-spun linen for the warp, and a filling of fine copper wire. The thick-and-thin irregularities of the hand-spun linen create a random pattern or silhouette. The textiles in Figs. 102 and 103 were designed and woven by Marjatta Metsovarra-Nystrom, a Finnish weaver.

A coating, Fig. 104, woven of black and white Orlon "ribbon" yarn, has a soft, luxurious hand, designed for Dior by Hurel of Paris. In this fabric the ribbon has been woven flat, but allowed to twist or "fold" on itself at random.

Contrast in fiber and twist gives strong textural quality to this experimental weaving in Fig. 105, which alternates bands of gauze and plain weave on paired warps. The warp ends combine high-twist cord with low-twist string. The filling in the gauze weave bands is of very loosely spun hemp; in the plain weave bands, the filling is raffia, an unspun material.

Weave, or Construction in Relation to Texture

If texture depends upon the character of fiber and yarn, it derives also from the kind of weave. Plain weave is relatively flat and smooth, whereas twills create alternate ridges and depressions, with more highlight and shadow than plain weave. In the process of interlacing, some yarns are raised to the surface while others recede into shadow. This three-dimensional breakup of light and shade, which serves to accentuate a fabric's texture, is inherently decorative and is an important design consideration, both texturally and as regards color effects.

Waffle weaves, as well as seersuckers and pile constructions, exaggerate fabric texture in varying degree and, for this reason, are especially valuable in developing texture from simple, smooth yarns.

FIG. 102. *Heavily grouped filling picks of hemp and raffia on a loosely spun, widely spaced hemp warp give interesting texture to this floor matting. Designed by Marjatta Metsovaara-Nystrom. Photo, Pietinen.*

FIG. 103. *Distinctive texture results from the use of unusual materials in a fine screening woven with a single yarn of hand-spun linen for the warp, and a filling of fine copper wire. Designed by Marjatta Metsovaara-Nystrom. Photo, A. Fethulia.*

FIG. 104. *A soft, luxurious hand distinguishes a black-and-white coating in "ribbon" yarn of Orlon, a Du Pont acrylic fiber, designed for Dior by Hurel of Paris.*

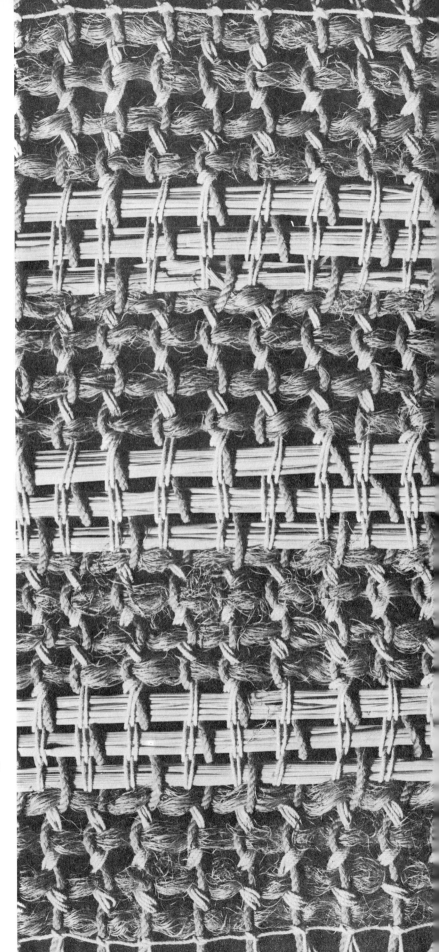

FIG. 105. *Contrast in fiber and twist gives strong textural quality to an experimental sample which alternates filling bands of gauze and plain weave on twisted warp ends. Warp combines high twist and low twist cord; filling in gauze weave bands of loosely spun hemp; plain weave bands of raffia, an unspun material. Designer, Bill Knox. Photo, Ferdinand Boesch.*

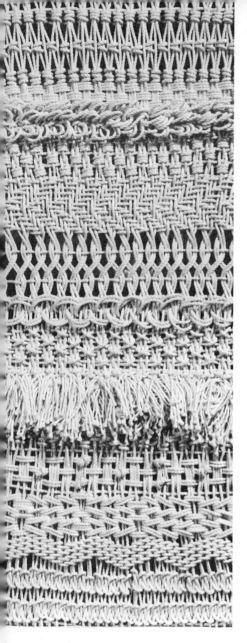

FIG. 106. *Combined gauze-weave techniques develop variety of texture with sculptural relief in a single tone of cotton cord. Designed by Carolyn Hopkins. Photo, Ferdinand Boesch.*

Combining Weaves for Texture

Most, if not all, constructions on harness looms already have been invented. A major area of cloth construction open for exploration, however, is that of combining weaves.

A logical occasion for combining weaves occurs when the weaver is manipulating a silhouetted pattern, as in the Jack Larsen casement, Fig. 107, page 173. Here, a complex stripe in plain weave and basket weave gives a surface of contrasting areas, translucent and opaque, reflecting the sheen of linen and silky Egyptian cotton as played against the grainy sections of plain weave and the random, shaggy goat hair floats.

In Fig. 106, a bit of experimental weaving combines bands of basket weave, twill, leno, and other gauze techniques—areas of density contrasting with lacy bands—for an interesting variety of textures in sculptural relief. It was designed and woven by Carolyn Hopkins in a single yarn of cotton cord, in one color.

Many combinations of weave are done quite simply. A brocade pattern, for instance, may be more interesting if it is centered on a warp stripe, or outlined with a skip-dent stripe, as in Fig. 83, page 129, by Girard. This kind of addition or combination requires no extra weaving time or material.

Importance of Sett in Varying Textures

Sett, or the manner of sleying the warp ends in the reed, affects the hand and density of a cloth, its strength, its roughness or smoothness. Skip-denting and cramming warp ends in the reed alternately create bands of sheer open areas and closely packed ones.

Silhouette is the word used here to describe this visual aspect of texture which becomes apparent when the fabric is seen against the light. The silhouetted pattern of opaque and transparent areas dominates both surface texture and color. In screens, casements, and lampshades it becomes the predominating pattern, determined by the size and character of the yarns, and by their spacing—whether the sett is close or

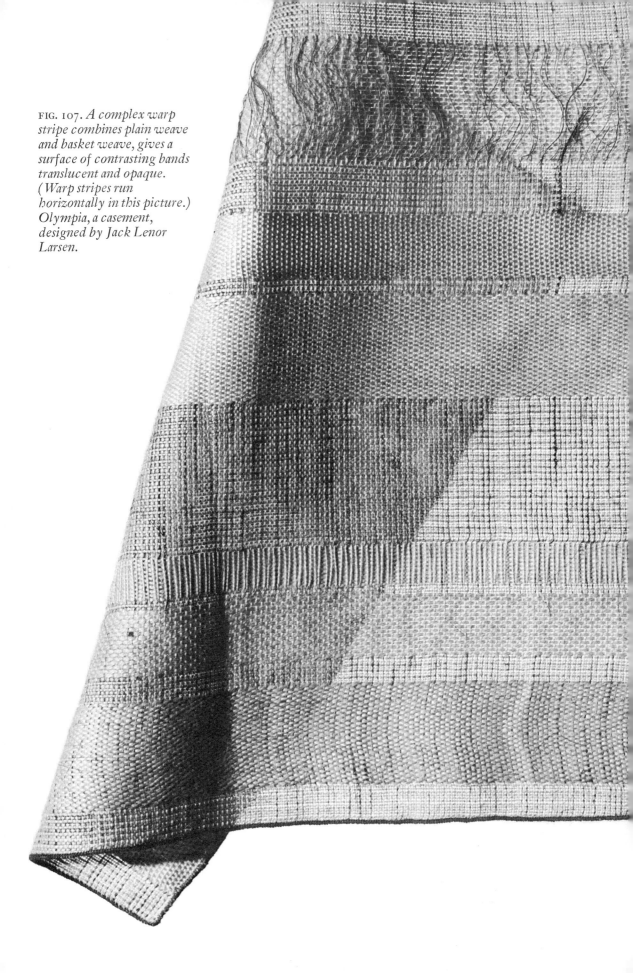

FIG. 107. *A complex warp stripe combines plain weave and basket weave, gives a surface of contrasting bands translucent and opaque. (Warp stripes run horizontally in this picture.) Olympia, a casement, designed by Jack Lenor Larsen.*

sparse and open, whether it is regular or random. Such effects may be likened to grille work on a fine scale. See Fig. 136, page 207.

The ten samples in Fig. 108 demonstrate vividly the different textural effects produced by variations in sett and the grouping of yarns. These are plain-weave derivatives, woven in 10/2 wet-spun linen for both warp and weft.

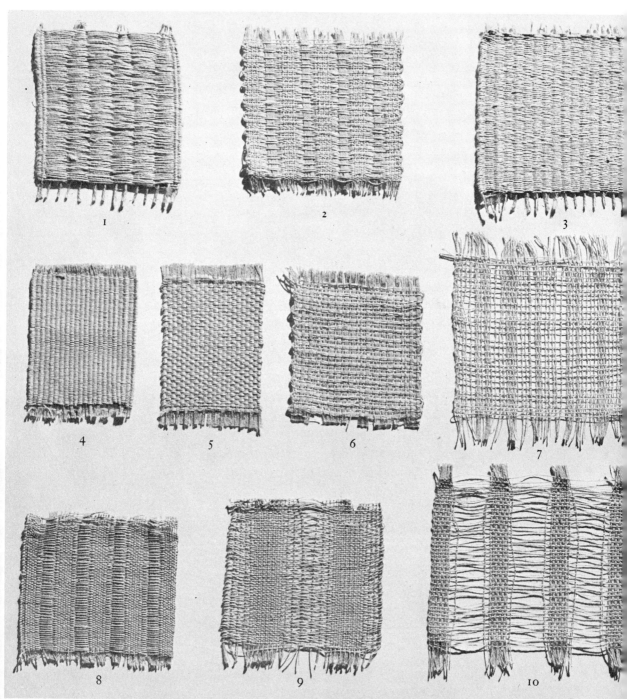

(1) A skip-dent filling-faced rib weave in which two warp ends on opposite sheds are sleyed in the same dent at intervals of half an inch, set 4 ends per inch. In Japan this is called tatami weave and is used for floor matting.

(2) Plain weave with warp and weft groupings; at intervals of 1 inch, 8 warp ends are grouped as one, set 12 ends per inch. Groups of 4 filling picks alternate with 3 single picks.

(3) Simple filling-faced repp woven on a warp which is openly spaced, set 5 ends per inch.

(4) Filling-faced rib weave on paired warp ends— 2 ends carried as one—with a closer sett, 15 ends per inch, to produce a firmer fabric than No. 3.

(5) Warp and filling are grouped, 4-and-4, to make a basket weave, set 15 ends per inch.

(6) Warp ends are grouped in blocks alternating with single ends to form a soft stripe, set 15 ends per inch. In the filling, 3 yarns are grouped as one, alternated with single picks.

(7) A warp, skip-dented at random, and an irregular filling beat-up make an irregular grid of opaque and transparent areas. Set 10 ends per inch, occasional ends are paired for further variety.

(8) Vertical stripes, formed by a group of 3 warp ends interlacing as 1, alternate with a group of 12 ends interlacing singly; set 18 ends per inch.

(9) A closely sleyed warp of paired and single ends —12 ends per inch—alternates with an openly set warp to produce vertical bands of opaque and translucent areas.

(10) A closely sleyed warp alternates with inch-wide open spaces; the warp is crammed for an inch and omitted for an inch. The crammed warp is made heavier, 18 ends per inch, by pairing the ends.

The effect of changes in texture by altering the sett is shown again in the five samples in Fig. 109, a plain weave fabric with the same yarn for warp and weft throughout. As the sley is altered, the change of hand from one sample to another is dramatic.

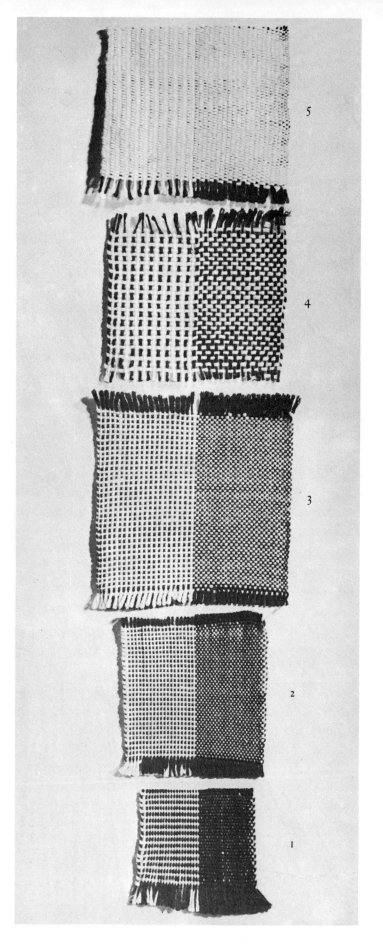

FIG. 109. *Again, five samples woven with same yarns for warp and weft, in plain weave, show the importance of changes in sett to vary texture. Read from bottom upward. Woven by Fan Mason.*

Note: The warp at left of each sample alternates black with white; at right, the warp is all black.

Reading upward from bottom:

(1) Canvaslike warp-faced cloth sleyed as closely as possible, 48 ends per inch. (2) Closely sleyed and predominantly warp-faced, 36 ends per inch. (3) Set 18 ends per inch, with warp and weft balanced. (4) Set with open sley, 6 ends per inch, a sleazy cloth, slightly filling-faced. (5) Set with open sley, 6 ends per inch; this cloth is a filling-faced repp.

A further example of loose and tightly packed sett is shown in Fig. 110, a casement woven in one yarn, natural wet-spun linen. The crossbar pattern of wide bands is made by cramming warp ends into the reed for several inches and then sleying single ends loosely.

FIG. 110. *Crossbar pattern for a casement is made by cramming the warp ends for vertical bands, then sleying loosely; filling picks are beaten in closely for cross bands. In natural wet-spun linen, designed by Alexander Girard for Herman Miller.*

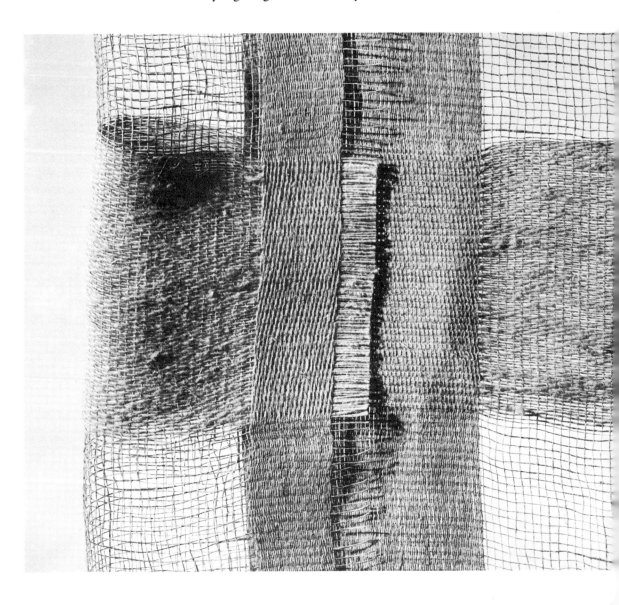

For the filling bands, the yarns are grouped three to the pick and packed in tightly with the beater to a width corresponding with the warp bandings; in the open areas the filling interlaces with the warp ends in evenly spaced plain weave.

Grouping of Yarns to Enhance Texture

Grouping is using several warp or filling yarns as one, an effective way of increasing the textural scale of a cloth. This is, of course, an extension of developing texture through fiber and yarn as explored on page 166. It is a means of adding fresh dimension, of enriching values in both texture and color. Combining single ends or picks with double or triple ones will seem to give variety of yarn size.

A grouped warp can be made in two ways: the multiple ends can be threaded in one heddle, or they can be threaded on separate heddles which are raised as one. The simplest example of this is the standard 2-and-2 basket weave, woven on four harnesses with a straight draw, in which the two ends are grouped whenever any two adjoining harnesses are raised. Such grouping is used to make a warp more versatile, so that both fine and heavy fabrics can be woven on a single warp. By grouping in this way, one could weave a dress fabric on a fine single warp and a companion coating with two, three, or four ends working as one heavy end.

Similarly, instead of making a warp of evenly mixed fine and heavy ends, a sequence of single-double, single-double could be used for a fine/heavy effect. Single-single-single-triple would give a more exaggerated texture. Groupings, of course, need not be regular; an occasional double end gives a random look, especially if combined with a random sleying.

A grouped filling is made either by throwing two or more filling shots through the same shed or by winding two or more yarns on one bobbin. Usually they are wound together on the same bobbin, and allowed to twist at random as they come off the shuttle to give a natural, uncontrived texture pattern. In the Metsovaara-Nystrom upholstery, Fig. 111, both warp and filling are of four grouped yarns differing in fiber and color. The twisting multiple ends and picks of worsted and goat hair, in closely related colors, provide a modulated surface texture that looks as though hand-spun yarns had been used.

A coating of hand-spun alpaca in natural, gray, and white, Fig. 112, shows a regularly varied alternation of dark and light paired warp ends, threaded in one heddle, and a filling with two yarns to the pick.

The wall covering of raffialike paper strands in Fig. 113, has warp ends in natural color, paired alternately with black and white. These ends twist at random concealing now the dark, now the light member, giving a wholly random effect. The filling has single picks, all in natural.

FIG. 111. *"King's Tweed," an upholstery fabric of worsted and goat hair in basket weave, with four different yarns grouped in both warp and weft. Designed by Marjatta Metsovaara-Nystrom for Jack Lenor Larsen, Inc. Photo, Pietinen.*

FIG. 112. *Coating in natural, gray, and white hand-spun alpaca with dark and light paired warp ends with two yarns to a heddle. Designed by Trude Guermonprez.*

FIG. 113. *Wall covering of raffialike paper strands, vinyl-treated with Du Pont Everset, has warp ends in natural paired alternately with black and white, twisting at random; filling is in natural. Product of Fabricraft, by Deltox, Inc., Oshkosh, Wisconsin. Photo, Ferdinand Boesch.*

Grouping of yarns also is used to create pattern blocks, a topic to be explored under the heading of Pattern, together with more information on forming texture patterns.

Texture and the Finishing Process

Finishing can subdue or exaggerate the texture of fibers. Simple finishing of fabric—washing and pressing—generally softens the hand of a cloth and also bulks it. Standard fabric finishes such as scouring and steaming will enhance texture by raising fibers to the surface. Brushing, or napping, will further expose the fiber, adding softness and increased warmth.

In Fig. 114, half of the cloth was first scoured and then steel-brushed in the finishing; the other half was left unbrushed, in a suiting designed by Azalea Thorpe. Brushing, or napping, is done to give the material a softer hand and additional warmth.

Other finishing processes which can transform the surface texture are calendering, embossing, and glazing. Polishing will add luster to a fabric with a smooth surface, such as satin.

Shrinking a cloth in the finishing may result in a crepelike or seersucker surface. The dress fabric, shown in Fig. 115, has been permanently pleated through an imaginative approach involving the selection of materials, the weave and the finish. It was woven on a spun silk warp, off-white, with a fine wool weft in pale gray on a herringbone threading. When it was washed, the wool shrank, giving it an accordion-pleat effect. For the flared skirt as shown in the picture, the material was simply pressed flat with a steam iron below the waistline.

FIG. 114. *In finishing, one half of this cloth has been steel-brushed after scouring, the other half left unbrushed, a suiting by Azalea Stuart Thorpe. Brushing, or napping, gives a softer hand or additional warmth.*

FIG. 115. *Section of dress material woven with a doupione, or spun-silk warp and a fine worsted weft on herringbone threading. When washed, the wool shrank, giving an accordion-pleat effect. Designed and woven by Mariel B. Collins.*

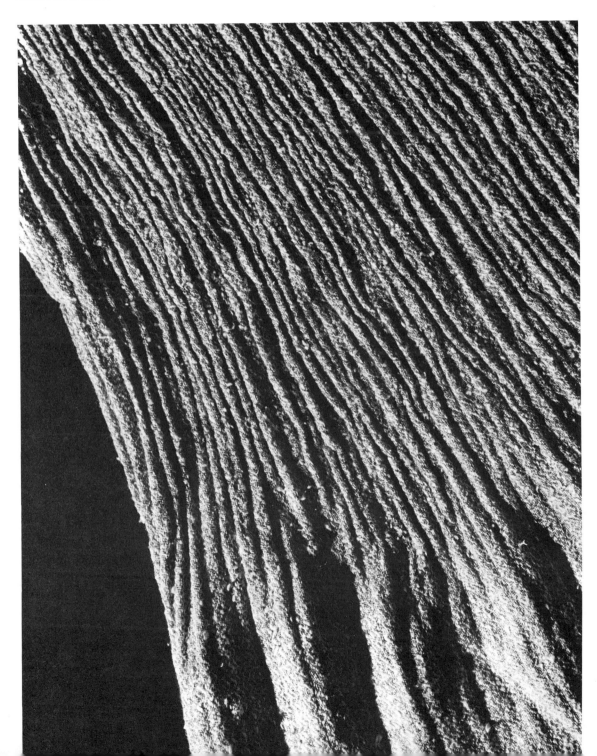

PATTERN

In passing from the aspect of texture to that of pattern in woven design, a significant example of *texture-pattern* serves to illustrate how inextricably these two elements are related. A casement, Fig. 116, has a checkerboard design which in one block has both warp and filling interlacing singly and, in alternate blocks, has five picks grouped as one followed by single picks to make a fine stripe. The character of the yarn—a wet-spun, single-ply linen, in natural—contributes as much to the silhouette interest as the pattern itself.

Many small-scale texture patterns can be produced by particular yarn sequences in contrasting yarns. Woven on straight or pointed draws, these are espe-

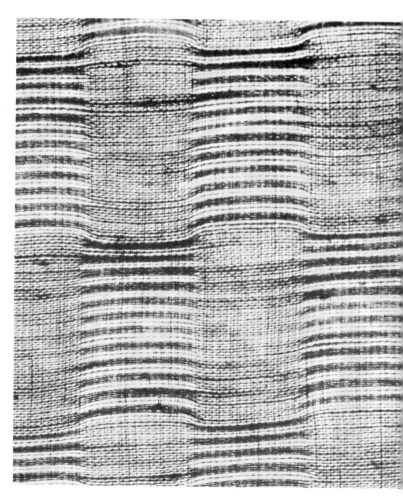

FIG. 116. *Texture and pattern are indivisible in this casement with its checkerboard of pattern blocks. In one block, warp and filling are woven singly in plain weave; in the striped block, five picks are grouped as one, alternating with a single pick. Designed by Marie Howell, Howell Design Associates, Providence 3, R. I. Photo, H. J. Greenwald.*

cially effective when a single, simple yarn is used. A provocative example of these is supplied in the black-and-white blanket sample shown in Fig. 77, page 124.

Stripes

Stripes are the simplest, most logical decorative outgrowth of the process of interlacing continuous and parallel materials. Stripes are one of the most obvious ways for a weaver to decorate cloth, the most direct way of combining colors, and they are flexible. Broad stripes become a pattern, fine striae in themselves create a texture pattern, border stripes add architectural definition to a fabric used as a hanging.

There are, of course, warp stripes, filling stripes, stripes of two colors, stripes of many colors, stripes of texture alone. For interesting examples of texture stripes which illustrate, in particular, the silhouetted pattern, see Fig. 117.

CLASSIFYING STRIPES: Since stripes are of utmost importance in weaving, and widely varied in nature, it is helpful to put them into categories so that the weaver can work with them comprehendingly. Whether a stripe is barbaric or refined and sedate, narrow or heroic in scale, depends upon its proportion as much as on the yarns used, or on color contrast.

Different striping systems are used in combination for variety. This works especially well when line stripes—usually one to four ends wide—are used with area stripes which are merely broad bands of color and texture. When warp and filling stripes are combined (making plaids, of course), the use of both line and area stripes is particularly successful.

(1) The Roman stripe, Fig. 117A, is in universal use, with its broad, evenly spaced bands, typically in bold colors of strong contrast such as black and white, orange, blue and gold, red and green—simple and vivid.

(2) At the opposite extreme to the regular, mechanical Roman stripe are the striae, Fig. 117B, very fine random stripes. The width of these stripes is no more than one, two or three yarns. The effect is

random and seemingly repeatless, even though there may be a repeat. Striae simulate natural rhythms found in grasses, in barks and in streaky cloths woven of hand-spun yarns. A strié pattern may be woven of different yarns or in different colors of the same yarn, closely related in hue or value, in order to convey the variety and depth inherent in hand-spun and hand-dyed yarns. These are usually wound in the warp.

An upholstery fabric of exceptional richness, shown in Fig. 118, is woven of silk and ramie in fine random stripes with occasional groupings of four ends in one heddle.

Random stripes, of course, are not limited to fine striae; random stripes may combine a variety of widths. Traditionally, the random stripe is woven without repeat—it is exciting to weave stripes without the monotonous precision required in counting a re-

FIG. 117. *A. Roman stripe. B. Striae, or fine random stripe. C. Composite stripe. D. Composite stripe— positive-negative repeat. E. Ombré stripe. F. Pin stripe, or chalk stripe.*

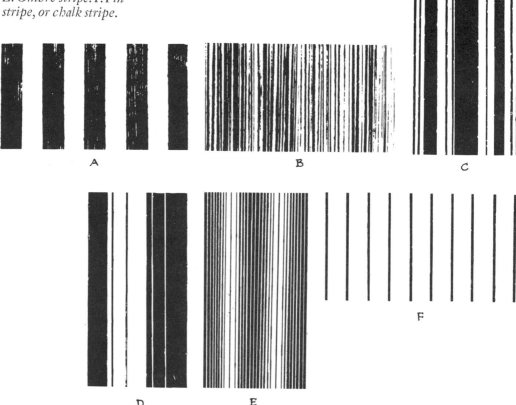

peat. Such stripes present an additional advantage in that they need not be matched. This obviates the common problem of inexact repeat.

(3) Between the simple Roman stripe and the versions of random stripe lies the composite stripe in which two or more colors are used in a regular repeat, (Fig. 117C). With this stripe the object is to create as much variety as possible while preserving a precise order. As often as not, composite stripes are symmetrical; the tartan is a classic example of composite stripes repeated in warp and weft. Fig. 117D shows a two-color composite stripe in which the spacing of the repeat remains identical but dark is substituted for light, and vice versa.

Fig. 119 shows composite stripes in a Mexican cotton woven in two colors, the third tone made by use of end-and-end area stripes.

(4) Ombré stripes result from gradation of color in which the change from one color to another is blended by slow transition, usually worked out in somewhat this manner: 6 ends of A, 1 of B; 5 of A, 1 of B; 4 of A, 2 of B; 3 of A, 2 of B; 3 of A, 3 of B; 2 of A, 3 of

FIG. 118. *A warp-face upholstery fabric woven in random striae of silk and ramie with occasional groupings of four warp ends. Designed by Edward Wormley. Photo, George Barrows.*

B; 2 of A, 4 of B; 1 of A, 4 of B; 1 of A, 5 of B; 1 of A, 6 of B. Ombré stripes are most used in face weaves, such as warp-face twill. These also are usually wound in the warp—to repeat them in the filling would be too tedious. (Fig. 117E)

(5) The pin stripe, or chalk stripe, is a fine line stripe, the width of a pin, against a band of contrasting ground. (Fig. 117F). The pin stripe is characteristically white against gray, brown or navy; the chalk stripe is tone-on-tone—light gray on darker gray, beige on brown, and so on.

(6) The outline stripe is useful in a variety of ways. It may be used as a transition from one kind of stripe to another, sometimes in a series, or with a pick-and-pick pattern between two outlines so as to give a ladder effect. The outline stripe is also a handy tool for connecting or outlining a spot weave or other similar pattern. The skip-dent stripe is another version of the outline stripe. The pattern is achieved simply

FIG. 119. *Composite stripes varied in color and width, in two colors with a third tone created by use of end-and-end in area stripes. A Mexican cotton for drapery or apparel, designed by Jack Lenor Larsen, woven by Bruce Rogers.*

by omitting one or more dents in the sleying; this may or may not be repeated in the filling by means of the beat-up.

PAINTED STRIPES: Painting, a medium unrelated to weaving, has been used to vary stripes. In Fig. 120, paint has been used to ornament warp stripes. Solid color and white stripes have been wound in the warp of the fabric, then some of the white stripes have been partly painted black. This is done on the loom; it is an economical way of producing variations in pattern.

Plaids and Checks

Checks and plaids are merely the combination of warp and filling stripes. The stripes may be identical in proportion and color, or the composition of the vertical and horizontal sets of stripes may be quite different. For example, a Roman warp stripe could be used with a random filling stripe. Or a line stripe can be woven across an area warp stripe.

FIG. 120. *This photograph shows a warp stripe fabric in which painting has been used to vary the stripe. Solid-color and white stripes were wound in the warp, then some of the white stripes were partially painted with black.*

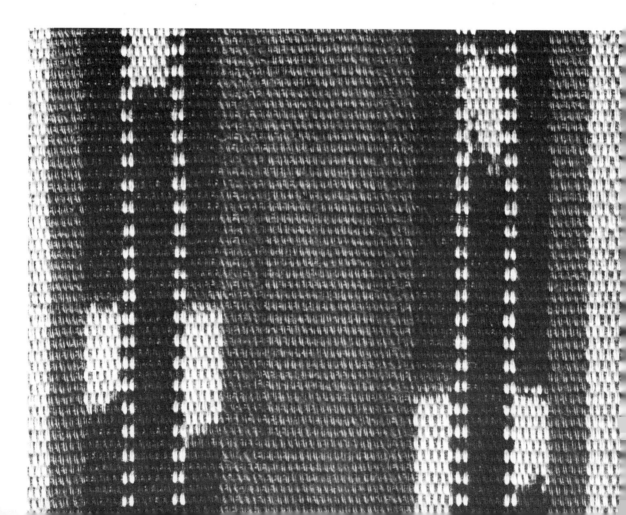

Creating Pattern Through Brocading

The several brocading techniques offer, possibly, the simplest and most versatile means for creating pattern in weaving. Often such patterns are geometrical; sometimes there is a repeat or alternation of motif. On the other hand, a brocading pattern may be free, repeatless, consisting of a random silhouette as in the casement by Hella Skowronski, Fig. 130, page 202.

In an ancient Peruvian brocade, Fig. 121, the brocading yarns form a pattern of vertical bars, alternating with bars with figure, possibly symbolic. These are repeated in two colors, to vary the design and relate it to the background. In Fig. 128, the extra, white brocade picks vary the long and short stripes.

In the four-harness warp brocade, Fig. 122, the motif is geometric, an orderly but changing play of rectangular forms in modulated sizes. From the minute modules of the warp floats to the large-scale supporting and dividing members of the composition, the success of the design stems from the subordination of all elements to the several gradations of the rectangle motif.

FIG. 121. *In an ancient Peruvian brocade, the supplementary filling yarns alternate stripes, in two colors, with repeated motif, for variety and to relate it to the brocade ground cloth.*

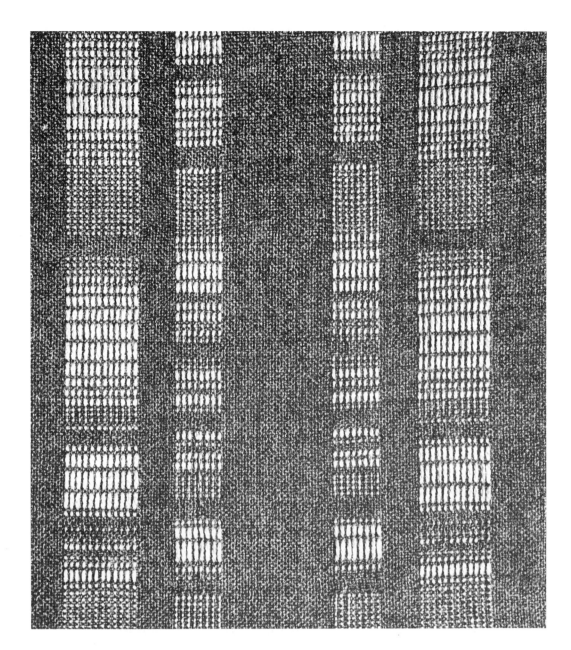

FIG. 122. *Four-harness warp brocade of mercerized cotton on gray wool ground; face floats are kept short for upholstery. The success of the design arises from the subordination of all elements to the gradations of the allover motif. Designer, Anne E. Cheavens.*

A flat-woven, filling-faced rug of plied rug worsted, in blue, orange, brown, and black, achieves a dark-light pattern and a change of scale and texture by combining bands of plain weave and rib weave. The pattern is dramatized by alternating the colors in the rib. The rug was designed and woven by Joseph Menta at the College of the Institute of American Indian Arts. (Fig. 123)

VARYING PATTERN IN BROCADES: Eleven ways of varying filling brocades on a common warp are shown on the strip, in Figs. 124 and 125. The warp for these woven samples is 8/4 white cotton, set 15 ends to the inch. The filling for the plain weave ground is the same yarn as is used for the warp, the supplementary brocade filling is 4-ply Germantown wool.

The variations described here are basic, but not exhaustive; combinations of these could render unending variety. All the samples shown are on a two-block threading draft, the same threading as is used for mock double cloth, Fig. 87, page 137. Block A is threaded 1-2, 1-2; block B is threaded 3-4, 3-4. These blocks are alternated in irregular widths.

FIG. 123. *A rug woven of plied worsted in blue, orange, brown and black brings about a change of scale and texture by combining bands of plain weave and rib weave. Designed and woven by Joseph Menta, Yuma Indian student, Institute of American Indian Arts, Santa Fe, New Mexico.*

(1) Beginning at pattern 1, bottom of Fig. 124, a stripe as shown there can be woven on any filling brocade draft by alternating a single brocade float with a ground weave pick.

(2) The use of two or more brocade shuttles is a primary step to varying brocades. The shuttles may change when the pattern block changes, or they may change within the pattern block, as shown in pattern 2.

(3) In pattern 3, the plain weave ground has been changed by using a contrasting color of filling yarn.

(4) In pattern 4, two supplementary filling yarns have been wound on a single bobbin and have been allowed to twist at random. This is but a variation of pattern 2.

(5) Pattern 5 has three picks of ground between the insertions of each brocade pick. This has changed the character of the design as compared with pattern 1.

(6) Floats in both block A and block B have been repeated, in pattern 6, to form separated brocade shapes.

(7) The striped color arrangement of both ground filling and supplementary filling form checks in pattern 7 (continuing to read upward from bottom of Fig. 125). The construction is the same as in patterns 1, 2, and 3, with one brocading pick alternating with one ground cloth pick.

(8) Pattern 8 is not a brocade, but the alternation of float A and float B without plain-weave binder picks. This is a rib weave, sometimes called "weaving-on-opposites."

(9) Block A and block B, in pattern 9, are woven with supplementary wefts of different colors. A more striking pattern would emerge if gray block A were made subordinate to black block B.

(10) Pattern 10 is a combination of patterns 1 and 8, except that here the narrow black bands are woven on opposites in the same color.

(11) Pattern 11 is a laid-in or discontinuous brocade. The pyramid motif is composed of squares consistent with the block threading of this warp.

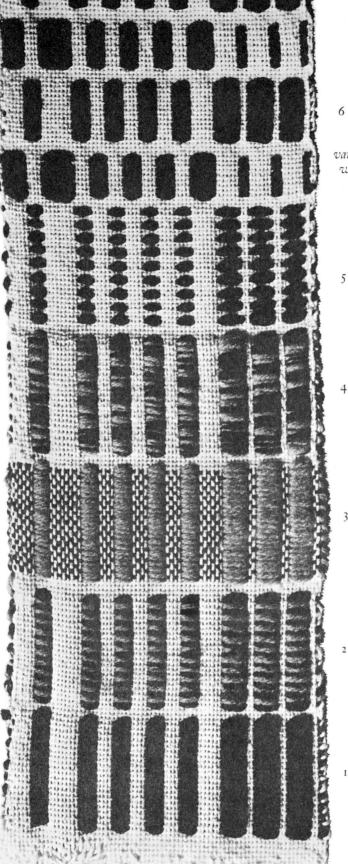

6

5

4

3

2

1

FIGS. 124, 125. *Eleven variations of filling brocades woven on a common warp. (See text). Read from bottom upward, as numbered. Photo, Ferdinand Boesch.*

11

10

9

8

7

WARPS DEVISED FOR VARYING FILLING BROCADES: Any brocade pattern can be changed by widening or narrowing the pattern blocks; the scale can be made larger or smaller. More important, perhaps, is the fact that a dominant and a subordinate block can be created, allowing one to use the brocading as an accent

FIG. 126. *Checkerboard filling brocade of wool on a linen ground. The principle in technique is the same as in No. 6 on the woven strip of brocades,* FIGS. *124, 125.*

on the cloth, or to use the brocaded area as an all-over surface with an accent pattern of ground cloth. This last is especially successful for upholstery and coverlets, as shown in Fig. 126.

On a dominant-subordinate block draft, two warp brocades of mercerized cotton on single-ply hemp ground were designed for casements emphasizing silhouette. Warp floats have been clipped to form opaque rectangles with chenillelike effect (left); a compound brocade (right) has both supplementary warp and filling which is not interwoven with ground but held under supplementary warp ends.

Other changes can be effected with a striped warp: the threaded pattern blocks can be of different colors, or they can be outlined by a contrasting stripe; or this stripe—and draft—can bear a casual relationship to each other. The striped warp can be plaided. In this case, the brocading may be sparse, incidental decoration on a plaid ground, as in Fig. 129.

The sett may be varied. Ordinarily, brocading is done with an even sleying and with balanced ends and picks. But this is not always necessary—the cloth may be warp-faced or filling-faced, and is especially effective if the ground cloth is striped, or if it is desirable to conceal contrasting tie-downs.

The sleying can be arranged in various skip-dent formations, such as one that forms a narrow drop-out stripe. Bands of tight and loose sleying could be alternated to conform to the threading sequence used for the blocks.

If the fabric is to be used against light, as in a casement, the weaver should take pains to keep the brocading pattern effective; in silhouette, a back float is exactly as important as a front float and is seen, against the light, as a straight line. In this case, clipping and discontinuous brocade become important devices. To remain distinctive, the brocaded pattern, or motif, should be placed on the closely sleyed, solid areas rather than on those which are loosely sleyed. Again, see Fig. 83, page 129.

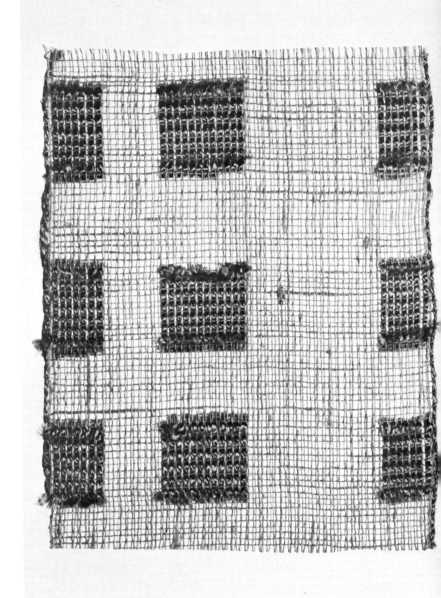

FIG. 127. *Two warp brocades of mercerized cotton on single-ply hemp ground, designed for casements. Example at left, the warp floats have been clipped to form an opaque rectangular pattern,*

*emphasizing silhouette. The
compound brocade at right
has both supplementary
warp and filling; the filling
is not interwoven with
ground, but is held down
under supplementary
warp ends.*

FIG. 128. *Warp and filling brocade woven on four harnesses, using two harnesses for ground cloth, two for brocading yarns. The extra, white brocade picks—sometimes single, sometimes double—add pleasing variety to the long and short stripes. Photo, Ferdinand Boesch.*

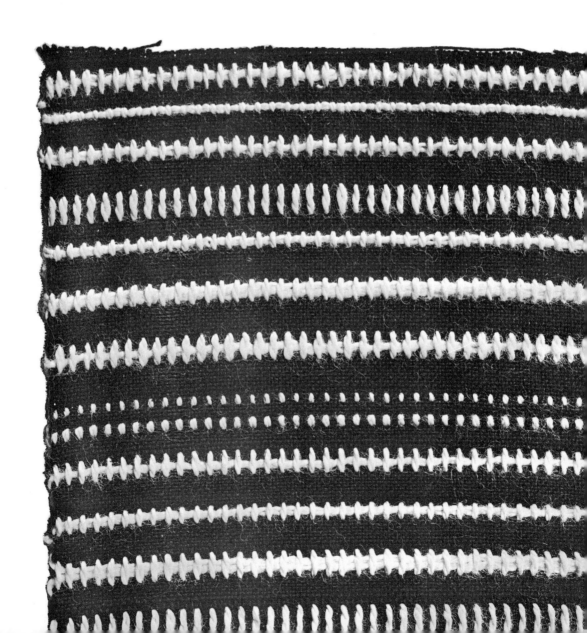

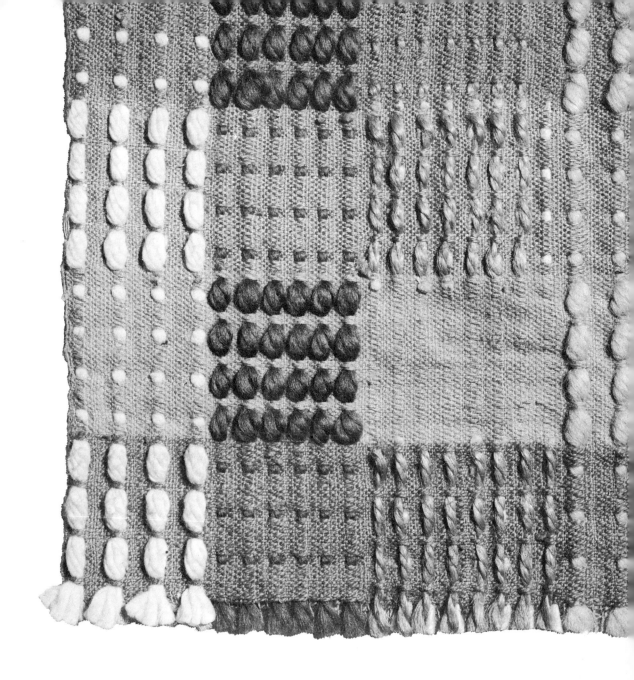

FIG. 129. *Four-harness two-block warp brocade using heavy-ply worsted brocade yarns but sparsely, on cotton ground. Color changes in the weft face stripes coincide with pattern blocks to emphasize the plaid. Underfloats are tied down to form reversible cloth. Photo, Ferdinand Boesch.*

202

FIG. 130. *Warp brocade casement cloth of spun silk on a sheer mohair ground. The warp take-up of the basic cloth produces the loose, wavy silhouette pattern, seemingly random, of the supplementary ends. Designer, Hella Skowronski.*

FIG. 131. *Experiment in color sequence, alternating black and white filling on a filling-faced plain-weave construction. Designed by Jack Lenor Larsen. Photo, Ferdinand Boesch.* (¼ scale)

FIG. 132. *Irregular widths of rigid filling in the heading exaggerate the symmetrical pattern which alternates two colors in a warp of dull viscose yarns. The fabric at top shows the pattern in normal scale. Designed by Lyn Van Steenberg.*

FIG. 133. *Warp-faced repp with pattern made by regularly varied alternation of black and white warp yarns; color sequence is a quarter-inch black, one-inch black and white set end-and-end, a quarter-inch white, one-inch black and white set end-and-end. Designer, Lyn Van Steenberg.*

FIG. 134. *Alternation of dark and light yarns changes at center to effect a staggered horizontal line; filling sequence of two dark to one light completes pattern. Designed in plain weave of hemp and silk by Jack Lenor Larsen.*

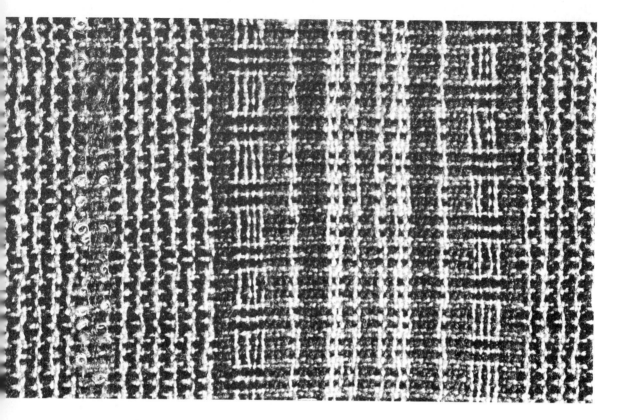

FIG. 135. *Worsted suiting in plain weave; pattern made by color alternation of both warp and weft. The long warp repeat carries a regular five-pick, two-shuttle filling sequence which causes the block effect in three of the warp stripes. Designed and woven by Azalea Stuart Thorpe for Einiger Mills, Inc.*

FIG. 136. *The repeat of an eight-end warp unit is clearly seen in this screening; five kinds of yarn, all of linen, vary in color and value (white, black and brown); and in size, twist, and profile. The natural, random character of yarns is emphasized by the skip-dented sleying. A rigid copper wire filling helps to stabilize the loose sett. Designed by Marjatta Metsovaara-Nystrom.*

COLOR

In weaving, color is radically different from most other applications of color. In painting, in interiors, color is ordinarily used in one area against another—a gold chair against a white wall, yellow flowers in a blue vase. But in weaving the interlacing of warp and weft creates contiguous color in quantities so minute that they appear as "broken color," somewhat as the pointillist painter applies colors to his canvas.

Of all things man-made, textiles most easily provide the broken color as seen in natural things, notably in sand, in skin, in a snowbank, in flowers, and in leaves. To ignore this broken color and its potential iridescence in woven design is to lose one of its most exciting aspects.

As with texture, it follows that color in weaving is not of the surface alone; it is both within the cloth and on it and is affected by fiber, yarn, and dyestuff. Color also is conditioned by the highlight and shadow of the weave as much as by the yarn colors and textures.

Learning about Color

Some expert colorists have had no formal training in color. Sensitivity to color and color relationships seems to be a matter of instinct. Take as examples of this the many primitive weavers, the Indians of the Western hemisphere, or the Berbers of North Africa whose weaving gives evidence of highly developed color sense.

However, color sense like any other can be developed by conscious observation, by exposure to it from every possible source such as painting, fruit and flowers, colored papers, the interiors that surround one. The weaver is fortunate who can have colored yarns arranged on open shelves, to be lived with day by day. On the spur of the moment, he can try out fresh combinations of color and texture. He can gain creative insight by arranging skeins of yarns in baskets, making still lifes and abstractions in color.

This is an appropriate exercise for the designer, but he should carry his study still further. Instead of juxtaposing skein to skein or cone to cone, he should experiment with single strands of yarn. Two skeined yarns which seem pleasant together may not be so when they are "fragmented" as they are in the actual web. The effect of combining yarns in weaving can be simulated by twisting the separate strands together in a spiral; this will break up color and texture on a scale similar to that in the woven cloth.

Spontaneous color work, on or off the loom, is good practice. The new weaver's great need is to plunge in freely and quickly, to experiment with color, producing color trials which can be compared, working generously with color from as many approaches as possible.

Paintings as a Color Source

Paintings provide a better training ground for the weaver than do textbooks; painters often are ahead of the scientific colorists. Persian painting, in particular, is a delight and a prolific source of inspiration to the weaver as is much of the color in Byzantine, Oriental, and Peruvian art. The post-Impressionists, and some painters of today also are a stimulating source of color.

Chroma, Hue, and Value

Controversies which have arisen as to whether there are indeed three, five, or six primary colors are academic and of small concern to the weaver. The aspects of color which are of first importance to him are *chroma, hue,* and *value,* and of these value is paramount.

CHROMA: Chroma may be defined as the relative intensity or brightness of color. Those which are a pure saturation of ungrayed color are called high chroma colors; those which are grayed by neutral or earth colors are said to have low chroma. An earth color is neutral by nature: it is grayed by, and therefore contains, several colors. An earth-colored tile red and an olive green have a great deal in common as regards chroma, and are thus related to the high mustard yellows and to earth violets.

209

Richest color effects repay the playing of muted earth colors, that is, colors of medium or low chroma, against colors of high chroma. The result is a depth and resonance through modulation, terms readily understood in music. In music, modulation is the passing from one key to another by means of related tones or chords.

All neutrals are modulators. With the exception of extremely rare pure blacks and whites, neutrals are colors too. A beige is a washed-out orange or red-orange. An ecru is a low-chroma, low-intensity faded gold. A pearl gray is a grayed, lightened purple. Ash may be a very much lightened and grayed blue, and so on.

Incidentally, a weaver's color sense can be gauged to a degree by his skill in working with neutrals. The novice sees these yarns as dull and colorless. To the experienced designer, they are the most powerful, though delicate, of shades. The colorist, perhaps intuitively, achieves brilliance by using a yellowed white against a complementary blued one, carefully balancing values to create interest "without color."

HUE: Hue is a shade or gradation within a color family. The weaver who understands hue appreciates that there are a thousand reds, each with its distinctive character. In some orange predominates, in others blue, or brown; some advance while others recede. In working out a color composition the designer thinks not in concrete terms of high chroma colors—red, blue, yellow and so on. Rather, he is seeking for a hard accent, or a sweet softness; for a warm neutral or a sour earth color. These can readily be found by comparing several charcoals, or browns or tans. A useful exercise is to describe by hue a hundred examples of white; or to arrange on a color wheel all the yarns in a studio, irrespective of chroma or value.

VALUE: For the weaver, the most important property of color is value, its dark-light aspect. Contrasts in value directly affect design in the woven cloth because value is closely related to scale; value contrast causes what is called "color effects." A knowledge of this, and skillful application of this knowledge, is a controlling factor in the consistent development of sophisticated color.

Strong contrast in values gives positive depth and movement which can easily add up to "busy-ness" if not expertly handled. Whereas colors close in value, such as flame and cerise, are brilliantly iridescent in either a large- or small-scale breakup, strongly contrasting values, such as royal and gold, which may fuse in a finely woven silk, can be blatantly busy in an average-scale weave.

All this has a particular bearing on patterned fabrics, for rugs, upholstery, table mats or covers which should "lie flat." In these, control of depth is essential to maintaining a horizontal plane.

Dominant contrasts, such as black and white or indigo and natural are strong and positive, as are many of the vibrant, close value relationships; but only very careful discrimination and skill in scaling values can save texture weaving which has contrast in both hue and value, as with royal blue and gold, for example.

Broken Color in Texture Weaving

For texture weaving which potentially exploits broken color to the utmost, experience suggests the following pointers:

(1) In combining colors, first look at the yarns together close up, then at a distance, and always in the scale in which they will be used—end next to end, or twisted together to simulate the breakup of weft over warp. The amount of contrast seen thus will, of course, be reduced in the web by the introduction of filling color and by the highlight and shadow of the interlacing process.

(2) The more intense the colors, the closer they should be in value.

(3) The more neutral the colors, the greater their tolerance of strong value contrasts.

(4) Close value can unify several different hues. Rather close values in analogous colors like blue, blue-

green, and green will tend to fuse and produce an effect of iridescence. Complementary colors such as blue and yellow will fuse only when values are approximately the same, as with an intense sky-blue and deep gold.

(5) The larger the scale of interlacing, the closer the values should be. Put conversely, a finely woven cloth allows of more contrast in values than a coarse one.

(6) The subtlety of dull-shiny relationships in yarns may be lost through too strong a contrast in colors. Highlight and shadow texture can be strengthened, or obscured, according to how contrasting values are handled.

(7) The greater the distance between eye and fabric, the more is contrast in chroma, hue, and value acceptable, even desirable.

(8) The closer a piece of weaving approaches to a definite pattern, the less these rules apply; a warp or filling-faced stripe, for instance, allows more latitude than a balanced mesh.

All these considerations are concerned with fusion, or simplification, of color within the eye. Subtle handling of color provides unity; results may be either subdued or brilliant. Such subtle handling of color, though it follows no set rules, produces harmony. Color used heedlessly and in defiance of appropriate scale, value, and texture becomes raw, obvious, and without distinction.

Color Myths

If there are no hidebound color rules to follow, there definitely are myths to dispel. The weaver knows that there are no beautiful colors, nor ugly ones, as such. Color is relative to the hues and values which lie next to it, to their proportioning and to the light that falls upon it. There are no colors which do not work with each other; a seeming lack of harmony may arise from wrong proportioning, or lack of modulation in changing from one color to another. Color divergencies can easily be drowned—particularly when they occur in the same family: there may be two blues which do not go well together, but it is impossible to find five blues that will not harmonize.

DESIGNING A WARP

First and last, the most important single step in the weaving process is designing the warp. The yarn selected for the warp, the threading pattern, and the sett will pretty well determine the quality and character of the cloth.

Because there are many far-reaching decisions to be taken in designing a warp, the weaver is strongly urged to regard this as a preliminary and fairly separate procedure, not concerning himself with filling materials and pattern development until these stages have been reached. The theory here is to work one step at a time, progressively, realizing that the imagination extends itself from the vantage point of each completed stage.

Selecting the Warp Yarn

In selecting the yarn or yarns for the warp, avoid tender ones even though they may look appealing; there are thousands of sturdy, resilient yarns to choose from. Testing the tensile strength of yarn for warping merely involves pulling briskly on a length of yarn about a yard long to determine its breaking point. This is usually done at several places because some yarns have weak spots due either to construction or the effect of rot. A yarn's resistance to abrasion can be tested by pulling down on it between thumbnail and forefinger. Severe roughing up, or fuzzing, automatically precludes its use for a warp, especially for close-set constructions.

The next question is whether this yarn alone should be used for the warp, or whether it should be combined with another yarn or yarns.

The sequence of the two yarns might depend upon their individual character. The similarity and natural texture of two slubby, single-ply yarns might tend to suggest a random threading. On the other hand, yarns of equal size, but otherwise in strong contrast, might suggest a regular, symmetrical sequence of threading. As a typical example, take two round, even yarns in black and white; here an end-and-end arrangement could be the logical one. This suggestion is, of course, purely arbitrary. There are no set rules. It is most important, however, that the weaver feel out the yarns he is working with and that he be imaginatively aware of their capacities.

Choosing a Threading Draft

When it comes to the threading draft, there is greater latitude of choice. Again, there are no rules to follow, but if the weaver is designing primarily from the character of the yarns themselves, the selection of a draft which accommodates a variety of weaves is a sensible one. On a straight draw, for instance, plain weave, rib or basket weave, and a number of twill variations can be woven. Although this is not the only draw that allows for variety of weave, it's a safe and simple one with which to explore.

THE SETT OF THE CLOTH

The sett of the cloth, as explained before, has to do with its density, with the closeness of the yarns. Sett also concerns the symmetrical or asymmetrical balance of warp and weft. In short, sett has three aspects: first is the density of yarns and weaves; second is the balance of warp and filling—in any construction this balance will affect the appearance and the hand of the fabric immeasurably. The third is the use of eccentric sett, meaning changes of density within the warp or filling. An irregular beat-up can effect this to some extent, but more drastic changes of density are determined in the sleying. Skip-denting is an example of this; so is cramming which means crowding more warp ends into some dents than others.

Most hand weavers greatly underestimate the importance of sett. (This is one thing that commercial weavers understand perhaps better than those textile designers who have been trained in art schools.) A keener appreciation of sett may dawn if the weaver reflects that broadcloth, batiste, cheesecloth, canvas are all in plain weave, all woven with much the same kind of cotton yarn. Thus it becomes clear that the manipulation of sett gives the designer one of his most versatile tools, adding scope to every weave.

When it comes to the selection of the reed, both the number of ends per inch and the size and character of the warp yarn have a determining influence. If the sett is twenty ends per inch, a twenty-dent reed would normally be used; but if the warp yarn tends to be fuzzy, to have loose slubs and frequent knots, there will be fewer problems in the weaving if sleyed two in a dent on a ten-dent reed.

Other Sett Considerations

With too soft or too open a sett, the fabric will lack body, it will be unstable and prone to sag. Too tight a sett makes a fabric boardy and diminishes its draping qualities. Also, yarns packed in too tight tend to lose their character.

Extremes in sett, on the other hand, can be inviting. An open weave, soft and pliant, is luxurious in a scarf even though it never could stand up to the cutting and sewing process. Crispness, as in canvas or taffeta, can be interesting, even challenging if used for certain types of garment; or for flat applications such as wall coverings, shades or place mats. With average-sized yarns, a casement may suggest an open sleying, whereas upholstery or suitings should be closely sleyed. Shirtings or blankets would fall somewhere in between these. Very soft yarns require closer sleying than do stiff or sticky ones. Another sett consideration is whether the sleying is to be regular and even, or spaced and perhaps random.

Testing the Sett

In testing a warp, an understanding of the rightness of the sett comes through trained fingers alone. A weaver feels the cloth; he feels it on the loom with the tension off. He will try the same construction over and over, with a few more or a few less picks. Before starting production, he will take the sample warp off the loom, wash and finish it to check the sett. This is because he knows that some fabrics will tighten and firm up in the finishing, others grow soft and sleazy. Perhaps more important still, he will have the courage to re-sley and retest the warp as often as is necessary to perfect the coordination of yarn, weave, and sett as these relate to the function of the cloth. A thorough grasp of this knowledge is in itself a goal worth striving for. It is the mark of the perfectionist. It is this that makes the difference between a sleazy cloth that stretches, slips at the seams, and wears out quickly, and a cloth that performs and serves the user well.

Looms

LOOM TYPES

A loom is a device or machine for weaving cloth. As such, it covers a broad range, from the simple devices described in Chapter 2, and in this section, to complete automatic, power looms for mass production.

Hand Looms

Hand looms, inherited from various cultures and eras, are those which are not power-driven. More typically, in America and England, a hand loom means a horizontal, foot-operated loom, similar to the one pictured in Fig. 29, or its more compact, table-based equivalent. The former is designated as a foot-powered hand loom, or floor loom, to distinguish it from the table loom. Basically, this hand loom is not unlike the horizontal loom developed by the ancient Greeks and brought to its present form during the Renaissance. With variations, it is common to the entire Old World and nowadays to the Americas as well.

Two-Harness and Four-Harness Looms

Two-harness looms often appear as table looms, originally imported for the use of children, and as rug looms. Although many types of rugs can be woven on two harnesses the authors recommend, rather, a sturdy, four-harness loom, wide and with double beams for general weaving. (See Warp Beams, page 222.

Table Looms

Table looms are commonly made with two, four, or more harnesses, up to twenty. In width they vary from 8 to 36 inches, but seldom are more than 20 to 24 inches wide. In quality, they range from inexpensive toys to professional equipment. Their chief advantage is that they are compact enough to transport and to store easily; and they are somewhat less expensive than floor looms of the same width. Table looms ordinarily are used in classrooms which must double for other courses and cannot therefore afford full-time floor space.

The table loom is valuable for sample-making. Because it saves space, and costs less, the table loom is particularly desirable for designers who may need many looms. But its greatest advantage, unquestionably, lies in the simplicity of its direct shed—no tie-up needed—when the weaver is experimenting with multiple-harness weaves.

DISADVANTAGES OF TABLE LOOMS: With table looms, because the shuttle must be dropped for each harness change, no rhythm is possible; without rhythm, the process of weaving becomes arduous and the product stilted. Clothmaking, therefore, should be learned on a foot-powered loom. The small table loom is not at all recommended for beginners.

Types of Foot-Powered Looms

There are three classifications of foot-powered looms, essentially the same except for their manner of creating the shed. All three of these may be wide or narrow, folding or rigid. The preference among weavers for one type as against another can elicit crisp differences of opinion. The three kinds are: (1) the counterbalanced, (2) the jack, and (3) the contremarche loom.

Counterbalanced Loom

The counterbalanced loom has an open shed. The opening shed is made by warp ends both rising *and* sinking from the closed position. This double, or up-

and-down, shedding motion is characteristic of the counterbalanced loom. Pairs of harnesses are suspended by a common cord over rollers or pulleys, or they may pivot from horses.

Counterbalanced looms now are made with two or four harnesses only. The four-harness types work best with balanced sheds, that is, two harnesses balanced against two harnesses. Raising three harnesses, or one harness, is inefficient as compared with the action of a jack loom. Counterbalanced looms tend to be sturdy and simple and, also, less expensive than jack or contremarche looms.

Jack Loom

The shedding motion of a jack loom is different from that of a counterbalanced or contremarche loom in that the rising harnesses lift from their closed shed position while the other harnesses remain stationary. There are no sinking harnesses. Actually, there are two styles of jack looms: those on which the harnesses are lifted from the top, and those on which the harnesses are pushed up from below.

Jack looms are available with four harnesses or more. Several new versions have metal harnesses. While steel harnesses produce a fine shed, they are noisy as compared with those of wood. (See Loom Noise, page 221.) Jack looms have a desirable flexibility in the matter of harnesses which can be added as the weaver needs them. Most table looms are jack-type looms. The authors recommend jack looms.

Contremarche Loom

The contremarche loom is really a counterbalanced jack loom. It has the double-action shed of the counterbalanced loom, and the clear, asymmetrical (three against one) shed of a jack loom. This is accomplished by using a double set of lams. The resulting tie-up, therefore, is a double one—difficult and tedious to effect and requiring great precision. Some skilled weavers prefer the contremarche to any other, but for general use, the newer types of jack loom seem to have superseded it. The complexity of the tie-up makes the contremarche a poor choice for teaching purposes.

CONSIDERATIONS IN BUYING A LOOM

The main considerations in buying a loom are: Its size, its width and weaving space, number and type of harnesses (including noise); its harness action, type of warp beam and, finally, cost.

SIZE AND WIDTH: Generally speaking the first, or major, loom should be as wide as possible; narrow cloth can be woven on a wide loom but, of course, wide cloths can be woven only on wide looms. Weaving cloth wider than 45 inches is a strenuous task, especially for those with short arms. In general, however, the loom selected should be as wide as can reasonably be accommodated.

Folding looms can be sturdy, but those with an X-form base rarely are. If portability is a consideration, either a small floor loom or a table loom is an excellent choice. This small loom may be used for experimentation, in addition to a wider loom for actual weaving projects.

In considering size, the height of the breast beam is a major factor. Generally, the higher the breast beam, the easier the weaving process; for a tall person this is especially important. Because looms with overhead beaters have tall superstructures, they may seem to be much larger than looms of the same size with underslung beaters.

Space requirements—and cost—are important considerations. As the *over-all* loom width is approximately 6 inches wider than the weaving width, and up to 10 or 12 inches wider than the maximum finished cloth, space becomes a decided factor. Dedicated weavers will, when necessary, turn a bedroom, living room, or play room into a weaving studio in order to have space for weaving.

The width of a loom is designated by the maximum width of cloth that can be set up on it. In other words, loom width is put in terms of the weaving width available, not the over-all width of the loom. Usually this is determined by the inside harness measurement, but may be limited by the reed slot or the cloth beam.

Standard widths for looms vary with manufacturers. Normally, looms can be bought in sizes ranging from 20 inches through 24, 30, 36, 40, 45, 48, 54, and up to 60 inches wide.

Finished cloth usually measures 4 or 5 inches less than the loom's width, so that standard width 29-inch suiting fabric would need to be set up on a loom at least 36 inches wide, or wider. Standard, finished width of shirting and dress material is 36 inches, requiring a loom at least 45 inches wide.

Minimum finished width of upholstery is 40 inches and would need to be set up on a loom 45 or 48 inches wide. A 48-inch upholstery would require a 54- or 60-inch loom, as would standard hand-woven drapery and upholstery of the same width.

The loom width required for rugs and blinds depends on the dimensions in which these items are to be woven. They often take the widest looms.

WEAVING SPACE: The term weaving space does not mean loom width. It is the distance from reed to breast beam which should be as deep as possible. A deep weaving space offers a better shed, generally speaking, and a more equalized tension. Moreover the cloth will have to be rolled forward less often, and more of the woven cloth can be seen at a glance. This final consideration is vitally important with fabrics in free patterns such as tapestries and rugs.

Number of Harnesses

Many cloths can be woven on four-harness looms, and most looms have four harnesses. However, looms with eight harnesses or more, allow for more complex patterns. Depending on what the weaver plans to do in the future, the considerably higher cost of these may be justifiable. Also some looms, such as the jack loom, can adapt to additional harnesses at a later date.

LOOM NOISE: The regular, measured sound of beating the weft into place is pleasant and usually tolerable.

But if limiting sound is important, a loom with metal jacks and harnesses should be twice considered. Applying felt or rubber pads at contact points of the loom between the loom and floor and using string heddles will reduce noise substantially.

WARP BEAMS: Some looms have pegged beams for sectional warping; far preferable to these are combination beams which can be reversed to allow for either sectional warping or the standard chain warping.

A large-diameter, or drum beam, will give better tension with less padding than a conventional, small-diameter beam. Heavy cords or ropes between the beam and warp stick are inferior to a canvas apron.

A double (second) warp beam often is useful for combining two yarns in a warp, for adding warp ends, and for special double-beam weave effects. Most looms can be ordered with two warp beams or with provision for adding a second beam later.

LOOM COSTS

Ordinarily, the value of standard looms depreciates slowly. The purchase cost should be considered an investment as well as an expenditure. Resale values are high. Secondhand looms are often "good as new" and may cost almost as much. Getting the right loom at the start, a good loom, and a loom large enough to carry on with is a reasonable investment to make.

Antique looms are usually too bulky and too warped to be useful. Parts missing from looms that have been dismantled and stored away may constitute a drawback serious enough to disqualify them. Lastly, building a loom is almost never a sound idea. Like sailboats, looms have subtle problems of balance between working parts that might confound even the most skilled cabinetmaker.

In weaving, the beginner, especially, needs a standard-quality, trouble-free loom. He also needs to have money left over to buy equipment for warping and bobbin-winding as well as other accessories.

LOOM ACCESSORIES AND EQUIPMENT

Bench or Stool

Many loom builders show benches of proper height for their specific looms; those which are adjustable in height are best. Generally speaking, the weaver should sit as high as possible over the weaving. In this position, treadling action is almost directly downward and therefore effortless compared with the diagonal movement of outstretched foot. Sitting high also gives the best view of the web and allows for maximum side-to-side stretch in weaving wide fabrics.

The authors prefer a stool to a bench; tall, sturdy, round-topped stools can be cut to the exact height needed. A stool is easier to move than a bench and less in the way when not in use. Some weavers now are using drafting stools which pivot and have an adjustable posture back. Also, they are padded and are certainly most comfortable.

LOOMSIDE TABLE OR CABINET: It is necessary to have some sort of table at hand to hold reed hooks, bobbins, extra shuttles and, perhaps, an ash tray. This can range from an orange crate to another stool or, for luxury and efficiency, an open-shelved cabinet on casters for easy handling.

THREADING STOOL: Because threading the warp should be done with the eye level close to the height of the heddle eyes, the threading stool should be low enough to make this possible. It must also fit in over the treadles. Depending on the loom, a camp stool, an artist's folding stool, or a low chair is the most suitable.

WARP WINDING EQUIPMENT

The warping reel pictured in Fig. 32 is a vertical floor reel. In addition to this kind, there are horizontal warping reels which can be turned easily and smoothly from a sitting position, but these reels are relatively hard to find. Both vertical and horizontal reels are made in apartment-size models and in space-saving collapsible versions which are the better of the two. The apartment-size reel is acceptable, however, for all but the longest warps.

Also widely used today are warping frames, mentioned in Chapter 3, which come in various sizes. The frame shown in Fig. 137 has a span of one yard between the pegs on one side of the frame and the pegs on the other side; it is shown with the warp started on the peg which allows for the winding of a 5-yard warp. The manufacturer's descriptions of such equipment usually give the number of yards of warp a board will accommodate.

The warping frame should be placed in an upright position, securely attached to a wall, so that it will not move during the warping process. The frame should be hung so that the pegs used for forming the cross in the yarns can be seen clearly whether the frame is hung with these pegs at the top or at the bottom. The procedure for winding a warp on a warping board is the same as for the reel. (See page 48.)

FIG. 137. *Warping frame, showing the cross in the yarns of the warp which has been started on the peg allowing for the winding of a five-yard warp. Drawing, Don Wight.*

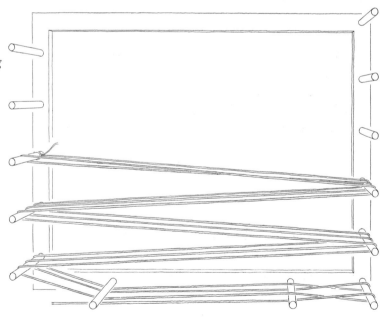

Constructing A Frame Loom

While the building of a standard four-harness floor loom is not recommended, the construction of a frame loom, such as was used in Chapter 2 for Project 1, is encouraged as an undertaking which will prove feasible and, at the same time, instructive to the weaver.

THE FRAME LOOM WITH COMPLETE SPECIFICATIONS AND INSTRUCTIONS FOR PUTTING IT TOGETHER

The dimensions of the weaving frame shown here were calculated on the following basis:

	Inches
Place mat, length	18
Allowance for loom waste and shrinkage (such as tying on and finishing), approximately 20 per cent	6½
Total distance required between inner edges of endboards	24½
Width of two endboards (2¾″ + 2¾″)	5½
Total length of baseboard	30
Place mat, width	12
Allowance for space between the two end nails and edges of the boards	4
Total length of endboards	16

As these calculations indicate, a baseboard 30 inches long and two endboards each 16 inches long are required for the frame. Fig. 138 shows that two blocks are nailed to each end of the baseboard and that the endboards are mounted on the blocks. Complete specifications and detailed directions for constructing the frame are given below.

Materials required:

1 baseboard, 30″ long × 5″ wide × ¾″ thick
2 endboards, 16″ long × 2¾″ wide × ¾″ thick
4 blocks, 5″ long × 2¾″ wide × ¾″ thick
8 - 1½″ finishing nails
8 - 2″ finishing nails
8 - 2½″ finishing nails
102 - 1″ finishing nails

Baseboard

Attach the first set of blocks to each end of the baseboard using the eight 1½-inch finishing nails as indicated by the four dots on each block, shown in Fig. 139.

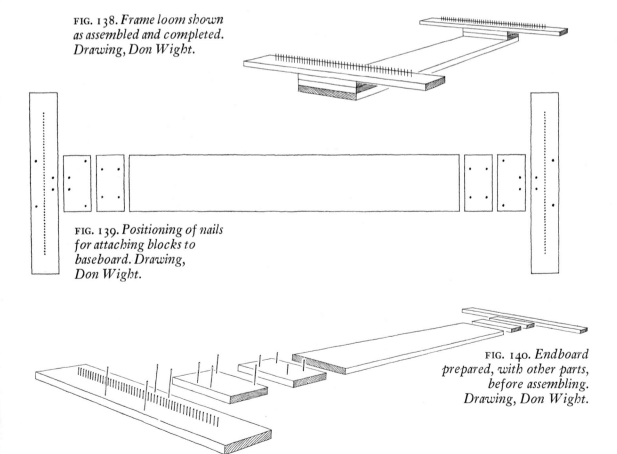

FIG. 138. *Frame loom shown as assembled and completed. Drawing, Don Wight.*

FIG. 139. *Positioning of nails for attaching blocks to baseboard. Drawing, Don Wight.*

FIG. 140. *Endboard prepared, with other parts, before assembling. Drawing, Don Wight.*

Nail on the second set of blocks using eight 2-inch finishing nails, placed as shown.

Before mounting the endboards on the blocks, prepare each of them as follows: Measure the width of the board and mark its center, first at one end and then at the other end. Make a ruled line from one mark to the other so that the line runs the complete length of the board at the center. Now find the center of this lengthwise line and mark it with a pencil dot.

From the center mark, measure 6¼ inches to the right and 6¼ inches to the left and at these points on the line make pencil dots. Between these two dots, a distance of 12½ inches, make a row of dots at ¼-inch intervals. The total number of dots will be 51. At each dot drive in a 1-inch finishing nail, allowing the nail to extend about ½ inch above the surface of the board (Fig. 140). An alternative system for placement of the 1-inch nails is to stagger them. This helps to prevent a lengthwise split in the board.

If this system is used, there will be two rows of nails at ½-inch intervals instead of a single row at ¼-inch intervals. The lengthwise lines marking the position of the nails should be ruled parallel to the center line and ¼ inch on each side of it.

TO MOUNT THE ENDBOARDS: Make a center mark on the outside end of each top block. Then, measuring lengthwise, mark the center of each endboard on the edge that is to line up with the marked block. Mount each endboard on a block, making certain that the center marks are lined up, and drive in four 2-inch nails as indicated by the large dots shown in Fig. 139.

Figure 141 shows the position in the baseboard of the twelve nails.

FIG. 141. *Positioning of twelve nails in baseboard before final assembling. Drawing, Don Wight.*

(It should be noted that the nailing arrangement for attaching the blocks and endboards to the baseboard has been carefully worked out to prevent one nail from interfering with another as each subsequent part is added. The dots indicating placement of these nails should be marked on all the blocks and the endboards before any of the parts are assembled.)

This loom can be constructed, also, with a nut and bolt assembly. However, although this method may be the easier of the two, it requires special tools for drilling and countersinking the nuts and bolts.

If this method is used, two holes must be drilled in the endboards, the blocks, and at each end of the baseboard. The parts then are lined up and bolted together with two nut-and-bolt assemblies at each end of the frame.

Yarn-Count Systems

Various counting systems are used to designate the size of yarn and to calculate the yards per pound. These systems vary by fiber and in different industries and countries.

The simplest of these, and one coming more and more into use, is based on *yards per pound*. This system has the advantage of being applicable to all yarns—even novelties and special twists, cut film, and straws. Also, it is completely accurate and not merely an approximation.

Most yarn dealers identify their samples with a *yards-per-pound label*. If neither yards per pound nor yarn number are known, yardage can be measured by making a skein of known length and size and weighing it. Alternatively, a skein of known weight may be measured. This measuring off, or skein making, can be done on a skein winder or a warping reel or frame.

NUMBERING SYSTEM

Yarn numbering systems give a standard number for the measuring of yarn. Except for reeled silk, natural fiber yarns are calculated by the ratio of length to a unit of weight. The higher the yarn number the finer the yarn. For instance, cotton count is based on a standard length of 840 yards a pound. The number of 840 lengths in one pound will give the yarn count: Thus, a No. 1 cotton has 840 yards per pound, and a No. 10 cotton, with 8400 yards a pound, is ten times finer than a No. 1 cotton. Cotton count can be written as No. 10, or 10's. It can also be written 10/1 (called a ten's single) with the figure 1 indicating a single-ply yarn. A 10/2 designation would indicate that two single 10's had been plied together; the yards per pound, 8400, is then divided by the second number to equal 4200. A 10/2 yarn is twice as heavy as a 10/1 yarn.

For 8/4 cotton, yards per pound are calculated by multiplying 840 by 8 to equal 6720 divided by 4 equals 1680. Spun silk and spun rayon are often calculated on the cotton system.

Linen Count

Linen is measured by the lea, or leas. One lea is 300 yards. The number of leas in one pound determines the count, so that 1-1/2 leas measure 450 yards; 7 leas measure 2100 yards; seven leas, 2-ply, measure 1050 yards per pound.

Woolen Count

Woolen count may be measured by two systems: the *cut system* and the *run system*. The cut system is based on 300 yards to one pound of No. 1's (or 1 cut) yarn. A No. 6's wool (or 6 cut wool) has 6 times 300 yards, or 1800 yards a pound.

The run system of wool count is based on the number of 1600 yard units in a pound of No. 1's. To find the yardage of a 6-run wool, multiply the standard of 1600 by the count of 6, which equals 9600 yards a pound.

Worsted System

There are 560 yards in one pound of No. 1's worsted yarn. A No. 20's (20 × 560) has 11,200 yards a pound. A No. 20's, 2-ply worsted has half that yardage, or 5600 yards a pound.

The Denier System

The denier, an old French coin generally of small value, is used as the weight unit to measure silk and the synthetic filaments and fibers. Unlike yarn counts for other fibers, the denier system is predicated on the basis that *the smaller the number, the finer (and longer) the filament.* A No. 1 denier filament yields 4,464,528 yards a pound. To determine the yardage of a (fine) 50-denier filament, divide 50 into 4,464,528 to get 89,290 yards a pound. A coarse denier, No. 900, yields only 4950 yards a pound.

Correction of Errors

In weaving, the correcting of errors is almost completely a matter of common sense. Every error can be corrected in one way or another and should be done in the way that involves the least work. If the weaver clearly understands the procedures in winding the warp, dressing the loom and tying up; if he understands, too, the relationship of the required procedures one to another, he will see that each fault has a direct and logical cause.

When the heading has been completed, examine it closely. If in spite of all precautions taken there are errors, analyze the nature of them coolly and make amends methodically, remembering that in making corrections it is all too easy to commit fresh errors. Make a careful check, examining the surface and the underside of the web, to see that all of the warp yarns are interlacing through the filling in correct sequence. Any yarn which has been interlaced out of sequence must be traced from its position at the fell of the cloth through the reed and the heddles to find the mistake and to decide how to correct it.

ERRORS IN THREADING

One of the most common errors made in threading is a skipped heddle. For example, if in working left to right on a 1, 2, 3, 4 draw, the warp ends in one unit were threaded 1, 2, 3, −, leaving the heddle on harness

4 empty, an incorrect sequence of interlacing would result, showing clearly as a fault in the woven cloth. To correct this, remove from the heddles all the warp ends threaded between the skipped heddle and the edge of the warp nearest to it, then rethread these warp ends correctly.

The incidence of such errors is greatly reduced when the heddles are grouped for threading, as explained on page 63. Grouping of heddles also greatly lessens the risk of threading heddles out of sequence. For example, if in working left to right on a 1, 2, 3, 4 draw, the first two warp ends were threaded correctly on harnesses 1 and 2, but were followed by an end drawn on harness 4 and, then, on harness 3, the sequence would be changed to 1, 2, 4, 3. Correction requires that the transposed warp ends be removed from the heddles and redrawn in correct sequence.

Picking up the warp ends at the lease sticks where the yarns are crossed in place is a help in avoiding the error of a skipped warp end. This occurs when all the heddles have been threaded, with none skipped, but leaving a warp end which has not been threaded through a heddle. If the warp is a simple one with only one kind of yarn as in Project 1—and since the error will have no effect on the interlacing—it can be corrected by pulling the yarn out of the lease sticks, free of the other warp ends, so that it can be dropped to the floor at the back of the loom. When the weaving begins, see that the extra end is pulled free of the warp as it moves toward the front of the loom. Since the only effect of removing this end is that the woven cloth will be one end narrower than planned, the labor of removing all the warp ends threaded between the skipped end and the nearest selvage, and then rethreading them, seems hardly justified.

Similarly, if two ends have been misdrawn through the same heddle, or through heddles on the same harness, the error can be corrected as above by simply removing the extra end, pulling it to the back of the loom and dropping it free of other warp ends. If it becomes necessary to make a repair heddle instead, the easiest way to make one is with the same type of wire or flat steel heddles on the loom. A heddle has a loop at each end; cut one side of this at the middle and spread the two halves so that they will fit over the heddle bar of the proper harness. Then flatten down the split halves, being careful of the sharp ends.

SLEYING ERRORS

A common error in sleying is that of crossing ends, that is, picking up two warp ends from the heddles in incorrect sequence. For example, in sleying a unit of four ends, from left to right, if the warp end on harness 2 is sleyed then followed, in the next dent, by the warp end on harness 1, the two ends will cross each other between the heddles and the reed. They can be detected by examining the shed from the side. Pull both ends out of the reed, follow them back to the heddles and resley them in correct sequence.

Sometimes crossed ends will so interfere with proper shedding that they will be noticed before the heading is woven. To prevent warp breakage, correct them as soon as they are found.

Two very common errors made in sleying are skipping a dent, and entering more warp ends than required in a dent. If the skipped dent and the over-entered dent are side by side, remove the end from the over-entered dent and transfer it to the empty dent. If the warp has been tied on, the group of warp ends in which the incorrectly entered dent is included will have to be untied to release it, then retied when the error has been corrected.

If the error is discovered after the weaving has been started, untie the group of warp ends which include it and check the sequence of the warp ends in the heddles to determine which one should be transferred to the empty dent. Grasp this yarn just above the fell of the cloth and gently work it out of the filling yarns, pulling it back toward the reed. When it has been freed, enter it correctly into the empty dent. Then weave the loose warp end into the cloth with a blunt-nosed tapestry needle, taking care that the interlacing relates correctly to the construction of the cloth.

When the yarn has been interlaced, pull it forward so that it is the same length as the other ends in the group. Retie the group of yarns onto the cloth rod, making certain that this group is at the same tension as the rest of the warp.

If the weaving done involves only the heading, the correctly sleyed end need not be rewoven. Instead, lay it on top of the woven heading, pulled to the same length as the other yarns in the group; retie the group onto the cloth bar, verifying the tension with that of the other groups, and proceed with the weaving.

If the error in sleying involves only a skipped dent, or only an over-entered dent, rather than both of these; or if both errors occur separately, with correctly sleyed warp ends lying between the two dents, the correction requires either the removal from the reed of all warp ends between the point of error and the edge of the warp that is nearest, or the removal from the dents of all warp ends between the incorrectly sleyed dents—whichever involves the fewest number of warp ends and, therefore, the least work.

If the weaving proper has been started, it is often easier to cut the filling yarns in several places across the warp and pull them out of the warp rather than take the time to unweave the filling from the warp. This is done by cutting the filling yarns between two warp ends with scissors or razor blade, taking care not to cut any warp ends inadvertently.

Obviously, it is well worth the time spent to make a careful check for errors before the weaving has been started and to make a second check when enough of the heading has been woven to make an error evident.

Abrasion Resistance. A fabric's surface resistance to wear; a yarn's resistance to roughing up by rubbing.

Acetate. Man-made fiber of cellulose acetate; name also applied to yarn and fabric of such yarn.

Acrilan, Acrylic fibers, usually crimped. Acrilan is the trade-mark name of Chemstrand Corporation for synthetic fibers made from a liquid derived from natural gas and air; other acrylic fibers are Creslan and Orlon.

Alpaca. Long, fine hair of the alpaca, one of the llama family, native to the Andes Mountains chiefly in Peru and Bolivia.

Angora. Long, fine silky hair of the domesticated goat of Asia Minor. When processed, this yarn is called mohair. Also the fine, long hair of the Angora rabbit.

Apron. A strong piece of cloth, the width of the warp, attached to the warp and cloth beams at front and back of the loom. The aprons provide the means of holding the warp in correct position.

Backstrap Loom. A simple, primitive weaving device. (See Chapter 2)

Bamboo. A variety of woody, treelike grass; split bamboo is sometimes used as rigid filler.

Bands. Area stripes. (See Borders)

Base Cloth. (See Ground Cloth)

Basic Weaves. (See Plain Weave, Twill Weave, Satin Weave)

Baskets. Primitive methods of weaving them, page 3.

Basket Weave. A derivative of plain weave, usually balanced, in which two or more filling picks are interlaced as one, over and under two or more warp ends, alternating on every second pick.

Bast Fibers. These include the woody fibers from plants such as flax, jute, ramie, hemp, and sisal.

Batten. (See Beater)

Beam. A loom part: at back of loom, back beam, and warp beam; at front of loom, breast beam, and cloth beam. (See Figs. 28 and 29)

Beater. A stick or sword, inserted in the shed between the heddles and the reed to press down the filling between each shot of the shuttle. Beating is the act of pressing down, or packing in, the filling.

Bobbin. A long, narrow spool on which the filling is wound so that there is an easy, continuous flow of yarn in weaving. When wound, the bobbin is encased in the shuttle for throwing through the shed.

Bobbin Winder. The winder, operated electrically or by hand, is for winding the yarn onto the bobbin.

Borders. Bands of color or texture; area stripes; may be in warp or in filling, or in both.

Bouclé. A novelty yarn. (See page 158)

Brocade. Brocade is a cloth in which a third decorative element of yarn or yarns is introduced onto the plain-weave two-element ground cloth; brocades may be filling-faced, warp-faced, discontinuous or laid-in. (See Chapter 5)

Broken Twill. A twill in which the characteristic diagonal progression is interrupted or taken out of sequence. (See Fig. 72, No. 9)

Burning Test. (See page 160)

Butterfly. A yarn device used to insert filling into the shed instead of a shuttle. The method of winding this is shown in Figs. 24-26.

Cable Ply. A firm, round yarn usually of eight or more strands twisted together.

Canvas. A heavy, firm plain-weave fabric of cotton (or linen).

Cashmere. Soft, luxurious yarn made from hair of goats native to Kashmir province, India; goats also raised in Tibet, Iran, and Southwest China.

Castle. Superstructure of loom framework from which harnesses are suspended.

Checkerboard. Pattern in which blocks of color or texture alternate and abut as on a checkerboard; often seen in brocades.

Chenille. (See Novelty Twists)

Cloth. Woven fabric or textile. (See Web)

Cloth Apron. Apron, usually of canvas, attached to cloth stick, or rod or beam, at front and back of loom, to hold warp in place.

Color. A hue, as contrasted with white, black, or gray. (See section on Color, page 208)

Comb. A loom accessory used as a beater.

Combed, Combing. Part of the process of grading and preparing a fiber for spinning.

Cone. Cone-shaped cylinder of cardboard or wood for winding yarn in convenient form or package for sale and use.

Cotton. Natural white cellulose fiber taken from seed pod of plant of the mallow family; most versatile and widely used of natural textile fibers.

Cotton Count. Cotton yarn is measured in terms of length per unit weight. No. 1 cotton has 840 yards per pound. (See Yarn Count Systems, page 229)

Dacron. A Du Pont trade-mark name for a synthetic polyester fiber notable for its crisp resilience.

Darning. (See Interlacing, page 2)

Denier. Originally a small French coin, the word denier now indicates the size or weight of silk filament or yarn, as well as man-made filaments. The denier of a filament is determined by the number of .05 gram weights to a standard skein of 450 meters; the higher the denier number, the coarser the yarn. (See Yarn Count Systems, page 229)

Denim. A strong cotton twill fabric.

Density. The hand of a fabric judged by the weight or compactness of the weave; more specifically, by the sett in the reed, and how the filling is beaten.

Dent. The opening, or space, in the reed through which the warp ends are drawn in sleying.

Derivative Weave. A derivative weave is a variation or extension of a basic weave which retains the essential order of interlacing.

Device. 1. A device for weaving, such as a loom; a piece of equipment used to perform a specific mechanical function. 2. Method or ways invented or contrived for varying or elaborating patterns in weaving.

Discontinuous Brocade. A brocading technique in which the brocade yarn does not go from selvage to selvage, but is laid in according to the requirements of a figure or motif; also called *laid-in brocade.*

Draft, Drafting. A draft gives directions for weaving a specific cloth or construction, plotted on cross-section paper. A comprehensive draft includes a weave draft, the draw-in or threading plan, and the harness and lam tie-up with treadling action.

Dukagang. Term for a Swedish version of discontinuous brocade.

End. A single strand of warp yarn.

End-and-End. Cotton fabric such as chambray woven with warp yarns alternating white with color. Sometimes called *end-to-end*.

Fiber. The smallest basic unit of a threadlike process capable of being spun into thread or yarn. (Fiber Classifications: See Natural, Man-made, Synthetic)

Fell. The fell of the cloth is at that point where the last filling picks have been woven.

Felling Marks. A pick or two of yarn, in a contrasting color to the cloth being woven, inserted into the shed at the end of the heading, or where the weaving becomes even. As the weaving progresses, the cloth is measured from the felling marks.

Filling. In weaving, the crosswise element of yarn or yarns which interlaces at right angles with the warp. (See Weft)

Filling-faced. A filling-faced cloth is one in which the filling picks predominate over the warp ends; the filling may conceal the warp completely.

Finger Lace. See Free Weaving.

Finishing. Process of finishing a fabric after it is off the loom; may be washing and pressing, scouring, bleaching, sizing, calenderizing, embossing; also the application of trade-marked processes for resistance to shrinking, wrinkling, fading, etc.

Float. A filling pick or warp end which goes over or under two or more warp ends or filling picks without interlacing with the structure of the cloth.

Fragmentation. Term used in connection with iridescence or minute breakup of color in the process of interweaving yarns of different fibers, colors, or values.

Frame. Framework of a weaving device for holding the warp taut; also harness.

Frame Loom. Primitive weaving device. (See Fig. 10)

Free Weaving. Weaves in which the pattern yarns are not loom-controlled but are manipulated with the fingers. Examples: discontinuous or laid-in brocade, tapestry; gauze, leno, and other open, lacy weaves, sometimes called *finger lace*.

Gabardine. Textile of plied worsted yarns, a warp-faced twill used for fine quality outerwear. Gabardine also is woven in cotton, wool, rayon, and nylon yarns, often blended or combined, for slacks, raincoats, and other casual wear.

Gauze. One of the open, lacy weaves which include leno; done in a free-weaving technique, sometimes called *finger lace*.

Germantown. A 4-ply wool yarn of slack twist, made in Germantown, Pennsylvania.

Glass. A fine, flexible filament made of glass, not a true fiber. See Fiberglas, an Owens-Corning product also available in staple form.

Grasses. Grass cloth is woven from fibers, reeds, and includes ramie, jute, hemp, and young bamboo.

Ground Cloth. Ground cloth, or ground yarns, are the basic warp and filling yarns, interlaced in the process of weaving and essential to the structure of the cloth. In brocading, the brocading yarns are added to the plain-weave ground cloth as is the case with tapestry. A double cloth ground has two sets of warp and filling.

Grouping. Grouping of yarns means warp ends or filling picks of two or more yarns used as one to produce textural or color effects; may be regular or random.

Hand Loom. Looms. (See page 217)

Hand Spun. Yarns spun by hand on a spinning wheel, a process rarely used today except in primitive countries. Hand spinning results in more irregular, unstereotyped yarns than machine spinning, hence in more interesting woven cloth.

Hand Weaving. Weaving done by hand without a loom, on a frame or backstrap loom, or a hand- and foot-powered loom.

Harness. A frame from which are suspended the heddles, through which the warp yarns are threaded; contrived to help hold the warp ends taut.

Heading, Hem. That portion of the web which is woven at the beginning of a new piece of weaving, and at the end. A hem is sometimes used to finish a fabric, made by folding back the edges and sewing them.

Heddle. One of a set of cords or wires suspended from a harness frame, with eyes through which the warp ends are threaded.

Herringbone. Twill weave, requiring a pointed draw threading, in which a vertical succession of diagonals, resembling the backbone of the herring, is produced by reversing alternately the direction of the twill. Sometimes called *chevron weave*.

Hue. A color, or shade or tint of a color. Shade implies a deeper version, tint a paler gradation of a color.

Interlace. To interweave the filling yarns with the warp ends to make the web, or woven cloth.

Iridescence. The close interplay of two or more colors or values in weaving.

Jetspun. Trade-mark name for American Enka Corporation's continuous filament rayon yarns, solution-dyed. (Dan River Dictionary)

Laid-In. Laid-in or discontinuous brocade is a free-weaving technique in which the brocade yarn does not go from selvage to selvage of the ground cloth, but rather is used to add pattern or motif much as these appear in embroidery.

Lams. The lams in a loom consist of a series of bars lying beneath and parallel to the harnesses. The final tie-up of the loom, before weaving begins, is done with cords connecting the harnesses to the lams which control them, then tying the lams to the treadles which activate them.

Lary Sticks. Two lary sticks, several inches longer than the *depth* of the loom, and strong enough to bear the weight of the lease sticks and the spreader which will rest on them during the beaming process.

Lease Sticks. Two lease sticks are inserted to hold the cross in the yarns as the warp is transferred from warping reel to warp beam. The lease sticks are held in place on the loom to hold the warp yarns in proper sequence for drawing-in or threading the heddles.

Linen, Line. Strong, lustrous yarn made from flax fibers; also the fabric. The longest of flax fibers is called line linen; these fibers are separated from the shorter linen fibers, the shortest of which are called tow.

Loft. The height or springiness of a yarn, or of the surface of a woven fabric.

Long Staple. In wool, fibers of a length suitable for combing. In cotton, fibers $1\frac{1}{8}$ to $2\frac{1}{2}$ inches in length.

Loom. A device, or a machine, for weaving cloth. (See page 217)

Man-made. All textile fibers other than natural ones; the synthetics, including those made by chemical synthesis such as nylon; those with cellulose base such as rayon, or protein base, such as Vicara; or mineral base (glass); and rubber (Lastex).

Mat, Matt, Matte. A smooth, flat finish without sheen; a dull or delustered man-made fiber or yarn.

Mercerized. A chemical and physical process which makes cotton lustrous, strong, moisture-absorbent, and more color-fast than natural cotton.

Merino. A breed of sheep that yields a fine grade of wool, considered by some the finest, used for high-grade woolen and worsted cloth.

Metallics. Yarns that have been fabricated in

sheets of film and slit into fine strips or ribbons, sometimes designated as monofilaments.

Mohair. The processed fiber of the long, silky hair of the domesticated Angora goat of Asia Minor.

Motif. A single, often a repeated, theme in a design; a small pattern; an element of shape or color in a design.

Multifilament. Two or more, often many more, filaments twisted together to make a yarn.

Multiple Harness. Designates a loom with 4, 6, or more harnesses; a cloth woven on a loom with multiple harnesses, such as an eight-harness twill, satin, damask, or figured double cloth.

Natural Fibers. Natural textile fibers are cotton and linen, wool and silk. Cotton and linen (and other bast fibers) have a predominantly cellulose base, wool and silk a protein base.

Noils. Wool noils, short fibers taken from long-staple woolen or worsted in the combing; noil silk, waste combed out of clean, even fibers of silk and spun into noil yarns used for blends and novelty effects.

Novelty Yarns. Yarns twisted for various novelty effects; these include bouclé, chenille, guimpe, ratiné, loop, and seed yarns. (See page 158)

Nylon. Term for a broad class of synthetic yarns in filament, staple, plain, or crimped fibers; nylon has high tensile strength and resilience.

Ombré. French word meaning shaded; ombré stripes are carefully graduated from one tone to another, also effective if randomly done.

Orlon. A Du Pont synthetic acrylic fiber, in staple and tow.

Paper. Fiber used in hand weaving, often in strips, for place mats, wall coverings, etc.

Pattern. Design woven into a cloth through a specific technique of interlacing, manipulation of threading or sett, and the use of color or values.

Pebble Weave. A fabric woven, according to a special technique, of novelty yarn or highly twisted yarns which shrink when wet.

Pencil Stripe. See Pin Stripe.

Persian Knot. Also called sehna or senna. A knot used in making knotted pile rugs.

Pick. A single shot of weft through the warp shed.

Pick-and-pick. Single wefts in two colors alternating through the loom shed in weaving.

Pile Weave. Raised loops which form the surface in pile fabrics and rugs. These may be cut or uncut.

Pilling. Little balls, or pills, produced by abrasion or wear on the surface of garments woven of wool, especially short-fiber woolens.

Pin Stripe. The narrowest stripe, about the width of a pin, used to decorate a fabric, running lengthwise. Especially appropriate in woolen or worsted goods for suitings; also used in silk, rayon, and satin materials. Pencil stripes are similar, about the width of a pencil. Both kinds, sometimes called chalk stripes, come in white against a dark ground or in a pale tint to contrast with it.

Plain Weave. The simplest basic weave, universally in use. (See Fig. 5)

Ply. A single fiber or strand of yarn. One or more strands plied together to form ply-yarns or plied yarns.

Raddle. Raddle or spreader, a tool used for spreading warp evenly.

Raffia. Fiber from the raffia palm, widely used for weaving mats, baskets, and hats. Synthetic raffia, simulating natural raffia, used for weaving as in Project 3.

Random. Weaving which may be without set pattern, color sequence or repeat; threading and sleying may be irregular; filling yarns may twist at random coming off the shuttle; random stripes, random repeat.

Ratchet. A ratchet wheel, having teeth which engage with a pawl, used to keep beams stationary and to control the supply of yarn at back of loom and the tension of the warp at the front of the loom.

Ratiné. A novelty in which a heavy-ply yarn zigzags between two fine binder yarns for a rickrack effect.

Reed. A frame with evenly spaced dents, at the front of the loom, through which the warp ends are sleyed; sometimes called the sley. The filling yarn is beaten back against the reed for a firm cloth.

Reeds. Grasses used as semi-rigid filling.

Reel. A revolving frame used for winding the warp, measuring the yarn and making the cross. (See Fig. 32)

Rep, Repp. A cloth which has a corded surface.

Resilience. Certain natural yarns, such as silk and wool, have the capacity to spring back after compression, as in the hand; the property of elasticity, ability to re-bound to original shape after stretching to capacity.

Rib, Ribbed Weave. Rib weave, a derivative or extension of plain weave. Extension may be vertical or horizontal; if vertical, warp interlaces alternately over and under groups of filling picks forming horizontal rib; if horizontal, filling interlaces alternately over and under groups of ends forming vertical rib. See Weaves, Chapter 5.

Ribbons. 1. Fabric woven in narrow strips of silk, cotton, velvet, rayon, nylon, etc. 2. Acetate fabrics woven in wide sheets and cut into very narrow strips; hot knife fuses the edges obviating selvages. 3. Woven fabric cut into narrow strips for weaving, usually with yarns or other materials.

Roving. Thick strand of cotton or wool fibers with little or no twist, usually heavy.

Selvage. The edges of a woven cloth, which, lying parallel to the warp, are often reinforced with extra warp ends. The filling wraps around these outside warp ends as it enters the web and prevents fabric from raveling.

Sett. Also Set. Spelled with one *t* here when used as a verb, with 2 *t*'s used as noun. Disposition of the warp ends in the dents of the reed or sley, determining the density of the cloth.

Shed. The space between the alternating warp ends made by the rigid heddle, or by the raising or lowering of harnesses, so that the filling can be passed through.

Shot. One filling pick cast through the shed.

Shuttle. Implement carrying the bobbin which is wound with the filling yarn through the shed. (See also Butterfly)

Silk. Natural, monofilament fiber unwound from the cocoon of the silk worm. Also doupione, broken or damaged silk which cannot be reeled but is carded and spun; called *spun silk*.

Silhouette. Pattern in sheer fabrics, stressing areas of opacity or translucence by using yarns of various thickness, in varied sequences of density and sparseness.

Skein. A length or yardage of yarn, usually twisted into a sort of knot.

Skip-Dent. In sleying the warp ends through the reed, certain dents may be skipped to conform with grouping of warp yarns, or to make a skip-dent stripe.

Sley, Sleying. To sley; sleying is drawing the warp ends through the dents in the reed. (See Reed)

Stria, strié. A stria is a very fine stripe, often irregular or random; striae is the plural of stria. Strié, pronounced stree-yay, is striated or striped.

Stripe. A pattern in weaving produced by parallel lines of color, texture or open spaces. (See Design)

Swift. Swift, or floor swift, is a weaving accessory, used for holding and winding skeins of yarn. See Fig. 30, No. 1; also No. 3, umbrella swift.

Synthetic. Generally, all textile fibers other than natural fibers. (See Man-made)

Technique. Used here to designate a specific

weave; the various steps or procedures used to produce a given construction on the loom.

Template, Temple. A devise used to prevent the cloth from pulling in too much at the selvages as the weaving begins and proceeds. (See Fig. 30, No. 6)

Terry Cloth. A plain weave cotton cloth in which loops are left rising above the face of the cloth; a pile weave with loops uncut for greater absorbency.

Texture. The characteristic look and feel of a fabric's surface—rough or smooth, shiny or dull, according to fiber texture, weave and finish. Often called *hand* or *feel*.

Thread. Thread is sometimes used instead of the word yarn; a single filling pick, a single warp end.

Threading. The prescribed order in which the warp ends are drawn-in on the harnesses as, for example, a straight draw or a pointed draw.

Thrums. The lengths of warp ends that remain unwoven after the cloth has been brought to completion.

Treadle. Treadle is that part of a loom which is attached by cords to a lam which, in turn, is attached to a harness. A treadle is depressed to accomplish the necessary shedding arrangement.

Twill. Twill weaves form the second basic classification of weaves. A twill weave characteristically forms diagonal lines across a fabric. Herringbone is a derivative of twill weave.

Vegetable Fibers. Natural fibers, largely cellulose in composition, such as cotton, linen, ramie, and other bast fibers; grasses and palm fibers.

Vicuña. Fine, soft fabric made from the wool or fur of the small, llamalike animal in the Andes Mountains; finest fiber classified as wool.

Viscose. One of the two processes by which rayon is manufactured; viscose rayon is made mostly of wood.

Warp. The lengthwise or vertical element in woven cloth is called the warp, composed of many strands, individually called *ends*.

Warping. The process of preparing the warp yarns for beaming, or putting warp on loom. For warping accessories see Fig. 30. Warping board (Appendix). Warping reel, Fig. 32.

Warp-faced. A woven cloth in which the warp yarns predominate over the filling yarns.

Weave. A characteristic interlacing of yarns, or construction, and derivatives thereof.

Weaver Bird. Finchlike bird of Africa or Asia that weaves elaborate nests by interlacing grasses, twigs, and other fibrous materials.

Web. The comparatively flat surface of fabric which results from interlacing warp and weft.

Weft. Horizontal or crosswise element in woven cloth, also called filling; a single strand of weft or filling is called a *pick*.

Wire. Semi-rigid filling or warp end usually made of fine copper wire.

Wool. A basic natural fiber for cloth making in virtually universal use.

Wool Counting System. See page 230.

Wool Noils. Waste or linters combed from the fine, long staple fibers.

Worsted. Yarn made from long-staple wool fibers, combed and laid parallel before spinning.

Wrapping. A technique used in making gauze, leno, or other lacy weaves; both weft-wrapping and warp-wrapping occur.

Yarn. Strand or thread of material spun for weaving; natural or man-made. (See Synthetic)

Yarn Count. (See Yarn Count Systems, page 229)

Yarn Sequence. Organization of two or more yarns used to create a pattern of texture, color or values within a weave; often referred to as *color effects*.

BOOKS ABOUT HAND WEAVING

Allen, Edith Louise. *Weaving You Can Do*. The Manual Arts Press, Peoria, Ill., 1947, 118 pp.

Atwater, Mary M. *Byways in Hand Weaving*. The Macmillan Company, New York, 1954, 127 pp.

————*The Shuttlecraft Book of American Hand Weaving*. The Macmillan Company, New York, 1951, 341 pp.

Becher, Lotte. *Hand Weaving—Designs and Instructions*. The Studio Publications, London & New York, 1955, 96 pp.

Black, Mary E. *New Key to Weaving*. The Bruce Publishing Company, Milwaukee, Wis., 1957, 571 pp.

Blumenau, Lili. *The Art and Craft of Hand Weaving*. Crown Publishers, Inc., New York, 1955, 136 pp.

Brown, Harriette J. *Hand Weaving for Pleasure and Profit*. Harper & Brothers, New York, 1952, 273 pp.

Davison, Marguerite P. *A Handweaver's Pattern Book*. M. P. Davison, Swarthmore, Pa., 1958, 228 pp.

Dean, Ida *Dressing the Loom*. I. Dean, San Mateo, Calif.

Kirby, Mary. *Designing on the Loom*. The Studio Publications, London & New York, 1955, 96 pp.

Mairet, Ethel. *Handweaving Today*. Faber & Faber, London.

Tidball, Harriet. *The Weaver's Book*. The Macmillan Company, New York, 1962, 173 pp.

Worst, Edward F. *Foot-Power Loom Weaving*. Bruce Publishing Company, Milwaukee, Wis., 1952, 275 pp. (Write Boris Veren, Big Sur, Calif.)

FIBERS AND YARNS

Bendure, Zelma, and Gladys Pfeiffer. *America's Fabrics*. The Macmillan Company, New York, 1946, 688 pp.

Birrell, Verla. *The Textile Arts*. Harper & Brothers, New York, 1959, 514 pp.

Hollen, Norma, and Jane Saddler. *Textiles*. The Macmillan Company, New York, 1955, 240 pp.

Potter, Maurice D. and B. P. Corbman. *Fiber to Fabric*. McGraw-Hill Book Company — Gregg Publishing Division, New York, 3rd edition, 1959.

HISTORICAL

Bauhaus: Weimar 1919–1925; Dessau 1925–1928. Walter and Ise Gropius, edited by Herbert Bayer. Charles T. Branford Company, Boston, 1957.

Bennett, Wendell C., and Junius S. Bird. *Andean Culture History*, Handbook Series No. 15, American Museum of Natural History, New York, 2nd edition, 1961.

Crawford, M. D. C. *5000 Years of Fibers & Fabrics*. Catalog of the Exhibition, 1946, The Brooklyn Institute of Arts & Sciences, The Brooklyn Museum, New York. 34 pp.

d'Harcourt, Raoul. *Textiles of Ancient Peru and Their Techniques*. The University of Washington Press, Seattle, revised & enlarged edition, 1962, 186 pp. Color plates.

Gropius, Walter. *The New Architecture and the Bauhaus*. Charles T. Branford Company, Boston, 1935, 112 pp.

Jayakar, Mme. Pupul, and John Irwin. *Textiles and Ornaments of India*, edited by Monroe Wheeler, The Museum of Modern Art, New York, 1956, 96 pp.

Kissell, Mary Lois. *Yarn and Cloth Making*, The Macmillan Company, New York, 1931.

Mason, Otis Tufton. *Aboriginal American Basketry: Studies in a Textile Art without Machinery*. Annual Report of The Smithsonian Institution, 1902.

Reath, Nancy Andrews, and Eleanor B. Sachs. *Persian Textiles*. Yale University Press, New Haven, Conn., 1937, 133 pp.

Weibel, Adele Coulin. *Two Thousand Years of Textiles*. Pantheon Books, New York, 1952, 168 pp.

RECOMMENDED READING

Allard, Mary. *Rug Making: Technique and Design*. Chilton Company, Publishers, Philadelphia, 1963, 192 pp.

Albers, Anni. *On Designing*. Wesleyan University Press, Middletown, Conn., 1961, 80 pp.

———*On Weaving*. Wesleyan University Press, Middletown, Conn., 1965, 226 pp.

Graves, Maitland E., *Color Fundamentals*. McGraw-Hill Book Company, New York, 1952, 206 pp.

———*The Art of Color and Design*. McGraw-Hill Book Company, New York, 1951, 439 pp.

Kepes, Gyorgy. *The Language of Vision*. Paul Theobald, Chicago, 1944, 228 pp. *Visual Arts Today*. Wesleyan University Press, Middletown, Conn., 1960, 272 pp.

Moholy-Nagy, Laszlo. *Vision in Motion*. Paul Theobald, Chicago, 1947, 377 pp.

Miles, Walter. *Designs for Craftsmen*. Doubleday & Company, Inc., Garden City, N. Y., 1962, 224 pp.

Mumford, Lewis. *Art and Technics*, Columbia University Press, New York, 1952, 162 pp.

Teague, Walter Dorwin. *Design This Day*. Harcourt, Brace & Company, New York, 1940, 291 pp.

Watson, William. *Textile Design and Colour*. Longmans, Green & Company, New York, 1954, 484 pp.

REFERENCE BOOKS

A Dictionary of Textile Terms. Dan River Mills, New York, 8th edition, 1960, 128 pp. Free.

American Fabrics Encyclopedia of Textiles, by the editors of *American Fabrics Magazine*. New York.

Encyclopaedia of Hand Weaving, by S. A. Zielinski. Funk & Wagnalls Company, New York, 1959, 190 pp.

Fabrics, by Grace Denny. J. B. Lippincott Company, Philadelphia, 8th revised edition, 1962, 163 pp.

The Modern Textile Dictionary, by George S. Linton. Meredith Publishing Company, Des Moines, Iowa, 1962, 772 pp.

PERIODICALS

American Fabrics, 152 East Fortieth Street, New York 16, N. Y.

Ciba Review, Basle, Switzerland. Not available to subscribers but back issues are to be found in libraries.

Craft Horizons, 16 East Fifty-second Street, New York 19, N. Y.

Handweaver & Craftsman, 246 Fifth Avenue, New York, N. Y.

Master Weaver, c/o Handicrafts, Fulford, Quebec.

Textile World, Man-Made Fiber Chart, edited by Wm. G. Ashmore and T. Benton Sevison Jr., and published biennially by Textile World, 330 West Forty-second Street, New York, N. Y.

BOOK SERVICES

Craft & Hobby Book Service, Big Sur, Calif.

Museum Books, Inc., 48 East Forty-third Street, New York 17, N. Y.

Joan Toggitt, 52 Vanderbilt Avenue, New York 17, N. Y.

Wittenborn & Company, Books, 1018 Madison Avenue, New York, N. Y.